D 21·1

Medievalism in Europe

Studies in Medievalism V

1993

Studies in Medievalism

Edited by Leslie J. Workman

Volume I

1. Medievalism in England. Edited by Leslie J. Workman. Spring 1979.

2. Medievalism in America. Edited by Leslie J. Workman. Spring 1982.

Volume II

1. Twentieth Century Medievalism. Edited by Jane Chance. Fall 1982. *(Out of print)*

2. Medievalism in France. Edited by Heather Arden. Spring 1983.

3. Dante in the Modern World. Edited by Kathleen Verduin. Summer 1983.

4. Modern Arthurian Literature. Edited by Veronica M. S. Kennedy and Kathleen Verduin. Fall 1983. *(Out of print)*

Volume III

1. Medievalism in France 1500-1750. Edited by Heather Arden. Fall 1987.

2. Architecture and Design. Edited by John R. Zukowsky. Fall 1990.

3. Inklings and Others. Edited by Jane Chance. Winter 1991.

4. German Medievalism. Edited by Francis G. Gentry. Spring 1991.

   Note: Volume III, Numbers 3 and 4, are bound together and cannot be ordered separately.

IV Medievalism in England. Edited by Leslie J. Workman. 1993.

Medievalism in Europe

Edited by

Leslie J. Workman

Studies in Medievalism V 1993

Cambridge

D. S. Brewer

First published 1994
D. S. Brewer, Cambridge

ISBN 0 85991 400 3

ISSN 0738–7164

D. S. Brewer is an imprint of Boydell & Brewer Ltd
PO Box 9, Woodbridge, Suffolk IP12 3DF, UK
and of Boydell & Brewer Inc.
PO Box 41026, Rochester, NY 14604-4126, USA

British Library Cataloguing-in-Publication Data
A catalogue record for this book is available
from the British Library

Library of Congress Catalog Card Number 93–46606

Printed in the United States of America

Studies in Medievalism

Editor	Leslie J. Workman
Associate Editor	Kathleen Verduin (Hope)
Editorial Assistants	Erin Dillenbeck, Richard A. Frontjes (Hope)

Corresponding Editors

Ulrich Müller (Salzburg)
T. A. Shippey (Leeds)
Toshiyuki Takamiya (Keio)
Domenico Pietropaolo (Toronto)

Advisors

Norman F. Cantor (New York)
Alice Chandler (NYSUC New Paltz)
Otto Gründler (Western Michigan)
John R. Zukowsky (Art Institute of Chicago)

Studies in Medievalism provides an interdisciplinary medium of exchange for scholars in all fields, including the visual and other arts, concerned with any aspect of the post-medieval idea and study of the Middle Ages and the influence, both scholarly and popular, of this study on Western society after 1500.

Studies in Medievalism is published by Boydell and Brewer, Ltd., P. O. Box 9, Woodbridge, Suffolk IP12 3DF, UK; Boydell and Brewer, Inc., P. O. Box 41026, Rochester, NY 14604, USA. Orders and inquiries about back issues should be addressed to Boydell and Brewer at the appropriate office.

Submissions and inquiries regarding future volumes should be addressed to the Editor, Studies in Medievalism, Department of English, Hope College, Holland, MI 49423 USA, tel. (616) 394-7626, fax (616) 394-7622. Contributors should submit the original manuscript and one copy with an abstract: unsolicited manuscripts should be accompanied by a stamped self-addressed envelope. When a manuscript is accepted for publication, copy on an IBM-compatible disk will be required.

Acknowledgments

The Editors make grateful acknowledgment for financial and other assistance to the Dean for Arts and Humanities, and the Department of English at Hope College.

The device on the title page comes from the title page of Des Knaben Wunderhorn: Alte deutsche Lieder, edited by L. Achim von Arnim and Clemens Brentano (Heidelberg and Frankfurt, 1806).

The epigraph is from an unpublished paper by Lord Acton written about 1859, printed in Herbert Butterfield, Man On His Past (Cambridge University Press, 1955), 212.

Studies in Medievalism

Medievalism in Europe

Editorial 1

Germany

Medievalism and Nationalism in   David E. Barclay   5
Nineteenth-Century Germany

The Prussian Royal House and Pictorial   Gerd-H. Zuchold   23
Representations of the Nibelung Saga

Medievalism in German Romantic Art: Hilary Braysmith   38
Reading the Political Text in the
Gothic Style

Nazi Medievalist Art and the Politics   Lisbet Koerner   48
of Memory

Medievalism as Modernism in Alfred   Richard J. Utz   76
Andersch's Nominalist *Littérature Engagée*

Italy

The Economic Decline and Reinfeudation   Thomas Barbiero   92
of the State of Milan in the
Seventeenth Century

Medievalism and Science in the Tuscany   Michael Lavin   101
of the Last Medici

Celluloid Criticism: Pasolini's   Carol L. Robinson 115
Contribution to a Chaucerian Debate

Eco on Medievalism   Domenico Pietropaolo   127

France

Medieval Nostalgia in France, 1750-1789:   Roland Bonnel   139
The Gothic Imaginary at the End of
the Old Regime

Ideology and Utopianism in the   W. Jay Reedy   164
Medievalism of Louis de Bonald

(Re)Creating a Medieval Parade: Jesse D. Hurlbut   176
La Fête historique in Douai

Modern Approaches and the "Real"   Laurence de Looze   183
Middle Ages: Bertrand Tavernier's
La Passion Béatrice

Other Countries

Spain's Medievalist Project in the   Theresa Ann Sears   200
New World

Medievalism in Serbian Painting   Ljubica D. Popovich   209
of the Nineteenth Century

Kazantzakis: Dante's Translator   Andreas K. Poulakidas   225
and Rhapsodist

Notes on Contributors   239

Volume V 1993

Two great principles divide the world, and contend for
the mastery, antiquity and the middle ages. These are
the two civilizations that have preceded us, the two
elements of which ours is composed. All political as
well as religious questions reduce themselves practically
to this. This is the great dualism that runs through our
society.

Lord Acton

Studies in Medievalism

Studies in Medievalism, Volume VI (Spring 1994), will be devoted to Medievalism in North America. **Studies in Medievalism**, Volume VII (Spring 1995), will return to Medievalism in England and is now under consideration. Abstracts or proposals will be considered until January 31, 1994, but should be sent as soon as possible. The deadline for completed papers will be May 1, 1994.

The Year's Work in Medievalism

From 1993, **The Year's Work in Medievalism**, a companion series to **Studies in Medievalism**, will be published annually. **The Year's Work** is based upon the proceedings of the annual International Conference on Medievalism, now in its eighth year, from which a substantial selection of papers will be published. Other papers will be included from time to time, but papers are not solicited. **The Year's Work** will also contain an annual bibliography, book reviews and surveys, notes on research sources, and similar matters in the field of medievalism brought to the attention of the editors. Volume V, based on the Conference in Kaprun, Austria in 1990, Volume VI, resulting from the Conference at the University of Delaware in October 1991, and Volume VII, from the Conference at the University of South Florida, will appear this year. The volumes outstanding from the first four Conferences are now being edited and will be issued as soon as possible. We expect that beginning with this year's Conference at the University of Leeds volumes will appear within twelve months of the Conference.

Those interested in the General Conference should request the SIM Newsletter.

All correspondence should be directed to

Leslie J. Workman, Editor
Studies in Medievalism
Department of English, Hope College
Holland, Michigan 49423
Tel. (616) 394-7626; Fax (616) 394-7922

Editorial

Our epigraph from Lord Acton provides *Studies in Medievalism* with a challenging thesis, but terms of reference which embrace the whole of modern European history are too broad to be helpful. We are left looking for a starting point, a point of attack.

One approach, still valid in the Wonderland of postmodern criticism, is to begin at the beginning, as the Queen advised Alice to do. Certainly medievalism begins with the term "Middle Ages" itself, since to use this and the cognate "Renaissance" as we are obliged to do is to adopt a critical position. To the Italian humanists who coined these terms, they meant certain quite specific things, such as the replacement of medieval by Ciceronian Latin, in which they were all too successful, and the condemnation of Scholastic philosophy, in which their victory was more of rhetoric than substance. Successive cultural movements found similar reasons to deplore the Middle Ages: for the Reformation scholar or politician, it was ecclesiastical tyranny; for the natural philosopher, it was received knowledge bolstered by authority but unsupported by observation or experiment. For the pundits of the Classical Age, which the French traditionally date from the Battle of Marignano in 1515 to that of Waterloo in 1815, it was ignorance of the rules of literary composition and appreciation which they fathered on Aristotle. Each defined the Middle Ages by reaction, and thus the consciousness of the Middle Ages as something definable began to emerge. To quote Wallace K. Ferguson (*The Renaissance in Historical Thought*, Cambridge: Houghton Mifflin, 1948), "By the second half of the seventeenth century, historians were beginning to look back upon the end of the intermediate period and the beginning of the modern age as something that had occurred in the past" (75).

However, the terms Renaissance and Middle Ages were in fact very little used until the late nineteenth century, and the idea that these earlier centuries were a continuation of the ancient world died very slowly: Gibbon perhaps was the last to employ it in English. Henry Hallam, in *A View of the State of Europe during the Middle Ages* (1818), cautiously introduced his subject as "the period usually denominated the Middle Ages." This term was just beginning to replace "Gothick," although it was not until almost the end of the nineteenth century that the "Middle Ages" became distinct from the "Dark Ages" in English usage. It is necessary to remind ourselves also that the antithesis of "Renaissance" and "Middle Ages" follows the publication of

Burckhardt's *The Civilization of the Renaissance in Italy* (1860), and the thinking that assimilates every new development in the fifteenth and sixteenth centuries, such as the development of printing or the opening up of the non-Western world, to a period in European history called "the Renaissance" is a product of the last hundred years and would certainly have confused a sixteenth-century humanist. The concept of historical periodization is a very recent one.

Clearly, then, we cannot, as René Wellek has so brilliantly (though sometimes misleadingly) done with the terms *Romanticism* and *Classicism*, define medievalism in an essay on terminology. This is a very fallible guide, unless we go into the detail of Ferguson's outstanding study, which, since the Renaissance is the Loathly Opposite of the Middle Ages, is still our best guide to medievalism.

A similar approach is the question of when the Middle Ages ended, with which historians have grappled from time to time, last and most wittily Fred C. Robinson in a Presidential Address to the Medieval Academy of America ("Medieval, the Middle Ages," *Speculum* 59.4 [1984]: 745-56). In fact, as historians have come to realize, it is scarcely a meaningful question: medieval patterns of thought and behavior ended at different times in different places and on different levels of society. Even Burckhardt was obliged to admit that he was writing about a very small segment of the Italian population: for most of Italy, the Middle Ages was still going on. There are even differences among intellectual disciplines. Though Ferguson may have been right about the historians, it was for example very different in the law, which ultimately codifies the thought of society and moves more slowly. French feudal law, swept away in France by the Revolution of 1789, survives today in the formerly French provinces of Canada, and a modern legal historian has pointed out that feudalism was not banished from the English statute book until the abolition of copyhold tenure in 1926.

The society which Spain planted in the New World was medieval by almost any definition, while, coming from a quite different level of society, the social ideas as well as the agricultural technology which the Puritans took to New England were similarly medieval. Few historical contrasts are more ironic than that between the complacent classicism of French culture and politics in the seventeenth century and what the French saw as the medieval parliamentary government of England, since in the eighteenth century England took the hegemony of Europe from France, setting the stage for the eighteenth-century Medieval

Revival (which we are now told to call Pre-Romanticism). There were of course powerful undercurrents of medieval culture in seventeenth-century France itself (for which *Studies in Medievalism*, Volume III, Number 1, may be consulted).

The complexities of survival and revival, then, limit the effectiveness of these approaches, and for the moment a brief overview may be more illuminating. Apart from the continuance of medieval institutions and ideas in different ways in different countries, there have been in every century since 1500, the textbook "end of the Middle Ages," different reasons for going back to the Middle Ages. In the sixteenth century the pamphlet wars of the Reformation which exceeded in virulence the political wars naturally drew their ammunition from the Middle Ages. Growing out of this the Catholic Counter-Reformation in France in the seventeenth century produced a vast systematic publication of medieval records by the Maurist and Bollandist Fathers (the second of whom flourish today) and out of this grew most of the ancillary sciences of history: modern historiography has its roots here in the study of the Middle Ages. English antiquarian researches in the seventeenth century, equally extensive though less systematic, and equally a direct reflection of the politics of the time, were devoted to legal and political rather than religious questions.

The nineteenth century had an enormous appetite for history, in which it sought guidance for every matter from religion to domestic decoration. For many reasons the bulk of the history written was medieval, and interest in the Middle Ages enjoyed the powerful reinforcement of politics and nationalism. In Germany the revival of medieval cultural unity was an conscious instrument of political unification: in France, conversely, what Michelet called "the epic of the people" served to compensate for political misfortunes after 1815. Contemporary politics also gave medieval studies a legal bias in Germany, an economic one in France, and a constitutional one in England. England not surprisingly preferred to attribute its power and prosperity to its medieval institutions rather than to seapower and the Industrial Revolution, but it was in England (closely followed and for similar reasons by the United States, as we shall see in the next volume of *Studies in Medievalism*), that under the impact of the Industrial Revolution interest in the Middle Ages first became social and economic as well as religious and political. Hence, the political and social collapse of medievalism between 1914 and 1918, in the form of the public school ethos of chivalry to which the Establishment was strongly committed, was most traumatic in England, as Mark Girouard has so brilliantly revealed in *The Return to Camelot: Chivalry and the English Gentleman* (New Haven: Yale University Press, 1981).

In the twentieth century, then, medievalism declined as a social force, except in the form of fascism, running the gamut from Bulldog Drummond to Adolf Hitler, but conversely, as Norman Cantor has now outstandingly shown in *Inventing the Middle Ages* (New York: William Morrow, 1991), medieval studies flourished as never before.

Finally, after the Second World War, there occurred what I have referred to as the "realization" of the Middle Ages. After two hundred years of scholarly inquiry, medieval art and literature became a fully accessible part of modern culture. *The Canterbury Tales* has became a musical, public radio stations play medieval music, medieval myth and society have captured the media at all levels, particularly since fantasy was readmitted to critical respectability at the end of the Sixties. And if we no longer look to the past for answers, as the nineteenth century did, Cantor has suggested that the idea of the Middle Ages is vital to our thinking about the future.

It is, then, clearly impossible to offer a systematic coverage of European medievalism in one volume of *Studies in Medievalism*, but it is to be hoped this overview will provide a context for the papers collected here, which richly illustrate an appropriate diversity of topic and approach. Medievalism is a new field of very great scope and significance in which much of the basic exploration is still to be done before a real philosophical and critical appreciation can emerge: to dismiss it as a Victorian fantasy, as a few still do, is an indefensible frivolity. We might envy the more advanced state of related fields like Romanticism if we did not value the challenge.

II

It is a pleasure to acknowledge editorial advice with this issue from specialists in different fields, all good friends of *Studies in Medievalism* for many years: David E. Barclay, Professor and Chair of History and Director of the Center for Western European Studies at Kalamazoo College; William Calin, Graduate Research Professor of French at the University of Florida; and Domenico Pietropaolo, Associate Professor of Italian and Academic Coordinator for the Graduate Centre for the Study of Drama at the University of Toronto. Like other volumes of *Studies in Medievalism*, this one owes its editorial quality to the critical acuity of Kathleen Verduin.

Medievalism and Nationalism in Nineteenth-Century Germany

David E. Barclay

At first glance, the link between medievalism and nationalism in nineteenth-century Germany seems clear and easily demonstrated. The large literature on nationalist movements in Central and Eastern Europe has always emphasized the extent to which nationalist intellectuals attempted to draw upon real or imagined national histories or traditions in their efforts to establish the moral and political legitimacy of their cause.[1]   In the case of German nationalism, the rediscovery of the Middle Ages was one way to assert Germany's distinctive national character and destiny in the wake of the French occupation of the country. Moreover, in the context of the country's continued political fragmentation after 1815 the Middle Ages could act both as a reminder and as an admonition for patriots who yearned for the unification of their nation.   As Peter Paret has written in an important recent study, "The dream of German unity found models and inspiration in the Hohenstaufen empire and its Carolingian and Ottonian predecessors; for every schoolboy in Germany, Barbarossa . . . became a symbol of what had been and would be again." The Middle Ages, with their "magical, demonic character," thus came to be a source of deeply emotional identification for many German nationalists.[2] In the words of another scholar, the Middle Ages

> were idealized as an age of religious commitment, of confessional unity, of a powerful, self-sacrificing faith, and of the development of a Christian-German spirit. They were regarded as the heyday of German art and poetry, and as the epoch of German imperial greatness. National hopes and expectations were ignited by the Middle Ages, while contemporary phenomena were measured against them. As

the supposed golden age of German history they affected the self-consciousness of the nation; their patterns of existence and their accomplishments were regarded as repeatable. Those people who linked the national renascence and the fulfillment of national yearnings with the medieval past created traditions and invested the nation with an aura of age and historical profundity. . . . The avowal of the nation expressed itself as an avowal of its history.[3]

Accordingly, it is not surprising that medieval themes figured prominently in the writings of some of the first major proponents of the German national movement in the nineteenth century. One of the best examples was Joseph Görres (1776-1848), a native of Koblenz who began his long career in political journalism as a fervent Jacobin and admirer of the French Revolution. His actual experience of Napoleonic France, however, transformed him into an impassioned German patriot. In the pages of his journal *Der Rheinische Merkur* (1814-16), Görres called upon his fellow Germans to cast off the French yoke and build a new nation, based on the true unity of the people and the establishment of constitutional structures. At the same time, Görres called the attention of his readers to the glories of the German Middle Ages, when the unique folk genius and identity of the German nation had most clearly revealed themselves. Görres went on to argue in several important articles that to commemorate their deliverance from Napoleon, contemporary Germans should complete the construction of Cologne Cathedral, a "torso" which had remained unfinished since 1560. Now, he contended, the cathedral should be completed and consecrated as a worthy monument to Germany's national greatness.[4] As W. D. Robson-Scott has remarked about sentiments of this kind,

If one were to try and sum up the main differences between the Gothic Revival in Germany and England, the most striking surely would be the extent to which the German movement was bound up with the reawakening of the national spirit under the Napoleonic yoke. . . . And so in Germany the reawakened interest in the monuments of the Middle Ages was part and parcel of the nationalist reaction to Napoleon in a way for which there is no parallel in England.[5]

Moreover, the connection between medievalism and nationalism seemed to persist throughout the nineteenth century; this is suggested by the lavish attention devoted to the construction or restoration of such "national monuments" as Cologne Cathedral (finished between 1842 and 1880), the Marienburg in East Prussia, the Wartburg in Thuringia (restored between 1847 and 1891), the medieval Kaiserpfalz in Goslar (restored after the 1870s), or the Barbarossa Monument at the Kyffhäuser (erected in the early 1890s).[6]

Upon closer inspection, however, the relationship between medievalism and nationalism turns out to be exceedingly complex and ambiguous, and historians would do well to rethink that relationship. The complexity stems from the fact that there are several kinds of "medievalism" in Germany after 1780, and thus it is necessary to draw attention to the relationship between each of those medievalisms and the evolution of German nationalist opinion.[7] It is in fact possible to identify essentially five kinds of medievalism in the period: (1) "cosmopolitan," pre-nationalist medievalism; (2) "Christian-German" or "national-conservative" medievalism; (3) "national-liberal" medievalism, with "national-democratic" medievalism as a variant; (4) "escapist" medievalism; and (5) the "official" medievalism of the late nineteenth century.

Cosmopolitan medievalism. The emergence of German medievalism in the form of the Gothic revival antedated the development of any kind of coherent nationalist movements in that country; accordingly, the medievalism of the period before 1806 can only be described as essentially "cosmopolitan" in nature. Some of the earliest and most important examples of the Gothic Revival in German architecture, for example, reflect the cosmopolitan tastes of German rulers who were utterly innocent of the nationalist enthusiasms of later decades: the Nauen Gate in Potsdam, built in 1755 at the behest of Frederick the Great; the "Gothic House," built between 1773 and 1809 in the famous Wörlitz Park for Duke Frederick Leopold Francis of Anhalt-Dessau, or a neo-Gothic church erected nearby between 1805 and 1809; the artificial Gothic ruins constructed in 1784 for Duke Carl August in the palace gardens at Weimar; or the neo-Gothic Franzensburg near Vienna, completed between 1798 and 1836 for the last Holy Roman Emperor, Francis II (later Francis I of Austria).[8] Indeed, before the dissolution of the Empire in 1806 it is difficult to find examples of writers, rulers, or statesmen who consciously

connected the aesthetic values of medievalism with incipient German
nationalism.   Perhaps the best examples of a developing linkage
between medievalism and nationalism before 1806 can be found in
some scattered remarks and observations of Friedrich Schlegel, but
above all in a 1799 essay by "Novalis" (Friedrich von Hardenberg),
*Christianity or Europe: A Fragment (Die Christenheit oder Europa. Ein
Fragment)*.[9]

In that essay, completed seven years before the Holy Roman
Empire's disappearance, Novalis evokes a brilliant image of "this
splendid Empire" in the Middle Ages, but that evocation emphasizes its
universalist character: "They were wonderful, brilliant times, when
Europe was a Christian land, when *One* Christendom resided in this
part of the inhabited world; *One* great, common interest bound
together the most remote provinces of the vast, sacred Empire." But
that Empire dissolved as a consequence of the Reformation, Novalis
contends, and belongs irretrievably to the past.   Now, in an age of
revolutionary upheaval, Germany faces a new world-historic task, in
contrast to the other peoples of Europe: "In Germany, however, one
can point with complete certainty to the signs of a new world. Slowly
but surely Germany is advancing beyond the other peoples of Europe."
But what is Germany's special mission? It is to create a "higher epoch
of culture," to prepare the way for a new universalism to replace the
extinguished universalism of the Middle Ages: "Christendom must again
become infused with energy, and again become a visible Church
beyond borders . . . ."[10]   As Friedrich Meinecke has written, for
Novalis the German nation as a concrete entity "dissolved" into
humanity as a whole (55); thus, in Kurt Borries's view, Novalis
essentially remained an adherent of a rather diffuse "patriotic
cosmopolitanism."[11]

As these examples demonstrate, before 1806 German medievalism
remained linked to older, cosmopolitan and universalist values. After
that date, though, the situation changed markedly, as Napoleon erupted
into Central Europe, shattering both the Habsburg Monarchy and
Prussia, erasing the Holy Roman Empire, and creating the
"Confederation of the Rhine" as a French satellite. The gradual
evolution among German writers and intellectuals of a nationalist
response to these circumstances has been amply documented; but what
kind of relationship developed between the new national feeling and
medievalism? As we have already noted, the Gothic Revival and
nascent German nationalism have often been associated with each

other, but that connection is in fact more ambiguous than has often been realized. To illustrate this contention, let us turn to a consideration of "Christian-German" or "national-conservative" medievalism, and then to what I have called "national-liberal" medievalism with its democratic variants.

Christian-German medievalism. In the years after 1806, intellectuals' reaction to the French occupation took the form of a repudiation of allegedly "French" and "cosmopolitan" values and an affirmation of the historical uniqueness and mission of the German nation. One well known aspect of this development was, of course, the tendency to identify the Gothic style with German traditions, to proclaim that Gothic was *vaterländische Kunst.* The politicization of the Gothic Revival in Germany had a number of interesting consequences. For example, after 1810 many conservative publicists, politicians, and rulers began to appropriate the medieval symbols of the national movement on behalf of their own avowedly monarchist and restorationist causes. On occasion this appropriation took the form of rather crude attempts to divert newly aroused patriotic energies into the service of traditional political institutions and structures. In other cases, though, rulers' decisions to support the neo-Gothic style, especially in architecture, seem to have been more or less politically neutral, a reflection of the popular taste for the Gothic between 1810 and 1820. Both elements seem to have played a role, for instance, in Karl Friedrich Schinkel's neo-Gothic design for the Kreuzberg war memorial in Berlin, approved by Fredrick William III and completed in 1821.[12] Other conservatives, however, embraced medievalist values in a genuine attempt to fuse nationalist ideals with anti-liberal, anti-parliamentary, anti-secular, and monarchical principles. Two Prussians and two Bavarians can serve as examples of this "Christian-German" medievalism: the Prussian writer Friedrich de la Motte-Fouqué; Frederick William IV, King of Prussia from 1840 to 1861; Ludwig I, King of Bavaria from 1825 to 1848; and the Bavarian jurist and Gothic enthusiast Friedrich Hoffstadt.

The Romantic writer Fouqué is largely forgotten today, but during his lifetime his aesthetic and ideological influence was considerable.[13] The descendant of Huguenot *réfugiés* who had settled in the Mark Brandenburg after 1685, Fouqué often drew on legends and fables of his native region for his tales of the German Middle Ages, which after 1810 enjoyed a brief if important vogue throughout the country. The painter Caspar David Friedrich once said that Fouqué could "sing of nothing else but religion, chivalry, and courtly love . . .";[14] and with his novel *The Magic Ring* (*Der Zauberring*), published in 1812, he enjoyed a tremendous popular success.   The story concerns a wandering Swabian knight named Hugh von Trautwangen, the sire of numerous offspring who become involved in convoluted struggles with each other.[15] The story is full of swordplay and courtly romance, but also manages to convey a subtle ideological message with two important components: the historic mission of Germany to save Europe from revolutionary chaos, and a vision of political order based on "the existence of a patriarchal order, God-given differences among social ranks, and a people intimately bound to its dynasty by love, loyalty, and obedience."[16] Fouqué's notions had a powerful impact on a whole generation of young Germans who came of age during the Napoleonic occupation and the Liberation War, among them the Crown Prince of Prussia, the future Frederick William IV.[17]

More than any other German of his era, Frederick William IV (1795-1861; reigned 1840-1861) embodies the spirit of Christian-German medievalism. From an early age he developed an intense love for the German Middle Ages, a passion that was sustained by his reading of Fouqué, his wartime experiences, and his travels through the Rhineland between 1813 and 1815. On one of those occasions he met the distinguished art collector and Gothic enthusiast Sulpiz Boisserée, who fired his enthusiam for the patriotic proposal to complete Cologne Cathedral; and after his accession to the throne in 1840 Frederick William played a decisive role in finally getting that project underway.[18] He was also directly involved in the restoration of other Gothic edifices, including Stolzenberg Castle near Koblenz on the Rhine, Hohenzollern Castle near Hechingen in southwestern Germany, and the Altenberger Dom in the Bergisches Land northeast of Cologne. To be sure, Frederick William's devotion to Gothic architecture was sporadic at best, and in his maturity his tastes ran to neoclassical and Renaissance villa designs as well as to the basilica style of church architecture.[19] Still, his medievalism was intense and enduring, and it was bound up with a lifelong ideological program: to devise a dynastic, conservative alternative to the liberal model of German nationalism. His patriotic feeling was deep and genuine, and set him apart from many of his conservative contemporaries. But he was certain that Germany's national destiny could only be defined in terms of an affirmation of the country's legitimate dynasties and of historically evolved, "organic" traditions. In Germany, he believed, there could be no room for "artificial," "mechanical," "French" innovations like parliaments or written constitutions. Thus he supported the corporative representation of estates rather than the parliamentary representation of individuals; moreover, he insisted, only a Christianity which had been rejuvenated and renewed in the spirit of the old *Reichskirche* could immunize Germans against the blandishments of "alien" doctrines from France.[20]

Frederick William's national feelings were thus strongly legitimist and restorationist; and it was entirely logical that he should yearn for a restoration of the old Holy Roman Empire, which in his view encompassed all that was most noble and most sacred in Germany's national tradition. As a thoroughgoing legitimist, he resisted the notion that the Imperial crown should rest on the head of anyone except a Habsburg; and during the turbulent months of revolution in 1848-49, he diverted himself with a variety of plans to restore the Empire, with the King of Prussia to serve as the Emperor's first vassal and supreme warlord. Usually, though, he realized that such ideas were chimerical, as he noted in a revealing letter to his brother-in-law, Ludwig I of Bavaria, at the time of a war scare with France in 1840. He was almost hoping for a French invasion of the Rhineland, he asserted,

> for then the German Confederation will step forth for the first time as a European power, and what a power, for with its two comet tails it represents a population of sixty-six million!!!!!! And if *they* are *united* (and oh! may God grant that they will be), then no power of the earth can triumph over them, while they will be able to triumph over *many*. The thirty million Germans at the heart of this central power in Europe will again *undeniably* constitute the *world's leading nation*. Scold me for being a dreamer. It is sweet to dream of the greatness of Germany's princes and peoples! I shall dream further about outer forms of splendor and glory. For on the head of the mightiest German prince, the hereditary President of the Confederation, . . . I would again like to see what is incontrovertibly the world's most important crown, the crown of Charlemagne. I would like to hear it proclaimed that the Austrian monarch only as Roman Emperor . . . would be President of the Confederation, the first Prince of Germany, the greatest leader of Christendom.

But let us awaken. I'll now jump with both legs back into reality.[21]

In early 1849 Frederick William had the opportunity to become German Emperor himself, when the Frankfurt National Assembly offered him the Imperial crown of a constitutional state; but the King of Prussia could never accept a crown which would make him a "serf of the Revolution of 1848," he proclaimed; and, as is well known, he rejected the offer in the spring.[22]

Frederick William IV was not the only German monarch of the *Vormärz* period to be influenced by the values of Christian-German medievalism. His brother-in-law Ludwig I, King of Bavaria (1786-1868; reigned 1825-1848), shared a number of Frederick William's views and interests. He too had been inspired by patriotic feeling during the Liberation War and subsequently supported the Cologne Cathedral project. Like Frederick William he also encouraged the restoration of a number of medieval churches. His medievalism was limited by a wide and eclectic range of intellectual and aesthetic concerns, but at the same time it helped to define his political agenda. In Ludwig's case this consisted of establishing and sustaining Bavaria's unique position as a medium-sized state within Germany. As a thoroughgoing *cultural* nationalist who regarded the possibility of Germany's *political* unification with skepticism, Ludwig hoped to encourage among his subjects a sense of loyalty to the Wittelsbach dynasty and to Bavarian particularism. At the same time, though, he remained faithful to larger German patriotic concerns, as evidenced by his sponsorship of such things as the "Valhalla" project, a neoclassical memorial to famous Germans located near Regensburg.[23]

A similar ambiguity was reflected in the ideas of his fellow Bavarian Friedrich Hoffstadt (1802-1846), who was perhaps the most tireless devotee of the Gothic style in nineteenth-century Germany. As a law student in Landshut, Hoffstadt's obsession with the German Middle Ages had earned him the sobriquet "Gothicus," and that obsession sustained him throughout his brief lifetime.[24] In 1831, Hoffstadt and a group of close friends created an organization in Munich called the "Society of the Three Shields for the Study of German Antiquity," a group that played a major role as propagandist for the Gothic style. Pledged to the "maintenance of the purity of German art and its redemption from the domination of foreign art and classical antiquity," the Society completely rejected the traditions of classicism and neoclassicism as un-German and contrary to the spirit of the nation. Hoffstadt lauded Gothic as the true German style, a style that was at once national and Christian, "growing in and from the nation and from Christianity, not artificial or the product of individual invention, but rather a style that has evolved and grown" (quoted in Erichsen and Henker, 266). To recover the sense of selfless communitarian endeavor which Hoffstadt believed had typified the High Middle Ages, the Society acquired a house in Munich where its members were to live and work. There they built up an important collection of medieval documents and art; at the same time they developed their skills in such things as Gothic design and architectural restoration. Not surprisingly, the Society was especially interested in the preservation and restoration of Gothic buildings, while it also hoped to make the Gothic style normative for nineteenth-century architecture. After 1840 Hoffstadt began to produce a monumental *Gothic ABC Book, or Principles of the Gothic Style for Artists and Artisans (Gothisches A.B.C.-Buch das ist: Grundregeln des gotbischen Styls für Kunstler und Werkleute)*; based on years of intensive research, it was essentially a technical manual for artists and artisans (Erichsen and Henker, 274). The *Gothic ABC Book* was probably Hoffstadt's greatest achievement, but by the time it began to appear the Society itself had dissolved, largely as a result of Hoffstadt's transfer in 1843 to a new government job outside Munich.

Hoffstadt's medievalism emphasizes the Christian quality of the Gothic style; indeed, as Walter Schmitz has written (429-30), for Hoffstadt the principal function of art was to serve and glorify religion, in contrast to the tendency of many Romantics to regard art itself as a kind of religion. Certainly medievalism seems not to have had quite the same political implications for Hoffstadt that it had for a Frederick William IV (or, for that matter, a Joseph Görres); like Ludwig I, Hoffstadt adhered to an essentially cultural rather than an overtly political nationalism. But this merely suggests that there was considerable variation of emphasis among the Christian-German medievalists. What they all had in common, though, was more important: a commitment to the "organic" and "historic," as opposed to the "mechanical" and "artificial"; an abiding hostility to the legacy of revolutionary France; a determination to encourage "truly German" institutional and cultural alternatives to that legacy; and a fusion of Christian religious belief with German patriotic sentiment.

National-liberal medievalism. Until the 1850s or 1860s, however, most German nationalists continued to argue that the German national cause was inseparable from the triumph of genuinely representative and parliamentary institutions. At the same time, many of those nationalists looked to the German Middle Ages for patriotic inspiration. Curiously, "national-liberal" medievalism appears to be a little-investigated problem, despite the oceans of ink that have been spilled on the subject of German nationalism. There are several important examples of liberal medievalists who embraced the Gothic style for political and ideological reasons, especially before and during the revolutions of 1848. The Swiss architect Johann Georg Müller (1822-1849), for instance, shared Hoffstadt's distaste for classical antiquity as well as his enthusiasm for the Gothic; for Müller, however, what defined the Gothic style as "patriotic" was its "national-democratic quality," the idea that the great monuments of Gothic art represented the collective achievements of ordinary people.[25] A similar notion was shared by those liberal nationalists who saw in the Cologne Cathedral project a symbol of what Thomas Nipperdey has called a national unity "grounded in the German people and not based solely on princes and states" ("Kölner Dom," 598). To be sure, most liberals who were inspired by the Middle Ages were more cautious in their views than Müller, and were worried about what they perceived to be the dangers posed by republicanism and the radical demands of the lower classes. This was certainly the point of view of the artist Alfred Rethel (1816-1859), well known for his Charlemagne frescoes in the town hall of Aachen and for his series of woodcuts, *Another Dance of Death*, on the Revolution of 1848 (Paret, 79-92, 104-30; see also Kerssen, 110-11).

As Müller's example suggests, a variant of "national-liberal" medievalism might be described as "national-democratic" medievalism. The remarkable Rhenish politician and art publicist August Reichensperger (1808-1895) is perhaps the most interesting example of a man who combined thoroughgoing medievalism with a complex political doctrine composed of nationalist, conservative-organicist, and democratic tendencies. As a young man he had originally been inspired by the example of the aging Görres, who in the 1830s and 1840s had become a fervent champion of Catholic interests and a fierce opponent of Prussia. Although he was a Prussian subject who held high administrative posts in the Prussian Rhineland, Reichensperger always yearned to free his region from Hohenzollern domination. One of the initiators of the famous *Kölner Dombauverein* in 1841, Reichensperger spent decades propagating the idea of the Cologne Cathedral as a German national monument. Politically active until 1885, he became a leader of the Catholic Center party after 1870. He always sought to combine his deeply religious and patriotic views with democratic values and a commitment to Catholic social doctrines.[26] For Reichensperger, the Gothic style was the only style appropriate to the nineteenth century. As Heinz Gollwitzer has written of this indefatigable friend of Montalembert in France and Pugin in England, "If he had had his way, one would have only built Gothic town halls in Germany, and in Berlin a Gothic Reichstag palace" ("Fragenkreis," 7).

Escapist medievalism. Among the five categories of nineteenth-century German medievalism, the fourth, which can be called "escapist" medievalism, is probably the vaguest and thus the most problematical. Some nineteenth-century Germans turned to medievalism to avoid dealing with the difficult issues posed by that century. For them medievalism was a way to escape the traumas of industrialization, urbanization, a new mass society, and unsettling political change. The most important example of an "escapist" medievalist is Ludwig II (1845-1886), King of Bavaria from 1864 to 1886.

Before we turn to Ludwig's medievalism, however, an important digression is necessary. "Escapist" medievalism, and indeed the other categories of medievalism delineated in this article, should not be confused with what might be called the "historicist" eclecticism of so many Germans in the nineteenth century. An individual could look to the Middle Ages for various kinds of inspiration, without, however, really being a medievalist. An architect like Karl Friedrich Schinkel, for example, designed several Gothic buildings, but he was never a thoroughgoing medievalist; among his best-known achievements were neoclassicist structures and even severely functional edifices that anticipate twentieth-century architecture. But perhaps the best example of a nineteenth-century German who, though influenced by the Middle Ages, cannot really be regarded as a medievalist is Richard Wagner.[27]

The case of Wagner presents real difficulties for the student of medievalism, as indeed for the student of every other aspect of his life and work. Of his intense German national feeling there can, of course, be no doubt, just as there can be no doubt of his conviction that art and the resurgence of German nationalism were linked. Moreover, most of Wagner's works are set in the Middle Ages and emphasize "medieval" or "Christian" values: *Tannhäuser, Lohengrin, Tristan und Isolde, Der Ring des Nibelungen, Parsifal*, and perhaps *Die Meistersinger von Nürnberg.* Moreover, as Volker Mertens has observed, Wagner contributed in important ways to the popularization of the Middle Ages: "Wagner's works aroused and stimulated interest in the Middle Ages not only in the late nineteenth century but also in the twentieth."[28] Nevertheless, Wagner should probably not be included in any of the categories of medievalism outlined here.[29] For one thing, his politics are too murky and paradoxical; for another, one can question just how central the Middle Ages really were to Wagner's artistic and cultural vision. To be sure, he had early on been inspired by Friedrich Raumer's history of the Hohenstaufen emperors;[30] but the undeniable medievalism of much of Wagner's work is only one aspect of an astonishingly eclectic *mélange* of forces and influences that shaped his messianic vision of himself and his *Zukunftsmusik.*[31] Martin Gregor-Dellin warns us that Wagner defies attempts at systematization;[32] and any attempt to fit him into one of the categories of nineteenth-century medievalism is not very helpful.

With Wagner's royal patron Ludwig II, categorization presents fewer difficulties.[33] That tragic monarch's desperate attempts to escape from the modern world have been amply documented; and of course architecture was central to his effort to find a refuge from modernity. Even as a teenager he had been inspired by Hohenschwangau in the Bavarian Alps, a medieval castle which had been restored by his father, Maximilian II, after 1833. In a letter to Wagner, Ludwig once described Hohenschwangau as a "paradise on earth," and it was in the vicinity of that edifice that he later built his own castle, the famous Neuschwanstein, which he intended to be full of "reminiscences of Tannhäuser . . . and Lohengrin."[34] Ludwig's architectural escapism was not, however, limited to the Middle Ages; it extended to other epochs, including both the Renaissance and the Baroque. Indeed, his attempt to build a new Versailles at Herrenchiemsee is perhaps the best example of his escapist eclecticism.[35] Moreover, Ludwig's views on German unification also demonstrate that in the second half of the century it was still possible to combine medievalism with indifference or even hostility to modern nationalism. The King of Bavaria disliked Bismarck, regarded the new Germany of 1871 with distaste, and deplored Prussia's dominant role in it. That dominance, Ludwig feared, would lead inexorably to the loss of Bavaria's own identity and traditions. As he put it in another letter to Wagner, "I am disgusted to the greatest possible extent by the wretched German Reich in the form that, unhappily, it has taken thanks to the prosaic and unimaginative

Prussianism of the Junker from the Mark."[36] (The latter reference, of course, is to Bismarck.)

Official medievalism. Finally, a fifth category of nineteenth-century German medievalism might be called the "official" medievalism of Imperial Germany after 1871 and especially of Wilhelmine Germany after 1888. The utility to Germany's rulers of "medieval" and especially neo-Gothic architecture for asserting the values of official, monarchical nationalism after 1871 is fairly obvious. As Paret observes, "medieval and quasi-medieval motifs were used so widely in the last third of the century that they turned into cultural and stylistic clichés" (147). Even today Germany is full of turn-of-the-century train stations, post offices, town halls, and factories built in neo-Romanesque or neo-Gothic styles that celebrate the unity of the German nation and its supposed historical foundations. The political and ideological functions of post-1871 "official" medievalism were most clearly and obviously expressed in the numerous monuments and memorials built throughout the country during those years. One especially interesting exmaple was the "national monument" at the Kyffhäuser in central Germany. Erected between 1892 and 1897, it was a memorial both to Frederick Barbarossa and to "Barbablanca," Emperor William I (1797-1888), the younger brother of Frederick William IV who had acceded to the Prussian throne in 1861 and to an Imperial title in the unified *Reich* ten years later (Kerssen, 97-105).[37] Even more revealing, perhaps, was the restoration of the medieval Kaiserpfalz in Goslar, which Hermann Wislicenus (1825-1899) decorated between 1879 and 1897 with a series of frescoes depicting legendary scenes from the history of the old Empire. The series concluded with an apotheosis of William I, accompanied by the figures of Charlemagne, Louis the German, Otto the Great, Henry I, Henry III, Henry IV, and Frederick Barbarossa (Kerssen, 105-9).[38]

By the end of the nineteenth century, medievalism in Germany had become "domesticated." The German Middle Ages had been emptied of any "demonic," mysterious, or emotional quality with which they may have been invested earlier in the century. Instead, they were now serving to justify and legitimize the new Imperial system, which was frequently portrayed—especially after the accession to the throne of William I's grandson, the erratic and bombastic William II (1859-1941; reigned 1888-1918)—as the legitimate and direct descendant of the old *Reich*.[39] As several recent studies have suggested, however, Wilhelmine society remained deeply divided, and in the years after 1888 the reservoir of popular monarchical sentiment was steadily drained. Accordingly, the efforts of monarchical elites to appropriate Germany's medieval past for contemporary political ends enjoyed at best a mixed success.[40]

Considering the tentative categories of nineteenth-century German medievalism that have been sketched here, what can we say about the relationship between those medievalisms and German nationalism? Above all, we see that the linkage between these phenomena is not at all clear or unambiguous. As the first category demonstrates, modern German medievalism antedates the emergence of any kind of coherent body of nationalist thought in that country. As other categories show, after the first decades of the nineteenth century a wide range of German nationalists and patriots could use medievalism for a large number of different purposes. Medievalism could lend itself equally well to the Christian-German patriotism of a Frederick William IV, the Bavarian-influenced cultural patriotism of a Hoffstadt, the democratically tinged Catholic nationalism of a Reichensperger, the escapist particularism of a Ludwig II, or the aggressive bombast of William II's Germany. For many German nationalists, medievalism was a logical consequence of that discovery of the national past and the "invention" of traditions which typified so many nationalist movements in nineteenth-century Europe.[41] Still, medievalism seems not to have been a necessary ingredient of nationalist thought in Germany. While, for example, many adherents of "Christian-German" conservatism were intense German patriots and fervent medievalists, many other "Christian-German" conservatives were neither medievalists nor especially patriotic. Many liberals seem to have been medievalists, but many were not. And, just as many medievalists were nationalists, others adhered to non-nationalist or anti-nationalist views.

In short, these tentative findings suggest that, like Romanticism, medievalism in Germany was a complex and distinctive cultural tendency, something that has to be understood and studied on its own terms, rather than as an epiphenomenon of conservatism or nationalism or Romanticism. But as these remarks also demonstrate, a great deal of work needs to be done before historians will recognize medievalism as a distinct and useful analytical category.

NOTES

An earlier version of this essay was presented at the Third Annual General Conference on Medievalism, Chicago, 13-15 October 1988. The research for this article was made possible in part by a fellowship from the Alexander von Humboldt Foundation, Bonn-Bad Godesberg.

1. For recent examples of studies that consider the role of nationalist intellectuals in Central Europe, see Miroslav Hroch, *Die Vorkämpfer der nationalen Bewegung bei den kleinen Völkern Europas. Eine vergleichende Analyse zur gesellschaftlichen Schichtung der patriotischen Gruppen* (Prague: Universita Karlova, 1968), 24-5; Thomas Nipperdey, "Der Kölner Dom als Nationaldenkmal," *Historische Zeitschrift* 233 (1981), 602, and *Deutsche Geschichte 1800-1866. Bürgerwelt und starker Staat* (Munich: Verlag C. H. Beck, 1983), 300-13; Hagen Schulze, *Der Weg zum Nationalstaat. Die deutsche Nationalbewegung vom 18. Jahrhundert bis zur Reichsgründung* (Munich: Deutscher Taschenbuch Verlag, 1985), 58-70; Geoff Eley, "State Formation, Nationalism, and Political Culture: Some Thoughts on the Unification of Germany," in his *From Unification to Nazism: Reinterpreting the German Past* (Boston: Allen & Unwin, 1986), 63-4; Hans-Ulrich Wehler, *Deutsche Gesellschaftsgeschichte*, 2 vols. (Munich: Verlag C. H. Beck, 1987), 1:512; and especially James J. Sheehan, *German History 1770-1866* (Oxford: Oxford University Press, 1989), 371-8.

2. Peter Paret, *Art as History: Episodes in the Culture and Politics of Nineteenth-Century Germany* (Princeton: Princeton University Press, 1988), 147.

3. Ludger Kerssen, *Das Interesse am Mittelalter im deutschen Nationaldenkmal* (Berlin and New York: Walter de Gruyter, 1975), 12-13.

4. For biographical details on Görres, see, *inter alia*, the entries in *Allgemeine Deutsche Biographie* 9 (1879; Berlin: Duncker & Humblot, 1964), 532-6. On Görres and the Middle Ages see Kerssen, 19; Sheehan, *German History*, 374-5; and Thomas Nipperdey, "Auf der Suche nach der Identität: Romantischer Nationalismus," in *Nachdenken über die deutsche Geschichte. Essays* (1986; Munich: Deutscher Taschenbuch Verlag, 1990), 141.

5. W. D. Robson-Scott, *The Literary Background of the Gothic Revival in Germany: A Chapter in the History of Taste* (Oxford: Oxford University Press, 1965), 301.

6. For details, see Kerssen.

7. Inevitably, I shall have to pass lightly over several areas and issues that have been more extensively treated elsewhere (e. g., the relationship of Goethe or of the Nazarenes to medievalism).

8. Among others, see Robson-Scott, 30-2; Heinz Biehn, *Residenzen der Romantik* (Munich: Prestel, 1970), 31-9, 82-95.

9. Friedrich Meinecke, *Cosmopolitanism and the National State*, trans. Robert B. Kimber (1907; Princeton: Princeton University Press, 1970), 50.

10. "Novalis" [Friedrich von Hardenberg], *Fragmente und Studien. Die Christenheit oder Europa*, ed. Carl Paschke (Stuttgart: Reclam, 1984), 67, 81-2, 88.

11. Kurt Borries, *Die Romantik und die Geschichte. Studien zur romantischen Lebensform* (Berlin: Deutsche Verlagsgesellschaft für Politik und Geschichte m. b. H., 1925), 131.

12. On the political implications of the Kreuzberg memorial, see Thomas Nipperdey, "Nationalidee und Nationaldenkmal in Deutschland im 19. Jahrhundert," *Historische Zeitschrift* 206.3 (1968), 541; see also Michael Nungesser, *Das Denkmal auf dem Kreuzberg von Karl Friedrich Schinkel* (Berlin: Verlag Willmuth Arenhövel, 1987).

13. On Fouqué, see Arno Schmidt, *Fouqué und einige seiner Zeitgenossen. Biographischer Versuch* (1958; Zurich: Haffmans Verlag, 1987).

14. Quoted in Johannes Erichsen and Michael Henker (with Evamarie Brockhoff), eds., *"Vorwärts, vorwärts sollst du schauen . . ." Geschichte, Politik und Kunst unter Ludwig I. Katalog zur Ausstellung* (Munich: Haus der bayerischen Geschichte, 1986), 267.

15. Friedrich Baron de la Motte-Fouqué, *Fouqués Werke*, Part 3, *Der Zauberring*, ed. Walter Ziesemer (Berlin, n. d.).

16. Frank-Lothar Kroll, "Politische Romantik und romantische Politik bei Friedrich Wilhelm IV.," in *Friedrich Wilhelm IV. in seiner Zeit. Beitrage eines Colloquiums*, ed. Otto Büsch (Berlin: Colloquium Verlag, 1987), 97.

17. Ernst Lewalter, *Friedrich Wilhelm IV. Das Schicksal eines Geistes* (Berlin: Gustav Kiepenheuer Verlag, 1938), 107-9; Kroll, "Romantik," 96-8.

18. For Frederick William's involvement with the Cologne Cathedral project, see Norbert Trippen, "Das Kölner Dombaufest 1842 und die Absichten Friedrich Wilhelms IV. von Preußen bei der Wiederaufnahme der Arbeiten am Kölner Dom. Eine historische Reflexion zum Domfest 1980," *Annalen des Historischen Vereins für den Niederrhein insbesondere das alte Erzbistum Köln* 182 (1979): 99-115; Thomas Parent, *Die Hohenzollern in Köln* (Cologne: Greven Verlag, 1981), 28-30, 34-42, 50-76; and especially Ursula Rathke, "Die Rolle Friedrich Wilhelms IV. von Preußen bei der Vollendung des Kölner Doms," *Kölner Domblatt* 47 (1982): 127-60; 48 (1983): 27-68; 49 (1984): 169-73.

19. Ludwig Dehio, *Friedrich Wilhelm IV. von Preußen. Ein Baukünstler der Romantik* (Munich: Deutscher Kunstverlag, 1961), 19.

20. For recent work on Frederick William, see Büsch; Frank-Lothar Kroll, *Friedrich Wilhelm IV. und das Staatsdenken der deutschen Romantik* (Berlin: Colloquium Verlag, 1990); Walter Bußmann, *Zwischen Preußen und Deutschland. Friedrich Wilhelm IV. Eine Biographie* (Berlin: Siedler Verlag, 1990); Dirk Blasius, *Friedrich Wilhelm IV. 1795-1861. Psychopathologie und Geschichte* (Göttingen: Vandenhoeck & Ruprecht, 1992); and David E. Barclay, *Frederick William IV and the Prussian Monarchy 1840-61* (Oxford: Oxford University Press, forthcoming).

21. Frederick William IV to Ludwig I, 19 December 1840, Bayerisches Hauptstaatsarchiv, Munich, Abteilung III: Geheimes Hausarchiv, Nachlaß König Ludwig I., 85/3/2. I am grateful to S. K. H. Herzog Albrecht von Bayern for

permission to quote from this source. See also Kroll, *Friedrich Wilhelm IV.*, 118-20.

22. For Frederick William's ideas about German nationalism, the Holy Roman Empire and the Imperial title, see Kroll, *Friedrich Wilhelm IV*, 108-42.

23. On Ludwig, see, *inter alia*, Heinz Gollwitzer, *Ludwig I. von Bayern. Königtum im Vormärz. Eine politische Biographie* (Munich: Süddeutscher Verlag, 1986); Gottlieb Leinz, "Ludwig I. von Bayern und die Gotik," *Zeitschrift für Kunstgeschichte* 44 (1981), 399-444; Jochen Zink, *Ludwig I. und der Dom zu Speyer* (Munich: Haus der Bayerischen Geschichte, 1986); David E. Barclay, "Medievalism and Monarchy in Nineteenth-Century Germany: Ludwig I and Frederick William IV," in *Selected Papers on Medievalism*, eds. Janet Goebel and Rebecca Cochran (Indiana, PA: Indiana University of Pennsylvania, 1988), 2:124-35.

24. Walter Schmitz, "' . . . Daß der teutsche Styl das ganze Leben der Teutschen umfassen möge'. Die 'Gesellschaft für Deutsche Altertumskunde von den Drei Schilden': Ihre Vorgeschichte in Franken und ihr Wirken in München," in *"Vorwärts, vorwärts sollst du schauen . . . ": Geschichte, Politik und Kunst unter Ludwig I. Aufsätze*, eds. Johannes Ehrichsen and Uwe Puschner (Munich: Haus der Bayerischen Geschichte, 1986), 420. See also the biographical entry in *Allgemeine Deutsche Biographie*, 12 (1880; rpt. Berlin: Duncker & Humblot, 1969), 618-9.

25. Heinz Gollwitzer, "Zum Fragenkreis Architekturhistorismus und politische Ideologie," *Zeitschrift für Kunstgeschichte* 42 (1979), 6.

26. For biographical information, see, among other things, the entry by Georg Kaufmann in *Allgemeine Deutsche Biographie*, 53 (1907; Berlin: Duncker & Humblot, 1971), 276-81; and Franz Schnabel, *Die religiösen Kräfte*, Volume 4 of *Deutsche Geschichte im neunzehnten Jahrhundert*, 3rd ed. (Freiburg: Verlag Herder, 1955), 200-2.

27. It should be emphasized that we are defining "medievalism" on the basis of three categories which Leslie J. Workman has identified: "the study of the Middle Ages, the application of medieval models to contemporary needs, and the inspiration of the Middle Ages in all forms of art and thought" (Editorial, *Studies in Medievalism* 3.1 [Fall 1987], 1).

28. Volker Mertens, "Wagner's Middle Ages," in *Wagner Handbook*, eds. Ulrich Müller and Peter Wapnewski, trans. and ed. John Deathridge (Cambridge: Harvard University Press, 1992), 266. This essay is the best available discussion of the place of the Middle Ages in Wagner's work.

29. For a divergent point of view, see Edward R. Haymes, "Two-Storied Medievalism in Wagner's *Die Meistersinger von Nürnberg*," *Studies in Medievalism* 3.4 (Spring 1991): 505-13. As Haymes argues, "Richard Wagner was almost certainly the most famous German practitioner of what we today call medievalism. Everything he wrote after *Der fliegende Holländer* was based directly or indirectly on stories from the Middle Ages, most of them from the thirteenth century" (505).

30. Curt von Westernhagen, *Wagner: A Biography*, trans. Mary Whittall, 2 vols. (Cambridge: Cambridge University Press, 1978), 1:69-70.

31. On Wagner's modernity as well as his messianism, see "Introduction," *Wagnerism in European Culture and Politics*, eds. David C. Large and William

Weber in collaboration with Anne Dzamba Sessa (Ithaca, NY: Cornell University Press, 1984), 19.

32. Martin Gregor-Dellin, *Richard Wagner: His Life, His Work, His Century*, trans. J. Maxwell Brownjohn (San Diego: Harcourt Brace Jovanovich, 1983), 459. For a somewhat different point of view, and one which rightly calls attention to the problems of categorization, see Francis G. Gentry and Ulrich Müller, "The Reception of the Middle Ages in Germany: An Overview," *Studies in Medievalism* 3.4 (Spring 1991), 402-3.

33. On Ludwig's relationship to Wagner, see Manfred Eger, "The Patronage of King Ludwig II," in Müller and Wapnewski, 317-26.

34. Michael Petzet, "Architektur als Kulisse—Die Kunst Ludwigs II., " in Martin Gregor-Dellin *et al.*, *Ludwig II. Die Tragik des "Märchenkönigs"* (Regensburg: Verlag Friedrich Pustet, 1986), 31-2.

35. On Ludwig's castles, see, *inter alia*, Ludwig Hüttl, *Ludwig II. König von Bayern. Eine Biographie* (Munich: C. Bertelsmann, 1986), 224-99.

36. Quoted in Franz Herre, "Das Ende der Souveränitat—Ludwig II. und die Reichsgründung," in Gregor-Dellin *et al.*, 57.

37. See also Michael Stuhr, "Das Kyffhäuser-Denkmal—Symbol und Gestalt," in *Historismus—Aspekte zur Kunst im 19. Jahrhundert*, ed. Karl-Heinz Klingenburg (Leipzig: VEB E. A. Seemann Verlag, 1985), 157-82, 261-4.

38. See also Rudolf Pfefferkorn, *Die Berliner Secession. Eine Epoche deutscher Kunstgeschichte* (Berlin: Haude & Spener, 1972), 13.

39. On the *"embourgeoisement"* of medievalism after the 1870s, see Paret's discussion of Joseph Viktor Scheffel and his historical novel *Ekkehard*, which enjoyed tremendous success after the foundation of the new *Reich* (133-48, especially 147-8).

40. For example, see Isabel V. Hull, "Prussian Dynastic Ritual and the End of Monarchy," in *German Nationalism and the European Response, 1890-1945*, eds. Carole Fink, Isabel V. Hull, and MacGregor Knox (Norman: University of Oklahoma Press, 1985), 13-41; Bernd Sösemann, "Der Verfall des Kaisergedankens im Ersten Weltkrieg," in *Der Ort Kaiser Wilhelms II. in der deutschen Geschichte*, ed. John C. G. Röhl with Elisabeth Müller-Luckner (Munich: R. Oldenbourg Verlag, 1991), 145-70. Wolfgang Hardtwig reminds us, however, that "symbolic" political socialization during the Kaiserreich may have been more successful than I am suggesting here; the new national state, defined as a Kleindeutschland and without much reference to the constitutional issues of 1848-49 or of the era of the constitutional conflict after 1861-62, had clearly established itself as a focus of popular loyalty and sentiment by the turn of the century ("Nationsbildung und politische Mentalität. Denkmal und Fest im Kaiserreich," in his *Geschichtskultur und Wissenschaft* [Munich: Deutscher Taschenbuch Verlag, 1990], 264-301).

41. See Eric Hobsbawm and Terence Ranger, eds., *The Invention of Tradition* (Cambridge: Cambridge University Press, 1981).

The Prussian Royal House
and Pictorial Representations
of the Nibelung Saga

Gerd-H. Zuchold

The first known reaction of a Prussian monarch to the Nibelung saga was negative. In 1782 Christoph Heinrich Müller edited in Berlin the first completed version of the *Nibelungenlied* based on what subsequently came to be called *Handschriften* A and C.[1] He asked the Prussian king, Frederick the Great, to honor him by including his edition in one of the royal libraries, but the king answered, "You overestimate the value of poems from the twelfth, thirteenth, and fourteenth centuries whose publications you have proposed and that you regard so highly as enriching the German language. I think that they're not worth a penny and they don't deserve to be salvaged from the dust of the past. In my library at least, I will not tolerate that kind of miserable stuff, but throw it out."[2]

That this classically educated and Francophile king reacted so negatively is not surprising, since he had an aversion to everything German, at least in literature and the fine arts. Yet only one year later, Johannes von Müller, professor of history in Kassel, pointed out that "the Nibelungenlied could become the German Iliad."[3] In 1804 Müller went to Berlin, stayed until 1807, became a member of the Prussian Academy, and was mainly occupied with describing the life and work of Frederick the Great. In Berlin he met another admirer of the *Nibelungenlied*, August Wilhelm Schlegel, who had asserted in an 1803 lecture, "These heroic sagas demonstrate that the human race at that time was far superior to following generations, not only in physical strength, but also in greatness and purity of ideals. In liveliness and immediacy of portrayal and the greatness of passion and characters the Song of the Nibelungen is comparable to the Iliad."[4] One of the most important and interesting Romantic writers in Prussia, Friedrich de la Motte Fouqué (1777-1843), attended Schlegel's lectures. In 1803, inspired by Schlegel, he wrote a drama related to the Nibelung theme, the dramatic scene *Siegfried in der Schmiede* (*Siegfried in the Smithy*).[5] He followed this piece in 1808 with the drama *Sigurd, der Schlangentöter. Ein Heldenspiel in sechs Abenteurn* (*Sigurd the Dragonslayer: An Heroic Epic in Six Adventures*), which he in turn expanded in two subsequent works: *Sigurds Rache* (*Sigurd's Revenge*) and *Aslauga*. In 1810 he published all three works under the title *Der Held des Nordens* (*The Hero of the North*).[6]

Fouqué wrote his first work directly after the defeat of Prussia at the hands of Napoleonic France in 1806-7. He was interested not only in the portrayal of the Nibelung theme in the language of his time but also in the significance of the material for his time. In this connection it should be pointed out that Fouqué's forebears were Huguenots who had suffered religious persecution in their homeland. They were given a new, secure home in Prussia by the Tolerance Edict of the Great Elector of Brandenburg in 1688. Their descendant now fought the French conquerors with his poetry, creating a work whose purpose was the contemplation of national, that is, German values. Thus it is not surprising that he fought actively on the side of Prussia against Napoleon and also sought to become politically effective for Prussia through his writings.

Yet Fouqué was not the only one at that time who tried to emphasize the contemporary relevance of the Nibelung saga. Friedrich Heinrich von der Hagen gave lectures in 1810 at the University of Berlin concerning the epic, about which he later wrote: "In the most humiliating time of my country it was a great consolation for me and my friends, a true encouragement and a great indication of Germany's return to global splendor [*Wiederkehr deutscher Weltherrlichkeit*] that did not deceive us."[7] Von der Hagen valued Fouqué's writing highly and wrote to Friedrich Tieck that Fouqué was the "new Volker," that is, the new bard of the Germans.[8]

Von der Hagen moved on to the University of Breslau. His successor in Berlin was Johann August Zeune, who also wanted the Nibelung saga to serve the national interest. Zeune wrote about his lectures, "For the past two hundred years, one piece after another of our holy German empire has been nibbled away by the wicked dragon, or rather, by the wicked lily [i. e., the emblem of the French]: Metz, Toul, Verdun. . . . Yet the mighty dragonslayer has risen and our holy

German soil is again pure and free from the foreign dragon. For that we are grateful and thank God."[9]　The connection to Fouqué's work is clear and underscores its significance.

Franz Grillparzer, the Austrian who despised Prussia, also had Fouqué's popular Nibelung saga in mind when he wrote ironically about a *"literarischem Landsturm,"* that is, "a popular literary militia," with whose help the Nibelung advocates sought to demonstrate that the German "nation had already been superior to all others in the distant Middle Ages" and now was taking control of its "inalienable rights."[10]

Fouqué had a close personal relationship with the Crown Prince, later King Frederick William IV (ruled 1840-1861), who thought highly of his friend's writings. But Frederick William III, his father, Prussian king since 1797, did not participate in the Nibelung vogue with quite as much enthusiasm. That indefatigable chronicler of his times, Karl August Varnhagen von Ense, once reported a converstion of the king with the General Director of the Royal Theater, Count Brühl, concerning a tragedy called *Der Nibelungen Hort* (*The Nibelung Treasure*) that had premiered on January 8, 1828, in the Berlin Schauspielhaus;[11] the author was the fashionable dramatist Ernst Raupach (1784-1852), at the time a resident of Prussia's capital city.[12] The king was not at all pleased with Hagen's deceitful murder of Siegfried. When Brühl noted that the murder had taken place upon the king's command, Frederick William III corrected him: "Just because the king commands something like that, it must not happen."[13] The king's judgment is a moral one and demonstrates the nature of Frederick Wiliam III's enlightened concept of governance based on law.

Critics, however, reacted differently. The reviewer for the *Haude und Spenersche Zeitung,* one of Berlin's most influential newspapers, wrote of Raupach's work:

> We see before us the life and actions of the Germans in that point in time of the great episode of world history that reshaped Europe, the tribal migrations. We see Attila and his powerful kingdom, the fame that the Germans share with him, not the fame of the destroyer of world order, but the irresistible power against a decayed order, thus the beginning of a new German culture [*Bildung*] . . .

The review goes on to describe the extraordinary popularity of that play.[14]

In contrast to his father, the Crown Prince responded enthusiastically to the Nibelung theme. This enthusiasm was shared by the members of his inner circle. Christian Carl Josias von Bunsen (1791-1860) is perhaps most important, because he had the greatest influence on the Crown Prince and later monarch. One of his many interests was the Nibelung saga. From 1818 to 1837 Bunsen was active in the Prussian mission to the Vatican, eventually becoming head of the mission himself. In that capacity he had directed the attention of the artistically inclined Crown Prince to the importance of early Christian and Byzantine art. In 1828 he served as the Crown Prince's *cicerone* during the latter's extended tour of Italy; and because of his extraordinary interests in contemporary art he has also developed close connections with the German artists' colony in Rome, which at that time included such important painters as Peter von Cornelius. Bunsen's mentor Barthold Georg Niebuhr, the famous historian and Prussian emissary to the Vatican from 1816 to 1823, was another influential devotee of the saga. Between 1812 and 1817 Peter von Cornelius created twenty-one drawings of the Nibelung saga, six of which were published in Berlin in 1817 and were dedicated to Niebuhr (Figure 1).[15] We can assume that the members of the royal house were familiar with these drawings.

With the drawings of Cornelius, artistic representations of the *Nibelungenlied* moved from the purely literary to the pictorial. In 1826 Karl Friedrich Schinkel arranged a series of *tableaux vivants* in the Hohenzollerns' Berlin palace which were repeated several times in the *Schauspielhaus*.[16] One tableau depicted "Siegfried's Leavetaking from Chrimhild, after a Drawing by Cornelius. . . Accompanied by a Medieval German Love Song."[17] According to a letter by Amalie von Helvig to Count Brühl of March 10, 1826, the backdrop of this scene depicted the Rhenish castle ruin of Stolzenfels, which had been presented to the crown prince in April 1823 by the town of Koblenz.[18] To be sure, the arrangement of these *tableaux vivants* shows that the *Nibelungenlied* was not being exploited here exclusively for political propaganda, but was only one topic among many others.

But the saga had become significant in yet another German residence, to which Prussia had close political and family ties: Munich. In 1825 the brother-in-law of the Prussian Crown Prince acceded to the Bavarian throne as King Ludwig I. Count August von Platen wrote an ode in honor of the new monarch:

Looking back you see flames, war and murder
Yet gently you carry the pure sword on your belt
And stand as that devout Dietrich
Above the corpses of the Nibelungen.[19]

In 1826 the new monarch ordered Julius Schnorr von Carolsfeld to decorate the ground floor of a new extension of the royal residence in Munich with paintings depicting scenes from the *Nibelungenlied*. Schnorr began the work in 1828 and in the following year sent a preliminary sketch to his friend Bunsen with the dedication "To my dear Bunsen as testimony of his activity in the fatherland."[20] In his work Schnorr von Carolsfeld connected the representation of Germanic-pagan heroes with Christian iconography. He portrayed the victorious Siegfried returning from the war against the Saxons and Danes, carrying a banner showing St. Michael, the dragonslayer. The viewer sees, experiences, and is strengthened by the parallel portrayals of the biblical archangel and the Germanic hero.[21]

When the Prussian Crown Prince visited his brother-in-law's palace in 1833, he saw the first complete Nibelung hall and was greatly impressed. The sculptor Christian Daniel Rauch, who accompanied the Crown Prince, wrote to the Munich architect Leopold von Klenze that Frederick William had "been deeply moved by everything. The royal palace, surpassing every expectation, impressed him both in detail and in its entirety."[22]

Schwerin, in Mecklenburg, was the second important royal residence connected to Prussia where Nibelung themes are present. Carl Georg Christian Schumacher (1797-1869) was court painter of the Grand Duke Frederick Francis of Mecklenburg-Schwerin (1756-1837), whose grandson Paul Frederick assumed the throne after his death. Paul Frederick had married Princess Alexandrine of Prussia, a sister of the Prussian Crown Prince, in 1822.[23] The painter Schumacher had himself stayed in Rome from 1821 to 1825, where he came into contact with the Nazarenes, a circle of Romantic painters. In 1823 he painted "Siegfried's Leavetaking from Krimhild," later presented to the castle of Ludwigslust in Mecklenburg-Schwerin.[24] The Nibelung theme appeared only once more in Schumacher's work, when he created a folio of four etchings, "Depictions of the *Nibelungenlied*," between 1827 and 1830.[25] These pieces were probably known at the Prussian court, since the close relationship of Princess Alexandrine's brothers to their sister is well documented; they often visited Ludwigslust.[26]

Frederick William IV of Prussia used the castle of Stolzenfels as his residence whenever he visited the recently acquired Rhine province. In 1846 he arranged for a bronze statue of Siegfried by Johann Hartung to be placed near the fountain in the palace's winter garden.[27] Moreover, Frederick William IV was the most active among the German monarchs in encouraging the completion of the Cologne Cathedral, starting in 1841, directly after his enthronement. Since the beginning of the movement for German liberation from Napoleon, the Cologne Cathedral had served as a symbol of national unity. Just as the *Nibelungenlied* had been compared to a Gothic cathedral since the beginning of the century, now the *Kölner Dom* and the Nibelung saga were frequently coupled. One of the first who did so was Heinrich Heine, writing in 1822:

> It is even true that the study of old German art and historical monuments is presently scorned. . . . May the time come soon when the Middle Ages will receive their due . . . when the glories of the Middle Ages are recognized from their organic sources and compared only with themselves, and the Song of the Nibelungs will be called a poetic cathedral and the cathedral a Song of the Nibelungs in stone.[28]

On the occasion of the laying of the cornerstone to mark resumption of construction of the cathedral on September 4, 1842, Ludwig Bauer published a drama called *Barbarossa* as a poetic tribute to the event.[29] This drama, with its "patriotic-political orientation" and dedication to the Prussian king, identified the Nibelungs, the completion of the cathedral, and the Emperor Frederick Barbarossa as symbols of German unity. Frederick William IV, here seen as a new Barbarossa, is called upon to work toward German unity. Bauer portrays the original Barbarossa as "the knightly father of the German people, as a strict champion of right and order . . . ; under the banner of his personality art flourishes."[30] Frederick William IV could easily be identified with these traits and the monarch could also be flattered by recognizing himself in them. In 1846 Frederick William IV was again connected with to the Nibelung theme. Moritz von Schwind showed the king his sketch of the programmatic painting "The Rhine." The king was "highly pleased," and Schwind himself judged that the monarch had been "quite noticeably delighted."[31]

In these years the court of Saxe-Weimar began to play an important role in the development of new responses to the *Nibelungenlied*. Prince Karl of Prussia (1801-1883), the third son of King Frederick William III and Queen Luise, had married Princess Marie's younger sister, Princess Augusta (Isenburg, Table 54). In 1847 the princesses' brother Karl Alexander, heir presumptive of the Grand Duchy of Saxe-Weimar, developed a plan to restore the Wartburg. The architect Hugo von Ritgen, who received the commision for the restoration, wrote that one aim of the project should be to make visible "the history of one of the noblest princely houses" in Germany.[32]

Moritz von Schwind was commisioned to paint the rooms. He noted in a letter of May 1852 that the "duke had admirably designated the *Nibelungenlied*" for the "*Sängerlaube*" in the "*Pallas*" (that is, the grand assembly hall) of the Wartburg, although a year later this plan was canceled (*Briefe*, 292). Nevertheless, thematic references to the German heroic epic were still to be included in the project. Hugo von Ritgen had planned scenes from the German heroic epic for the capitals of the columns in the duke's rooms in the Landgrafenhaus. These, he wrote,

> portray the reciprocal loyalty between nobles and vassals . . . . It was important to link up with the old German epic, whose essential element is German loyalty, because the greatness of the heroes and the greatness of their deeds is so decisively determined by the concept of loyalty, that it appears everywhere as the most important poetic motif. Loyalty appears most beautifully and purely, even if less thrillingly than in the *Nibelungenlied*, in the ancient song of King Wolfdietrich.[33]

The Grand Duke Karl Alexander agreed, but expressed skepticism about the whole venture, writing in a letter: "It's always a dangerous thing to appropriate the past as a plan for the future."[34]

The Nibelungs found a real home in Potsdam, the main residence of the Prussian royal house, in 1848. In this year Frederick William IV arranged for eighteen frescoes on the Nibelungs to be painted on the colonnades of the late eighteenth-century Marmorpalais (Figures 2-3). Although executed by the painters Karl Lompeck and Osowsky, they were designed by Berlin's best known painter of historical scenes, Karl Wilhelm Kolbe the Younger, who in turn worked under the close supervision of Ludwig Ferdinand Hesse, the royal architect, and the king himself.

The core of the Marmorpalais had been built by Carl von Gontard between 1787 and 1791; and in 1797 it had been expanded with the addition of two wings, probably under the direction of Carl Gotthard Langhans, neoclassicist creator of Berlin's famous Brandenburg Gate. Between 1843 and 1845 those wings were further modified by Ludwig Persius and Ludwig Fredinand Hesse, and to them the Nibelung frescoes were added shortly thereafter.[35] Kolbe's sketches for the Nibelung frescoes are strongly influenced by Fouqué's earlier Nibelung drama; as early as 1806 he had illustrated Fouqué's *Sigurd the Dragonslayer*. Indeed, to his contemporaries Kolbe was "the Romantic of the North in art, as Fouqué was in literature." Both the sketches and the frescoes themselves must have been completed in a hurry. The former could be viewed at the annual Berlin exhibition in June 1848; although the finished products were not listed in the exhibition catalog, they must have been finished shortly thereafter, since the art journal *Kunstblatt* mentioned completion at the end of the year.[36]

A description of the frescoes in 1850 asserted:

> We owe this magnificent series of paintings to the educated spirit of our art-loving monarch and to his unique vision; truly patriotic, it faithfully preserves everything good and beautiful from our Germanic history. And the poetry depicted here belongs to the noblest and most glorious examples that German tales and poetry created and completed more than six hundred years ago in their noble simplicity and beauty, in wonderful sensitivity and in true depth of feeling. True appreciation for art and nobility of spirit and taste are only appreciated among an educated populace when it can possess those treasures that are accessible to most; to this belong national poetry and music, everything that a people owns in art and architecture . . . . And it is essential that we do not lose ourselves—in the upheaval of the times—in superficial daily tasks and at the same time lose everything glorious and great that our forefathers had.[37]

The younger brother of the king and heir presumptive to the throne, William, Prince of Prussia, was also interested in the Nibelungs in those years. When his palace at Babelsberg, close to Potsdam, was extended in 1850, "six bronze figures from the Nibelung saga were on the mantle of the marble fireplace in the tea salon"; they are now presumed to be lost.[38] This new interior decoration was largely the initiative of the Princess Augusta. Although it is not entirely clear whether she was responsible for bringing the bronze figures to Babelsberg, she very likely was, given the importance of the Nibelung motif at her home court in Weimar.

Not only for Frederick William IV but for the entire Hohenzollern family the "reciprocal commitment to loyalty between ruler and people" was a fundamental principle of government.[39] Precisely this concept was reflected in official interpretations of the Nibelung saga around the year 1850:

> It is the loyalty of the German people that has created an imperishable monument in these songs. With constant faithfulness the king is dedicated to his people, with equally constant faithfulness the people are dedicated to their king. Mildness—benevolent, abundant generosity, as long as he has anything to give—represents the king's gratitude, gratitude that only ends at death. For our beloved king and master everything will be done; battles will be fought truly, blood shed willingly, and death encountered joyfully. More will be done for him than the simple act of dying; for him our own children will be sacrificed with a strong heart. . . . These traits, of which I have chosen only some of the most notable, are the essential life element of the German people.[40]

When Frederick William IV mounted the throne in 1840, he was seen as a ruler who could bring about national unity and reconstruct a German state. The famous poet Georg Herwegh, for example, composed a poem for the new monarch that contained the demand to govern Germany under one scepter:

> That helplessly moves apart,
> My people shall move toward you;
> Stand up and speak: "I am the shepherd,
> The only shepherd, the only trustee,
> And heart and head, they are together!". . .
> You know for what the German yearns . . .
> You can still see true hearts

That gladly go with you to death,
To death and victory in holy battle.
You are the star to which one looks,
The last sovereign whom one trusts.[41]

Frederick William IV himself had encouraged the plan to become
ruler of a united German people by supporting the completion of the
Cologne Cathedral, a project that symbolized the emergence of a
unified nation. During the revolutionary tumults in Berlin on March
19, 1848, Württemberg's representative to Berlin wrote, "The king,
who yesterday had ambitious plans to be the leader of Germany, has
now been humiliated more than any other German prince."[42] Almost
two years later, on March 14, 1850, the royal adjutant general Leopold
von Gerlach wrote in his diary, "The king wants to be the head of
Germany and is unable to clear the garbage from his own door."[43] The
revolutions of 1848 had thus brought apparent humiliation and defeat
to a monarch who had embarked on his reign with grandiose plans of
monarchical restoration and national reconstruction.

That he found the time, after the revolutionary violence of March
1848, to have one of his palaces decorated with scenes from the literary
monument of the Germans, confirms once again the seriousness with
which he supported the idea of a unified nation and wished to regard
himself as its spokesman.   And he would probably have liked to
become Emperor of the Germans, if they had been ready to accept his
conditions.[44] As it happened, he turned down the throne of a unified
but constitutional-parliamentary state when it was offered to him by
representatives of the doomed Frankfurt National Assembly in the
spring of 1849.

He found that his thoughts and fantasies about German unity were
most clearly reflected in the writings of Fouqué, which he had
"absolutely devoured" as a young man. The Potsdam frescoes for the
Marmorpalais strongly confirm historian Frank-Lothar Kroll's assertion
that "the fact that Frederick William untiringly worked toward a
political realization of these 'dreams' since he assumed power, clearly
gives the relationship between him and Fouqué a significance crucial for
the understanding of the politics of Prussia between 1840 and 1860, a
relationship that extends far beyond the scope of a marginal intellectual
curiosity."[45]

In 1849 Frederick William IV once more turned to the Nibelung
saga. He gave his younger brother William, who had just suppressed

a popular revolt in Baden, a bronze copy of the monument by August Kiss in honor of the Prussian soldiers who had died in that conflict. The original stands in the cemetery in Karlsruhe. The subject of the monument is "Saint Michael in battle with the dragon"; the huge monument stands, surrounded by pseudo-Gothic architecture, on the Voltaire Terrace on the park side of Babelsberg palace (Poensgen, 31-2).[46] We have already alluded to the connection between the iconography of St. Michael and representations of Siegfried's struggle with the dragon. The Babelsberg monument corresponds in all essential charcteristics to the depiction of the same topic by Julius Hübner, who had prepared a drawing to illustrate the Leipzig special edition of the *Nibelungenlied* in 1840; it was also used for a new edition of the work in 1841.[47]

Frederick William's last known connections with the Nibelung theme can be found in the Rhineland city of Düsseldorf. Wilhelm von Schadow, director of the renowned Düsseldorf Art Academy, arranged for a series of *tableaux vivants* to be mounted during the King's visit in 1852. Schadow intended to provide the monarch with a review of art history, ending with a representation of the last scene from Peter von Cornelius's Nibelung cycle, "Chriemhilde views Siegfried's body." The picture was accompanied by a long poem. Schadow's decision to present this tableau, based as it was on a sketch from the year 1817, suggests something about Frederick William's love for this genre. In the following year the monarch again visited Düsseldorf, and again a series of *tableaux vivants* included a Nibelung theme.[48] In neither of these cases, however, is there any concrete evidence that the portrayal of those themes was linked to nationalist or legitimist tendencies.

That tendency remained important during the reign of Frederick William's successor, his younger brother William I. Surprisingly, perhaps, we do not yet know enough about the history of the Hohenzollern dynasty to reach any definitive conclusions concerning its cultural policies and inclinations. In connection with the theme of this essay, however, it is interesting to note that a *Rhineland Album* presented to William I for his silver wedding anniversary contained a depiction by Peter von Cornelius of "Hagen Sinking the Nibelung Treasure."[49]

After the foundation of the unified Empire in 1871, it was decided to construct a new National Gallery in Berlin on the basis of Frederick William IV's original proposals. He had called for the construction of a museum in the form of a Roman temple; and, given his penchant for direct and intensive involvement in architectural projects, it is quite likely that he strongly influenced the later museum's pictorial program. The lunettes of the cupola, in the main gallery of the building, are decorated with frescoes that depict scenes from the Nibelung saga (Figures 4-5). National mythology is used here to decorate a building officially dedicated "To German Art." These frescoes may well support the thesis that Frederick William IV's response to the *Nibelungenlied* must be understood within the context of nineteenth-century notions of a revived German national state.

In 1897 the sculptor Rudolf Maison completed a monument to William I in Aachen. It represents a conscious attempt to link the old Prussian King and German Emperor, who had died in 1888, to the Nibelung saga. Its base depicts Siegfried after slaying the dragon; the Rhine maidens are offering him the Nibelung treasure, the possession of which will lead to limitless and never-ending power: in other words, the old Emperor is himself being equated with Siegfried.[50]

Occasionally, Bismarck himself was also compared to the old German hero. The base of Bismarck national monument in Berlin (Figure 6), which was completed by Reinhold Begas in 1901 and still stands in that city, includes a depiction of Siegfried forging his sword.[51] In short, as these examples suggest, responses to the Nibelung saga were now being used to historicize and legitimize political power, and for the glorification of the individuals associated with the new Imperial system.

The *hubris* evident in such late nineteenth-century depictions is clear; for only two decades later that new *Reich*, whose eternal existence had been equated with the Nibelung crown, had ceased to exist. Moreover, in that doomed Reich the humanism and the high culture which had characterized the Prussia of the "classical" period before 1850 no longer enjoyed a privileged place.

NOTES

1. *Der Nibelungen Liet: Ein Rittergedicht aus dem XIII. oder XIV. Jahrhundert zem ersten Male aus der Handschrift ganz abgedruckt durch Chr. H. Müller* (Berlin, 1782).

2. Letter of Frederick the Great to Müller, 22 February 1784, quoted in Friedrich Zarncke, *Das Nibelungenlied* (Leipzig, 1875), xxxi-xxxii. The original of this letter can be found in the Bibliothek Zürich.

3. Johannes von Müller, *Geschichte der schweizerischen Eidgenossenschaft* (Leipzig, 1786), 2.2:139.

4. August Wilhelm von Schlegel, *Vorlesungen über schöne Litteratur und Kunst* (Heidelberg, 1884).

5. Friedrich de la Motte Fouqué, *Der gehornte Siegfried. Dramatische Scene*, in *Friedrich Schlegel's Europa 1803*, 2:82ff.

6. Friedrich Baron de la Motte-Fouqué, *Der Held des Nordens. Heldenspiel in drei Teilen* (Berlin, 1810).

7. Friedrich Heinrich von der Hagen, *Bedeutung, Die Nibelungen: ihre Bedeutung für die Gegenwart und für immer* (Breslau, 1819), 196.

8. Letter of Friedrich von der Hagen to Tieck, 12 March 1813, in Otfrid Ehrismann, *Das Nibelungenlied in Deutschland: Studien zur Rezeption des Nibelungenlieds von der Mitte des 18. Jahrhunderts bis zum Ersten Weltkrieg* (Munich: Beck, 1975), 1:268n.

9. August Zeune, *Das Nibelungenlied. Die Urschrift nach den besten Lesarten neu bearbeitet* (Berlin, 1815), 111-12. The Peace of Westphalia in 1648 had awarded Metz, Toul, and Verdun to France.

10. Franz Grillparzer, "Zur Literaturgeschichte," *Studien zur Literatur*, ed. Fritz Stein (Vienna, 1922), 8.

11. See the report in the *Berlinische Nachrichten von Staats- und gelehrten Sachen*, 7 (9 January 1828): "Königliche Schauspiele. Mittwoch den 9. Im Schauspielhause: Zum Erstenmale: Der Nibelungen-Hort, Tragödie in 5 Augzügen, mit einem Vorspiele, von E. Raupach."

12. Karl Goedeke, *Grundriß zur Geschichte der deutschen Dichtung* (Dresden, 1905), 8:646ff.; Wilhelm Koch, *Deutsches Literatur-Lexicon* (Bern, 1956), 3:2166ff.

13. Karl August Varnhagen von Ense, *Blätter aus der preußischen Geschichte* (Leipzig, 1869), entry for 7 May 1828.

14. Review in *Berlinische Nachrichten* 33 (8 February 1828).

15. See the title page of Peter von Cornelius, *Aventiure von den Nibelungen* (Berlin, 1817).

16. See *Berlinische Nachrichten* 57 (8 March 1826): "Am Mittwoch, den 8. Im Schauspielhause. Lebende Bilder. Hierauf: Laßt die Todten ruhen. Lustspiel in 3 Abtheilungen von E. Raupach." The individual tableaux were organized around the following themes: "(1) Bekränzung Apollo's. (2) Joseph vor dem Pharao nach Raphael. (3) Die Auffindung des Mose, nach Raphael. (4) Verkauf der Liebesgötter. (5) Wandgemälde aus Herculanum. (6) Der Prinz von Geldern. (7) Raphael und seine Geliebte. (8) Siegfrieds Abschied von Chrimhilden. (9) Der Violinspieler. (10) Französische Rekruten (nach H. Vernet)."

17. *Berlinische Nachrichten* 62 (14 March 1826). Schinkel is named here only as the designer of the first tableau. The picture mentioned here is the fourth illustration in Cornelius's Nibelung cycle.

18. Henriette von Bissing, *Das Leben der Dichterin Amalie von Helvig geb. Freiin von Imhoff* (Berlin, 1889), 378-9: "Chriemhildens Gesicht muß einmal, wie es auch Cornelius gedacht, aufgegeben werden; sie muß Siegfried ansehen, sonst ist alle Wirkung verloren. . . . Wäre es noch möglich, so müßte freie unruhige

Ansicht mit dem Hintergrund von Cornelius' Bild vertauscht werden; die Ruine des Stolzenfels, der doch damals kaum Neubau war, stören, indem die Umrisse in die Linien der Hauptpersonen eindringen." For details on Stolzenfels, see Ursula Rathke, *Burgenromantik am Rhein. Studien zum Wiederaufbau von Rheinstein, Stolzenfels und Sooneck (1825-1860)* (Munich, 1979), 46ff.

19. *Morgenblatt für die gebildeten Stände* 296 (1825), 1182.

20. Friedrich Nippold, ed., *Christian Carl Josias von Bunsen. Aus seinen Briefen und nach der Erinnerung geschildert von seiner Wittwe. Deutsche Ausgabe* (Leipzig, 1868), 258.

21. See Hans Wühr, "Julius Schnorr von Carolsfeld: Die Nibelungenfresken," *Die Kunst im Deutschen Reich* 6 (1942), 96.

22. Quoted in Carl Theodor Heigel, *Ludwig I. König von Bayern* (Leipzig, 1862), 332. The frescoes survived World War II, despite considerable damage to the Munich *Residenz*; see Alexander von Reitzenstein and Herbert Brunner, *Reclams Kunstführer, Baudenkmäler*, Vol. 1, *Bayern* (Stuttgart, 1957), 413.

23. See Wilhelm Karl Prinz von Isenburg, *Europäische Stammtafeln. Stammtafeln zur europäischer Geschichte*, Vol. 1, *Die deutschen Staaten* (Marburg, 1957), Table 123.

24. Friedrich von Boetticher, *Malerwerke des 19. Jahrhunderts. Beitrag zur Kunstgeschichte* (Dresden, 1901), 2:681-82; Andreas Andresen, *Die deutschen Maler-Radirer des neunzehnten Jahrhunderts nach ihren Leben und Werken* (Leipzig, 1867), 2:123-4.

25. Andresen, 127-8: "Nr. 2: Der Traum der Chriemhild; Nr. 3: Der Wettsprung mit Brunhilde; Nr. 4: Siegfried kämpft mit Alberich; Nr. 5: Hagen und die Meerfrauen." See also *Das Nibelungenlied. In den Augen der Künstler vom Mittelalter bis zur Gegenwart*, Staatliche Bibliothek Passau exhibition catalog (1986), 63-4.

26. Crown Prince Frederick William (IV) and his younger brother Karl were often guests at Ludwigslust; see the letters of Prince Karl in the Geheimes Staatsarchiv Preußischer Kulturbesitz, Berlin, Brandenburg-Preußisches Hausarchiv Rep. 59 I.

27. *Kunstblatt* 83 (1845), 348; Robert Dohme, *Beschreibung der Burg Stolzenfels* (Berlin, 1850), 14.

28. Heinrich Heine, "Über Polen (Reisebilder I)," *Sämtliche Werke in sieben Bände* (Stuttgart, n. d.), 3:197.

29. Ludwig Bauer, *Barbarossa. Dichtergabe zum Kölner Neubau* (Stuttgart and Tübingen, 1842); and reviews in *Literaturblatt zum Morgenblatt* 105 and *Deutsche Jahrbücher für Wissenschaft und Kunst* 237/239.

30. Albert Depiny, *Ludwig Bauer—Ein Dichterbild aus Schwaben* (Trieste, 1911), 55, 57.

31. Rauch to Ernst Rietschel, 26 December 1846, in Karl Eggers, ed., *Briefwechsel zwischen Rauch und Rietschel* (Berlin, 1891), 2:259; Schwind to Ludwig Schaller, 5 November 1846, in Otto Stößl, ed., *Die Briefe Moritz von Schwinds* (Leipzig, 1924), 204.

32. Max Baumgärtel, *Die Wartburg. Ein Denkmal deutscher Geschichte und Kunst. Dem Deutschen Volke gewidmet von Großherzog Carl Alexander von Sachsen* (Berlin, 1907), 304.

33. Hugo von Ritgen, *Der Führer auf der Wartburg. Ein Wegweiser für Fremde* (Leipzig, 1860), 163; see also Baumgärtel, 424.

34. Conrad Höfer, *Der Sängerkrieg auf der Wartburg. Eine Studie zur Geschichte und Deutung des Schwindschen Bildes* (Jena, 1942), 92.

35. *Die Bau- und Kunstdenkmale in der DDR. Bezirk Potsdam* (Berlin [East], 1978), 376-7.

36. *Kunstblatt* 44 (1848): 175. See also the remarks in the *Kunstblatt* 63 (1848), 252: "Zu den sehenswerthesten, in diesem Jahre hier vollendeten Kunstwerken gehören die Fresken an den Wandräumen zwischen und über den Thüren und Fenstern an den erst neuerlich ausgebauten, nach der Gartenseite des Königl. Marmorpalais hin gelegenen Flügelgebäude. Diese Wandegemälde bilden einen Cyclus von Scenen aus dem Nibelungenliede . . . ."

37. Wilhelm Riehl, *Die Freskobilder aus dem Nibelungenliede am Marmorpalais im Neuen Garten bei Potsdam* (Potsdam, 1850), 3-4.

38. Georg Poesgen, *Schloß Babelsberg* (Berlin, 1929), 40.

39. Leopold von Ranke, *Aus dem Briefwechsel Friedrich Wilhelms IV. mit Bunsen* (Leipzig, 1873), 128.

40. August Friedrich Christian Vilmar, *Geschichte der deutschen Nationalliteratur*, 3rd. ed. (Marburg and Leipzig, 1848), 76, 78.

41. Georg Herwegh, *Gedichte eines Lebendigen. Mit einer Dedikation an den Verstorbenen* (Zurich and Winterthur, 1843), 91-2.

42. Quoted in Veit Valentin, *Geschichte der deutschen Revolution von 1848-49* (Leipzig, 1930), 1:447.

43. Quoted in Hans-Christof Kraus, "Das preußische Königtum und Friedrich Wilhelm IV. aus der Sicht Ernst Ludwig von Gerlachs," in *Friedrich Wilhelm IV. in seiner Zeit. Beiträge eines Colloquiums*, ed. Otto Büsch (Berlin, 1987), 75.

44. See Erich Brandenburg, *Die Reichsgründung* (Leipzig, 1922), 1:209-10.

45. Frank-Lothar Kroll, "Politische Romantik und romantische Politik bei Friedrich Wilhelm IV," in Büsch, 97, 98.

46. See also Carl Graeb, *Album von Schloß Babelsberg* (Berlin, 1872), title vignette.

47. *Der Nibelungen Lied. Abdruck nach einer Handschrift des Freiherrn Joseph von Laßberg* (Leipzig, 1841).

48. Wilhelm von Schadow, *Der moderne Vasari. Erinnerungen aus dem Künstlerleben* (Berlin, 1854), 64, 199, 227.

49. Hermann Riegel, *Cornelius—der Meister der deutschen Malerei*, 2nd ed. (Hanover, 1870), 42; Ernst Förster, *Peter von Cornelius—Ein Gedenkbuch aus seinem Leben und Wirken* (Berlin, 1874), 2:382.

50. See *Deutsche Kunst und Dekoration* (1898), 1:9ff.

51. *Reclams Kunstführer Deutschland*, Vol. 7, *Berlin* (Stuttgart, 1977), 330.

Medievalism in German Romantic Art: Reading the Political Text of the Gothic Style

Hilary Braysmith

From the Renaissance well into the nineteenth century, Europeans viewed the Middle Ages as a German phenomenon. In fact, Gothic architecture was not merely ascribed to the Germans, it was blamed on them.[1] In general parlance, when one referred to the Gothic, the terms "medieval," "barbarian," and "German" were all synonymous.[2] However, in "Von Deutscher Baukunst" (1772-3), Johan Wolfgang von Goethe enthusiastically affirmed that the Gothic was a German achievement, setting up that association which combined Gothic architecture and German nationalism and finding in the German past a patriotic and aesthetic ideal.[3] Thus, by the early nineteenth century, the negative view of the Gothic had been converted to a positive one. Gothic as national humiliation was replaced by Gothic as national triumph.

A very broad common denominator for the different camps of German Romanticism was that all of them saw the Gothic style in national and spiritual terms. It was seen as the sublime Christian manifestation with its transcendental vertical thrust and soaring vaults (Honour, 156-8). Thus, while facing the Napoleonic threat, any German artist citing the Gothic style meant it to symbolize a reanimation not only of that Christian spirit and insight peculiar to the medieval German people but also a resurrection of the culture and glory of the German nation. In order for Germans to repeat the glories of their past, they were enjoined to imitate its national and spiritual or Christian virtues. After Napoleon's defeat in 1815, Romantic artists continued to utilize the Gothic style to advocate a recommitment to the national, medieval *Weltanschauung*. Where these Romantics differed was in their definition of this *Weltanschauung* and their explanations as to how this medieval Christian civilization was achieved. The German Romantics can be divided into two major groups—those who viewed the Middle Ages as a princely accomplishment (the reactionaries) and those who saw it as the result of the collective effort of the German people (the liberals). For both groups, however, the Gothic served their purposes admirably, as an examination of selected paintings of the period will show.

Both liberals and reactionaries employed the Gothic style to advocate a revitalizing of the contemporary Christian state and its citizenry politically as well as religiously. Those in favor of reactionary policies feudalized the Gothic style and its attendant culture, that is, they co-opted it for absolutist purposes of propaganda. This involved placing the Gothic style within a medieval context or tradition presented as the Golden Age of German history. All the prosperity, social harmony, religious devotion, and cultural achievement projected onto the medieval period were seen as resulting from feudal political and social structure. Feudalizing eliminated all grass roots and populist movements and ideas from participating in collective cultural accomplishments, emphasizing that these accomplishments were princely in origin, gifts from benevolent rulers to their subjects.

The reactionaries did not vary their tactics or imagery in the Napoleonic or the Restoration periods, though their emphases were sometimes different. The monarch's Christian virtues and fulfillment of feudal obligations to defend the poor or lower social classes are portrayed by Carl Russ in the painting *Rudolph von Habsburg Reprimands the Watch for Denying the Entry of the Poor* (*Rudolph von Habsburg verweist der Wache die Verweigerung des Zutritts der Armen*, 1811 [Figure 1]). The contemporary application is obvious: as the king defends the poor, so will he defend all his downtrodden subjects from the Napoleonic threat. By dating the activity in the era of supreme national cultural achievement—the Middle Ages—and placing the figures in a Gothic architectural setting, Russ emphasized the inherent Germanness and Christianity of feudalism.

Ludwig Kohl's *Gothic Hall with Knights of the Holy Feme* (*Gotischer Saal mit Rittern der Heiligen Feme*, 1812 [Figure 2]) strengthens the viewers' trust in the military abilities of the contemporary nobility by reminding them of the traditions of German Christian knighthood. The work also reawakens confidence in the feudal system of governance and justice. The *Feme* was a system of jurisprudence operated by nobles. Setting the image of feudal justice within Gothic architecture not only implies Church sanction, it transforms feudal justice into a religious activity because of the Gothic's association as the emphatically Christian style. The viewer is again reminded that the German Golden Age is founded on the feudal system, which is not only a divinely established order, but, just as importantly, typically German. The Germanness of the Middle Ages and its feudal system are here reaffirmed so as to eliminate any popular support for the constitutional safeguards or democratic bureaucracies often accompanying Napoleon's invasions.

In Restoration paintings by reactionaries, Gothic architecture remained the setting for royal medieval events which continued to convey a positive statement of royal authority and, by implication, the establishment of a *Pax Europa*. Josef Wintergerst, in *The Reconciliation of Ludwig of Bavaria with Frederick the Fair in 1325* (*Die Versöhnung Ludwigs des Bayern mit Friedrich dem Schönen, 1325*, 1816 [Figure 3]), depicts the harmonious reconciliation of two absolute Christian monarchs. Wintergerst renders visible the benefits of peaceful foreign policy for the subjects of both kings, demonstrating confidence in feudal monarchical harmony and brotherhood, implying that the current *Pax Europa* is also founded on feudal royal authority. The reconciliation here is of European kingdoms, rather than republics, in the post-Napoleon era. The Restoration period, then, means the restoration of peace through absolute monarchy.[4]

This is confirmed in Heinrich Olivier's painting *The Holy Alliance* (*Die Heilige Allianz*, 1815 [Figure 4]) in which the artist honors the "sacred agreement" of the three reactionary rulers, King Frederick William III of Prussia, Czar Alexander I of Russia, and Emperor Francis I of Austria, by depicting them as medieval knights inside a Gothic church. In this work, the Gothic style and medieval culture are again associated with strong, absolutist, Christian monarchism which forms the foundation for the *Pax Europa*.

Olivier's painting also reflects the contemporary royal point of view regarding the relationship of church and state. The question of who should be the final head of the church, the royal or ecclesiastical government, which had been settled in Protestant Germany, was raised again by King Fredrick William III of Prussia in a strikingly insensitive manner. In 1819 the king illegally forced the Lutheran and Reformed churches into one united Protestant church known as the Church of the Union. The creation of the Union in 1819 was largely due to the personal preferences of the Prussian king: Frederick William III was primarily interested in a uniform rite and display of religious objects rather than in dogma and theology, and he was similarly not interested in preserving the legal constitution of either church. The king was persuaded to create a Commission to look into these matters, but it was empowered only to make recommendations.[5] The Commission concluded that changes should not be introduced through royal fiat, but arrived at through the Presbyterian or synodal system, as was customary.

In 1822, and to everyone's surprise, the king arbitrarily ordered his own version of the liturgy to be used in all churches despite the fact that the synods had not yet met to discuss the matter. Many of the king's advisors had warned him against introducing this new liturgy before a legal one could be established by the synods, but the king refused to retract his order. Furthermore, the king required all ministers to swear to uphold the new liturgy as a part of their ordination oath and declared himself as the supreme Bishop of the Church. While Reformed ministers protested the introduction of religious symbols on the altar and Lutherans opposed the idea of an established liturgy because each congregation was entitled to decide this matter for itself, members of both churches agreed that the main point of contention was the legal question of the Church of the Union's creation and establishment (Foerster, 2:59, 63-4; 1:208; 2:80). Thus, by depicting the rulers without attendant clergy, Olivier effectively fused the political and religious, indicating the kings to be heads of church as well as state.

Caspar David Friedrich, representing liberal German thought, asserted the Gothic as a democratic style in such works a *Hutten's Tomb* (*Huttens Grab*, 1823 [Figure 5]). A "democratic style," in contrast to a feudalizing style, meant one associated with grass roots movements and achievements such as the conversion of his home state, Pomerania, to Lutheranism and the establishment of a democratic church constitution there. For Friedrich, the Gothic style and civilization resulted from populist efforts and participation. They derived from the German people. In *Hutten's Tomb*, Friedrich undermines attempts by the Prussian royal house to claim the Middle Ages as a monarchical and feudal achievement. He is also countering the royal attack on the traditional democratic functioning of German Protestantism. The iconography of *Hutten's Tomb* and Friedrich's definition of an ideal church combine to debunk the political and religious policies of the Prussian royal house.

1823 was the three-hundredth anniversary of Ulrich von Hutten's death, and Friedrich painted *Hutten's Tomb* as his own commemoration. The life of Hutten (1488-1523), a German patriot who died in exile, was seen by liberals as a historical parallel to the situation confronting them during the early Restoration period. Hutten was considered a champion of German freedom in general, and of political, individual, and social rights. He also represented German unity, for which he had fought.[6] In response to the Carlsbad Decrees of 1819, which brought an end to the hopes of a united Germany and eliminated political and intellectual freedom, liberal intellectuals, artists, and poets called on the German people to imitate the deeds of Hutten. Adolf Wagner (1774-1835) had written a poem in 1802 entitled "Hutten's Admonition," in which he described a pilgrimage to Hutten's grave where he extolled the virtues of Hutten and ended with the promise to imitate him by fighting for freedom. Ernst Münch, in his introduction to the complete works of Hutten (1821), expressed similar sentiments (Krueger, 45-9).

In Friedrich's painting, we see a figure bending over the coffin of Hutten. On the coffin are the inscriptions "Jahn 1813," "Arndt 1813," "Stein 1813," and "Görres 1821." These inscriptions indicate that Friedrich was commemorating not only Hutten but his intellectual descendants, the populist reformers of his own day. Friedrich Ludwig Jahn and Ernst Moritz Arndt were critics of Restoration politics, and Freiherr Heinrich Friedrich Karl von Stein had been a great reformer before the war. In 1821, as a result of Prussian reactionism, Joseph Görres, like Hutten before him, fled to exile in Switzerland. Moreover, the figure bending over the coffin paying his respects to Hutten can be identified by his costume as a *Demagoge*. The "demagogues" were also the heirs of Hutten. Dissatisfied with Restoration policies, they opposed prevalent reactionary politics and hoped for a more liberal future. They were seen by most German rulers as subversive and, after the Carlsbad Decrees of 1819, persecuted. They wore the so-called old German costume, which included long hair, a German coat, usually black, a weapon, and a beret as a sign of their disaffection.[7] This costume was outlawed at the Dresden Academy in 1819 where Friedrich was teaching.[8] These religious patriots saw themselves as prophets and saints, helping to implement Christ's redemption of the state.[9] Hutten's sarcophagus, replacing the altar, is the focus of the anonymous demagogue's devotion, underscoring the fusion of religious and political concepts of redemption and freedom.

The ideal state, then, is democratic, founded on the collective deeds and ideas of the people or grass roots movements such as that of the "demagogues." On one level, therefore, this painting forms a declaration of liberal politics. But, as noted above, the blending of political and religious realms was typical of early nineteenth-century German practice. In fact the Germans saw the defeat of Napoleon as God's judgment, and the Wars of Liberation were viewed as a religious movement. Even the language of preaching changed, giving political and national meaning to religious and biblical explications for beliefs such as redemption, rebirth and resurrection.[10] In this painting, accordingly, Friedrich also depicts his ideal church, which also is democratic. Friedrich viewed the Church Union as a royal undermining of the constitution because, in terms of the Pomeranian church constitution, any changes in liturgy by princely edict were illegal. Since 1534, all church laws, liturgy, ritual, and regulations were to be approved by the Diet and their introduction had to be administered by the duke. Thus, all change moved from Diet to prince, and not the reverse.[11]

Not only was king Frederick William III's creation of the Church of the Union unconstitutional, it subverted the spirit and tradition of the Protestant Reformation. Freedom and Protestantism were strongly allied in the popular mind. Karl Villers, in his *Versuch über den Geist und den Einfluß der Reformation Luthers* (1805), affirmed this political and religious alliance when he wrote that Protestantism, and especially Lutheranism, was synonymous with freedom in Germany. Furthermore, he stated that the Reformation was progressive and a people's movement, unlike Catholicism which was opposed to reform and princely: "Truly, it has long been noted that the Reformation moved more from below to above rather than the reverse."[12] Gottlieb Mohnike, another historian, writing in 1823, stressed the political and democratic aspects of grass roots Lutheranism. Lutheranism was a political revolution because the citizens fought for the new teachings against the wishes of political authority. He added that several historians had made this point (2).

Thus, liberal politics and a progressive theology were inseparable and the Reformation was a democratic grass roots movement (Heyden, *Greifswalds*, 88).[13] Furthermore, this progressive, Protestant tradition was founded on a system of synods through which the people made known their collective will to the prince, who then saw that it was executed. In other words, the Protestant church had princely defenders, but not princely heads. In fact, there was no absolute head of the church. This was the message of the headless statue of Ecclesia which adhered to and emerged out of the walls of the church in *Hutten's Tomb*.[14] At the core of the church—its center—is the freedom fighter, the "demagogue" who perpetuates the tradition of religious democracy.

In *Hutten's Tomb*, Friedrich depicts the "demagogue" making his pilgrimage to the relics of the fatherland's hero whose remains are enshrined in what Friedrich understands to be the ideal Christian church rather than a ruin. Many Northern Germans, including Friedrich, believed that nature was the language of God and that art, or human language, should merge with nature rather than remain distinct from it. They even believed in the idea of celebrating the sacraments, including Communion, in nature.[15] Here, Friedrich portrays his ideal church as the harmonious synthesis of nature (moss, foliage, sky) and art, depicting the celebration of a politico-religious Eucharist before the remains of the martyred Hutten. By using a Gothic church to enshrine the relics of Hutten and the motif of Gothic arches to decorate the coffin, and by placing a "demagogue" at the "altar," Friedrich opposed the feudalization of the Gothic.

In German art of the nineteenth century, then, the citing of the Gothic style could represent quite variant points of view. It certainly referred to the Christian vision of transcendent spirituality ascribed to the Middle Ages: and because of its ethnic origins it certainly symbolized German national achievement. But Germans themselves did not agree on the derivation of their collective triumph. The reactionaries maintained that the Gothic era naturally resulted from the feudal system as a manifestation of aesthetic, cultural, and spiritual *noblesse oblige*. The liberals, on the other hand, rejected the notion of the Gothic as a princely achievement, asserting that their national and spiritual Golden Age arose out of the grass roots urges and democratic cooperation of the German people.

NOTES

The research for this article was made possible in part by a Fulbright fellowship and a grant from the Germanistic Society of American Scholarship.

1. Heinrich Lützeler, "Die Deutung der Gotik bei den Romantikern," *Walraf-Richartz Jahrbuch* 2 (1925), 16; W. D. Robson-Scott, *The Literary Background of the Gothic Revival in Germany* (Oxford: Oxford University Press, 1965), 4. The notion of the Gothic as German can be traced to an anonymous Life of Brunelleschi attributed to Manetti (c. 1450-80, in manuscript form), in which the the author included a succinct history of the architecture of Greece and Rome and its destruction at the hands of the Vandals and Goths. The work is the first in which the Germans were seen as the creators of the Gothic style, a view repeated in many subsequent writings. In 1727, for example, the German origins of the Gothic were again substantiated by Johann Ulrich König in his "Treatise on Good Taste" (Robson-Scott, 11).

2. Hugh Honour, *Romanticism* (New York: Harper and Row, 1979), 4.

3. Erika Platte, *C. D. Friedrichs Jahreszeiten* (Stuttgart: Philipp Reclam, 1961), 84.

4. In the nineteenth century, neo-Gothic architectural style could also be associated with feudal monarchism. For example, a neo-Gothic monument, the *Kreuzbergdenkmal* (1818-1821), by the Prussian court architect Karl Friedrich Schinkel, was commissioned and erected at the command of Frederick William III. In fact, the king had three similar neo-Gothic monuments erected. Originally, the Kreuzberg memorial was to be a fullblown Gothic cathedral, but the project was canceled because it was too expensive to execute (Helmut Börsch-Supan and K. W. Jähnig, *Karl Friedrich Schinkel: Architektur Malerei Kunstgewerbe*. Orangerie des Schlosses Charlottenburg 13 March-13 September 1981 [Berlin: Nicolaische Verlagsbuchhandlung, 1981], 142-3). The *Kreuzbergdenkmal* glorifies monarchy and the principle of monarchical authority (Thomas Nipperdey, "Nationalidee und Nationaldenkmal in Deutschland," *Historische Zeitschrift* 206 [1968], 541).

The Prussian crown prince Frederick William was also quite taken with the Gothic style, even more so than his father. As a child and young man, he was more attracted to art than to politics and was especially taken with the Gothic or "Medieval German" style (Ludwig Dehio, *Friedrich Wilhelm IV. von Preußen: Ein Baukünstler der Romantik* [Munich-Berlin: Deutsche Kunstverlag, 1961], 9-10, 16-17). The extent of his endeavors along these lines was remarkable. In 1815, after visiting several medieval castles, the crown prince was so impressed that he planned to build a Gothic castle to house the new Order of St. George he was eager to found. In fact, both the crown prince and Schinkel executed drawings for the project. In 1823, the crown prince's devotion to the Gothic caused him to interfere with the renovation of the Werdersche Kirche in Berlin. He rejected the classicizing plans and requested Schinkel to build a Gothic church (Börsch-Supan,

135, 163). The other royal princes, William and Albert, also inclined to the Gothic style (Dehio, 90).

5. Erich Foerster, *Die Entstehung der Preussischen Landes Kirche* (Tübingen: Mohr, 1905-7), 1:200-6.

6. Karl Eberhard Krueger, "The Image of Hutten in German Fictional Literature," Diss. Michigan State University 1980, 44-5; Gottl. Christ. Friedr. von Mohnike, *Ulrich Huttens Jugendleben nebst Geschichte und Beschreibung der Urschrift der Klagen als Einleitung zu der Ausgabe und Übersetzung derselben* (Greifswald, 1816), Volume 1.

7. Peter Märker, "Geschichte als Natur: Untersuchungen zur Entwicklungvorstellungen bei Kaspar David Friedrich," Diss. University of Kiel 1979, 28, 37.

8. Tina Grütter, *Die Bedeutung des Gesteins bei Caspar David Friedrich* (Berlin: Reimer, 1986), 38.

9. Karl Kupisch, *Kirchengeschichte V. 1815-1945* (Stuttgart: Kohlhammer, 1975), 9. For example, the terms "patriotic faith," "patriotic reverence," "the proselytes of a political faith," "the immortality of saints and martyrs," "political relics," and "German patriotic Passion" began to be coined (Gerhard Kaiser, *Pietismus und Patriotismus im literarischen Deutschland* [Frankfurt a. M.: Athenäum, 1973], 42).

10. It is interesting that at the same time Hutten was "canonized" Luther also became a national political hero. "At the Wartburg festival of the *Burschenschaften* [student fraternities] which took place on October 18th and 19th, 1817, the synthesis of the religious and the patriotic was blatant because the festival was held in remembrance of both the Reformation and the Battle of Leipzig, and became at the same time a 'festival of the rebirth of freedom of thought' and a 'festival of the liberation of the Fatherland.' The reformer Luther became a German national hero. On the commemorative medals appeared the Wartburg fortress accompanied by the words with which Luther's hymn of comfort begins 'A mighty fortress is our God'" (*Münzen und Medaillen zur Reformation* [Hanover Kestner-Museum: Schlüter-Margildis, 1983], 128, translation mine).

11. Hellmut Heyden, *Die Kirchen Greifswalde und ihre Geschichte* ([East] Berlin: Evangelische Verlagsanstalt, 1966), 2:27.

12. T. G. P. Möller, "Vermischte Nachrichten," *Neue Critische Nachrichten* 40 (February 1805) and review of *Versuch über den Geist und den Einfluß der Reformation Luthers* by Karl Villers, *Neue Critische Nachrichten* 267 (August 1805).

13. See also Heyden's *Kirchengeschichte Pommerns*, 2nd ed. (Cologne-Braunsfeld: Müller, 1957), 1:212, 225.

14. On the whole, Friedrich scholars have accepted Gerhard Eimer's claim (*Zur Dialektik des Glaubens bei Caspar David Friedrich* [Darmstadt: Copy Shop, 1982]) that this is statue of Fides (179). Eimer maintains that Fides is a Protestant symbol, not Catholic, implying that Ecclesia is somehow a Catholic symbol (181) and ignoring medieval examples of the depiction of Ecclesia as a woman with a cross (see "Ecclesia," *Lexikon der christlichen Ikonographie* [1968]). He further overlooked the fact that in the seventeenth and eighteenth centuries the

personifications of Church and Faith were sometimes fused (see "Die Darstellung der Kirche," *Ikonographie der christlichen Kunst* [1976]). However, in coin imagery, the woman with the cross is almost always identified as Ecclesia and the woman holding the cross was a featured symbol in Reformation commemorative coins and specifically referred to the *Evangelische Kirche* or "Protestant" church. Examples of a woman with a cross identified as the Protestant church include the silver medals struck in Amsterdam and at Brandenburg-Ansbach in 1730 and the ducat struck in Lübeck the same year. All are reproduced in the Kestner-Museum catalog.

In 1818, Heinrich Gottlieb Kreussler wrote the text to the illustrations of several Reformation commemorative coins in *Martin Luthers Andenken in Muenzen nebst Lebensbeschreibungen merkwuerdiger Zeitgenossen desselben*. For example, the coin struck by the city of Heilbrunn in 1717, showing the woman with the cross, is identified with the Protestant church (56). Especially significant for *Hutten's Tomb*, Kreussler reproduces a coin struck by the Electorate of Brandenburg in 1717 in which the woman holding the cross is specifically identified as the Lutheran church of Brandenburg (33). Two of the earliest works Friedrich ever did are tiny coin-like etchings, *Landschaft mit dürrem Baum in Rund* (c. 1794) and *Zwei kahle Bäume im Rund* (c. 1794), which I think reveal that Friedrich was interested in coins and in adapting coin imagery in his work. Both are reproduced approximately full size in Börsch-Supan and Jähnig.

Another argument for the identification of the statue in *Hutten's Tomb* with Ecclesia is that the interpretation of a headless church fits into Friedrich's depiction of an ideal church, whereas the negative image of a headless Fides would not. Unlike Fides, the headless Ecclesia also functions as a symbol of democracy and corresponds to the other democratic symbols of the "demagogue" and the Gothic style. During the Catholic Counter-Reformation the woman with the cross stood for the Catholic churches, as in Claude Mellan's depiction (reproduced in the Hamburger Kunsthalle publication *Luther und die Folgen für die Kunst* [Munich: Prestel Verlag, 1983]). The headless Ecclesia as the ideal Protestant church—a church already historically associated with democracy—serves as an obvious contrast visually and essentially to the Catholic church.

15. Werner Sumowski, *Caspar David Friedrich—Studien* (Wiesbaden: Steiner, 1970), 12.

16. Klaus Lankheit, "Caspar David Friedrich und der Neuprotestantismus," *Deutsche Vierteljahrschrift für Literaturwissenschaft und Geistesgeschichte* 24 (1950), 447.

Nazi Medievalist Architecture and the Politics of Memory

Lisbet Koerner

While the writings of Germanic and Nazi ideologues have been analyzed in detail,[1] their visual work has only begun to be discussed. This essay looks at one such body of art objects, Nazi medievalist architecture.[2] First, it examines the architectural plans of the Weimar Republic's extreme right and their implementation in the Third Reich. Second, it discusses an important Nazi medievalist project: Wilhelm Kreis's plans, commissioned by Adolf Hitler in 1942, for memorial castles (*Totenburgen*) to German soldiers fallen in the Second World War. Modeled on the aging architect's Wilhelmine "Bismarck-Towers" (*Bismarck-Säulen*), the never-built Nazi memorials were designed in a simplified Romanesque. Kreis's *Totenburgen* demonstrate that as opposed to the Weimar extreme right, the Nazi elite did not consider medievalism a political program. It was, rather, a general idiom of reverence, a diffused nostalgia. Third, the essay concludes that today, as Germans return again to their past, one of postwar Germany's most successful artists, Anselm Kiefer, re-establishes this nostalgia.

In the Weimar Republic (1919-33), Germanic ideologues drafted a comprehensive medievalist program. It involved returning to Romanesque, Gothic, Teutonic, and vernacular styles; reviving craftsmanship in building; constructing community buildings; and dissolving cities in favor of rural settlements. Founded on a supposed need to "preserve the German race," this program was set out in tracts such as Paul Schultze-Naumburg's *Art and Race* (1928) and *Art from Blood and Soil* (1934), Alexander von Senger's *Crisis of Architecture* (1928) and *Moscow's Firetorch* (1931), Hans F. K. Günther's *Race and Style* (1926) and *Citification* (1934), and, in a milder vein, Wilhelm Kreis's *On the Relations between Culture, Civilization and Art* (1927).[3]

Its organizational outlets included the Nazi cultural organization *Kampfbund für deutsche Kultur* (KfdK);[4] *Bloch*, a professional architectural society;[5] far-right cultural leagues (originating in turn-of-the-century environmental and antiquarian groups) such as the *Bartelsbund, Deutschvölkische Schutz- und Trutzbund, Heimatbund*, and *Deutschbund*; and extreme right-wing political parties such as the *Deutschnationale Volkspartei* and the *Nationalsozialisten* (Nazis). Of course, not all medievalist architects belonged to the "folk movement" (*völkische Bewegung*), as Weimar's organizationally splintered far-right cultural alliance styled itself.[6] Nor did all politically reactionary architects build in medievalist styles.[7] Yet on the whole the Weimar extreme right subscribed to a unified architectural program, combining anti-Semitism, Caesarism, Green environmental sentiments, and an idealization of the German Middle Ages.

This program was anchored in German medievalists' fervent admiration of the medieval cathedral. In their view, the cathedral was a true community building (*Gemeinschaftsgebäude*), that had emerged collectively, intuitively, and spontaneously, and reflected the all-embracing faith of a premodern society. Like the Greek temple, the medieval cathedral to them at once conferred and expressed unity. Elaborating on the Nazi commonplace of the kinship between Greece in classical antiquity and the German lands in the high Middle Ages, Martin Heidegger explained, "Only from and in this expanse [of the cathedral and the temple] does the nation return to itself for the fulfillment of its vocation."[8] German medievalists regarded such a "fulfillment" as both peculiarly German and peculiarly medieval. Hence they frequently invoked "the Germanic Middle Ages" (*das germanische Mittelalter*). They especially treasured public buildings of the early Middle Ages, such as Theodoric's grave in Ravenna (A. D. 526), Charlemagne's chapel at Aachen (790-804), and the Romanesque cathedrals built in the time of Henry I (876?-936). But they also regarded France's Gothic cathedrals, for example Saint-Denis (finished 1140) and Chartres (1194-1506), as "an expression of the German character"[9] and models for "the German style of the twentieth century."[10] The German extreme right thus idealized medieval architecture over "Jesuit" Baroque, Rococo, and nineteenth-century historicism. Some even doubted Greece. Schultze-Naumburg, for example, dismissed the Doric revival as a "theory of art, drawn up by intellectuals" (quoted in Taylor, 109-10). They considered the medieval period *itself* as German, and indeed as the *only* truly German period.

If one respected architect, Theodor Fischer, had once rejected Gothic as "magnificent, but French" (quoted in Taylor, 94), did not the very term belie this?[11] As for Romanesque, wasn't a more correct term simply "German"?[12]

The German extreme right wing vehemently opposed Weimar functionalism as "clinical," "fit only for the robot,"[13] and dominated by "the department stores of a couple of Jews."[14] They vilified the 1927 Stuttgart Weissenhof exhibition, and slyly renamed it "little Jerusalem."[15] They also abhorred Walter Gropius's 1926 Bauhaus (Dessau) school of architecture and art. (Its motto, coined by Láslo Moholy-Nagy, was "machine, technology, socialism.")[16] The Nazi daily *Völkischer Beobachter* summarized the antifunctionalist campaign on 25 January 1933: "The new man is precisely no man, no he is an 'animal geometrique' he needs no apartment, no home but a 'living machine'! . . . and so 'settlements' arise, housing areas of wretched uniformity, in which everything, down to the last detail, is standardized."[17] Such articles further embittered small burghers living in city districts where, to cite Christopher Isherwood's Berlin stories, "street was leading into street of houses like shabby monumental safes crammed with the tarnished valuables and the secondhand furniture of a bankrupt middle class."[18] Perhaps because Weimar's Social Democratic city administrations constructed public housing estates not for them but for blue-collar workers, Weimar medievalists imagined that public housing, labor-saving technologies, and modern architecture were somehow "Jewish" and Communist.[19] (The *Völkischer Beobachter* in 1933 discussed the "Communist principle to industrialize housing construction" [quoted in Teut, 56].) They felt, vaguely but persistently, that functionalism both illustrated and furthered a world devoid of meaning.[20]

Weimar's medievalist and functionalist schools of architecture both regarded architecture as at once promoting and reflecting an ideology. Medievalists hoped for the mystical awakening of the "race," functionalists for the political awakening of the proletariat. Medievalists imagined that their "genuine Nordic-German," "German Nordic-Germanic," or "Aryan-Northern"[21] blood would be invigorated by supposed racial stereotypes such as the hut, the rectangular house, the angled roof, and the roof-overhang. Functionalist architects, often Social Democrats or Communists, instead projected a proletarian self-realization unfolding by architecture freed from historicist style-influences and engineered for the working class. The one saw architecture as the mystical expression of a biological urge: the other, as a social tool for reasoning people.

Weimar's Luddite and Romantic medievalists thus violently opposed the productive spaces and docile subjects of an industrial order. They preferred a mythical medieval past in which Germans were bio-historically rooted in their *Heimat, and* conquered new territories. As a boy's book from the early 1930s describes the Middle Ages,

> It was a wonderful time, a time which people [*Völker*] only experience very rarely in their artistic creativity . . . truly, a time of flowering, a time of the greatest creations! . . . it was also a time when the whole German people was on the move, so as to conquer for themselves the necessary living-space [*Lebensraum*] in the East and once again Germanize [*einzudeutschen*] the old Germanic lands. Unforgettable, imperishable great deeds of our people!

As incontestable evidence, it added, "After all, even Americans, who are so proud of their horrendous stone and concrete buildings, sense something of the inexpressible magic of an old German town, which the many yearly visits to Nuremberg, Rothenburg, etc., prove."[22]

Never at home in a democratic republic, most German medievalists greeted 1933 with joy. Often Nazi party members, they confidently expected the Nazis would implement their programs. KfdK founder Alfred Rosenberg, a former student of architecture and a confirmed cultural Luddite who once lived from selling sketches of medieval Baltic towns, was the Nazi party's leading cultural advisor in the early 1930s (Taylor, 55). At the very least, medievalists were sure the Third Reich would eradicate functionalism. Bettina Feistel-Rohmeder, author of a syndicated art column, pleaded with Germany's new masters in 1933:

> that in the future we don't have to see in our fatherland living-coffins, glass boxes on pillars, leaky oriental cave-apartments . . . prison archipelagos, supposed to be working class settlements. . . . that ways will be found to snatch back from these criminals who destroyed so much of our indigenous culture what they have stolen, and that every memory of this perverted period will be erased. (quoted in Teut, 79)

Other medievalists had grander plans. German Bestelmeyer, President of the Munich Academy of Art and an eclectic advocate of neo-Gothicism, Romanesque revivalism, and Bavarian folk building, hoped that the Nazis would resurrect "heroic castles at non-threatened borders" and "walled cities with large cathedrals and wide squares" (quoted in Teut, 128).[23] Paul Schmitthenner, Stuttgart professor of architecture, urged Germans to try for "a breath of the purity and greatness of the early Middle Ages . . . [and] again paint in their halls and carve stone saints and kings, heroes and mystical animals."[24]

But, as is well known, for public buildings the Third Reich favored a pared-down, blown-up version of international neoclassicism, from Paul Ludwig Troost's 1934 Doric revivalist Temple of Honor (*Ehrentempel*) in Munich, honoring the Nazis killed in the 1923 *Putsch*, to Albert Speer's 1938-45 plans for "Germania," the capital of the postwar "New Order." Thus the Nazis intended to intimidate Germany's "Pinneberg" or "little man" and convince other nations that, as Hitler pathetically explained to Speer, "we are not inferior" (141). Neither of these goals, the Nazi elite believed, could be achieved by medievalism's small-scale, organic, and rural architecture.

As Jeffrey Herf has argued, the modernist wing of the Nazi Party successfully incorporated the concept of modern technology into that ideological sphere of "culture" which its members, and indeed most conservative Germans since the Romantic era, favored over the sphere of "civilization."[25] By the mid-1930s, Nazis designed "organic-dynamic functionalist" (they looked like ordinary functionalist) utility buildings for the German industry, army, and air force. Nazi modernists stressed the "primacy of economy" and "the necessary return to the basics of industrial building" (quoted in Teut, 311).[26] There emerged a marked Nazi cult of modern technology and industrial efficiency, led by engineer Fritz Todt, from 1933 head of infrastructure and from 1940 Minister of Armaments. "We must rationalize, we must create standard types, we must mechanize" (quoted in Teut, 302).[27] The enthusiastic motorist added, "Our Nazi character corresponds to the new roads of Adolf Hitler. . . . Intersections we cross, unnecessary delays are alien to us. We will not yield, we create for ourselves enough road on which to proceed, and we need a road which permits us to maintain a speed congenial to us" (quoted in Taylor, 201).

A failed student of architecture, Hitler believed that "art is the clearest and most immediate reflection of the spiritual life of a people. It exercises the greatest direct and unconscious influences on the masses of a people."[28]· He was a Nazi "reactionary modernist," and dismissed Romanesque and Gothic buildings as "Asiatic." He admittedly admired the Strasbourg cathedral (1015-1505) and planned to turn it into a memorial to the unknown German soldier. But it was the size he liked. Otherwise, Hitler favored public buildings such as Rome's Colosseum (72-80) and St. Peter's Basilica (1503-1667), as well as Vienna's grand historicist structures on the *Ring*, the late nineteenth-century boulevard circling the city center (Lane, 48; Taylor, 33-9).[29] Afraid of being exposed as a crank, he proclaimed his racist creed as modern. "The sign of our meeting places is not the mystic darkness of the cult place but clarity and light. . . . National Socialism is a cool knowledge of reality, of sharp scientific insights."[30] Flipping through Rosenberg's *Mythos des 20. Jahrhundert*, the author of *Mein Kampf* dismissed it as "plagiarized, pasted together, nonsensical junk!"[31] Hitler also ridiculed SS leader Heinrich Himmler's mystical medievalism. "To think that I may someday be turned into an SS saint! Can you imagine it! I would turn over in my grave!" Nor did he like Teutonic Romanticism. "We really should do our best to keep quiet about this [primitive] past" (quoted in Speer, 141).

Aware of medievalism's popular appeal, Nazi leaders instead sought to show their commitment by propaganda. In 1933 they added angled roofs to Weissenhof's model homes and Bauhaus (Dessau). They also in the early 1930s constructed some five hundred showcase rural settlements, each housing about a hundred and fifty families (Teut, 252).[32] (Half-timber, a vernacular style of north Germany's treeless plains, now appeared in the forests.) Such numbers were wholly inadequate to solve Germany's growing housing crisis, and below Weimar numbers. Also, Nazi urban public housing fell short of Weimar achievements. The much-touted 1933 Munich Kochenhof settlement and the 1934 Regensburg Ramersdorf settlement were never translated into large-scale projects. Such suburban "mini-settlements" (*Kleinsiedlungen*) mimicked pre-modern villages. The Nazi regime built chunky, vaguely traditional apartment houses. Its public buildings involved tearing down existing housing. At times, it did not move beyond that point. They were also sometimes financed, as in Augsburg, by appropriating public housing funds (Speer, 242). After 1935, housing was constructed almost entirely for army personnel. Then, on 20 November 1939, the Nazi state forbade new construction (Petsch, 184).[33]

The Nazis frequently employed vernacular styles for minor public buildings, such as the 1936 German Labor Front's Horst-Wessel-Halle in Erwitte, an oversized Teutonic hut, and the projected 1937 Hamburg Hitler Youth Home (*HJ-Heim*), a monstrous thatched-roof cottage. They also built some high medievalist structures. In the mid-1930s the SS constructed three *Ordensburgen*, boarding schools for the future Nazi elite (Petsch, 126-84). These schools imitated the castles of the Order of the Teutonic Knights (1190-1525). The SS considered itself their descendants, called up to reconquer the Order's Eastern European colonies. The *Ordensburg* style was a modified Romanesque, the material stone and wood, and the location rural and sentimental. One, Crössinsee, was built on the remains of a medieval fortress.[34] Other medievalist Nazi teaching institutes included centers for regional Party leaders (*Gauburgen*), Labor Front schools (*Reichsschulungsburgen der Deutschen Arbeitsfront*), and freshman officer schools (*Adolf-Hitler-Schulen*). Himmler's projected East European SS castles (*SS Wehrburgen*) were however never built. Nor were the officer schools intended to imitate the Benedictine monastery Monte Cassino (529-) (the Danzig and Berlin *Kriegsschulen*).

As Robert Taylor has pointed out, the most inventive Nazi architecture harked back to Germany's Teutonic past. From 1934 to 1937, the Labor Front, commissioned by the Reich League for German Open Air and Folk Plays and the Propaganda Ministry, built *Thingstätten* (210).[35] These sought to amalgamate Greek amphitheatres and Germanic tribal law courts. They were situated in the countryside: ideally by a pagan cult site, a battlefield, or a medieval castle. The Heidelberg *Thing*, for example, was located on top of the forested hill Heiligen Berg, with a view over the Neckar River, and next to a ruined abbey.

The *Thing* were places for a people's worship of itself. Heidegger stressed that the relation between the words *Thing* and *Ding* was not accidental. Bourgeois drama, like Goethe's *Faust*, was occasionally performed. More often, plays were customized to reflect "the communal spirit emanating from the [German] folk" (*das Gemeinsamme, das Volkische*).[36] *Sacred Earth, Man, The Border Is Burning*, and *Vaterland* are typical titles. These Nazi collective plays drew on medieval theater, like Oberammergau's passion plays, but also on radical Weimar *Totaltheater* (Petsch, 117).[37] They bored even Nazi viewers with their "simple but marvelous episodes," such as "the appearance of the dead soldier" (quoted in Taylor, 218). All agreed that the stylized military marches were the most impressive part. Since these were performed also at Party meetings, the *Thing* lacked a unique and popular form of national worship. Even Nazi reviews were resigned. "The miracle occurs . . . for several seconds, the *Volk* community is a living reality" (quoted in Taylor, 218). Twelve hundred *Thingsstätten* were planned, forty built. Propaganda Minister Joseph Goebbels withdrew his support in 1936: "One does not have to arrange a cultic feast as soon as five National Socialists meet. . . . I therefore wish that we for at least ten years removed words like 'cult' or 'Thing' or 'mystic' from our vocabulary" (quoted in Ruth and Karlsson, 343).

Baldur von Schirach located the Hitler Youth's leadership school in the Marienwerder Castle of the Teutonic Knights. SS leader Heinrich Himmler chose as his headquarters a medieval castle, Wewelsburg, and renovated it for thirteen million *Reichmark*. He believed he was a reincarnation of Henry I (Teut, 343). But plenipotentiary Hermann Göring's summer palace, Karinhall (1934), was the only major medievalist commission by a higher Party member. A lumbering thatched-roof building, its courtyard graced by a statue of a wild boar, it struck the American ambassador as a "medieval country gentleman's house, if there were gentlemen in those days."[38] It had a "Viking" hall, a "German" room, a "Byzantine" lounge, and a *Louis Quinze* dining hall. As a German aristocrat remarked, it was thus furnished according to the taste of "a typical German *Hausfrau*."[39] Göring received guests in a "medieval hunting costume" which, a visiting journalist dryly noted, "we could not sufficiently admire on account of its originality" (*Berlingske Tidende*, 6 March 1938). One evening, Göring turned up in a bearskin and with two leashed bison in tow, that then, to the "stupefaction" of the guests, mated in the living room. "So this is *Blut und Boden* ideology."[40]

Göring's over-dimensioned mongrel-Teutonic pleasure palace nicely symbolizes the fate of medievalist architecture in Nazi Germany. It found expression in a few buildings for blue-collar workers (the Labor Front's Strength Through Joy halls), women (pro-natalist settlements), children (Hitler Youth homes), students (Adolf Hitler schools and *Ordensburgen*), and the dead (*Totenburgen*). Medievalism also influenced interior decoration, private homes, and buildings for leisure. Some back rooms in Speer's neoclassical Berlin Chancellery had medievalist designs (Speer, 351). The stables and tennis courts of the 1936 Berlin Olympic Stadium were constructed with half-timbering and thatched roofs (Taylor, 138, 180). Hitler's Upper Bavarian retreat—but not his Berlin work-space—was furnished in what Speer called "bogus old German peasant style" (Speer, 81). Neo-Viking ornaments such as carved horns, horse skulls, and runic inscriptions became fashionable. So did pseudo-peasant furniture such as benches, long and angular tables, rag carpets, and rocking chairs. Viking, peasant, and medieval motifs appeared on murals, tablecloths, tapestries, china, statuettes, and so on.[41] In sum, the lesser a Nazi building or its purposes, the more likely it was to be styled in Romanesque, Gothic, Teutonic, or vernacular. That Nazi medievalism was relegated to marginal spheres of public life is also substantiated by the personal destinies of its theoreticians. They were made professors.[42] Medievalist Nazi architecture thus functioned as a female, domestic, *gemütlich* counterpart to male, public, terrorizing neoclassicist Nazi architecture. Together the two styles reflected Nazi idealist antimodernity, its quest for national redemption, and what already in 1925 Thomas Mann diagnosed as the German right wing's "sentimental brutality" (quoted in Stern, xxx).[43]

So far, this essay has focused on external reasons for medievalist architecture's failure to effect social and cultural reforms in Nazi Germany. Now, I turn to an internal analysis of Nazi medievalism itself. In particular, I look at the war memorials Hitler commissioned in 1942 from Wilhelm Kreis (1873-1955). By that time, Kreis was an aged and petulant *Wunderkind*. He had become famous overnight in 1895, at age twenty-two, by winning first prize in a design competition for a monument commissioned by the 45,000-member "German Patriotic Alliance for Erecting a Leipzig Memorial to the Fallen" (in the Napoleonic Wars).[44] The early German Gothic revival, expressed for example in Karl Friedrich Schinkel's small-scaled Berlin war memorial (1818), was richly detailed and complex. Kreis spearheaded the Wilhelmian turn towards large, iconographically simple, and primitivist monuments.[45] "I dedicated my sketches to Wotan, the norns, the ninth Symphony."[46] In the proposed 1895 *Völkerschlachtdenkmal* one statue alone (placed midway up the monument) was some forty feet high. In 1943, Kreis reminisced to a Nazi audience, "I was accused of Germanomania [*Teuschtum*] and barbarism. But the nationalists liked me."[47]

In 1898, Kreis shot to greater fame by winning first, second, and third prize in a Bismarck memorial competition. He submitted multiple anonymous sketches of stern, unadorned stone towers peering out from hilltops and mountainsides. Kreis then took on some fifty Bismarck tower commissions. He also designed the huge 1899 Eisenach *Burschenschaftsdenkmal* (a memorial to early nineteenth-century nationalist student fraternities), the enormous Stettin 1912-14 *Bismarckhalle*, and the massive 1908 Dresden bridge *Neue Augustusbrücke*, all medievalist structures.

Dominating the market and setting the style for late Wilhelmian monuments, Kreis was also a successful and well-respected architect in the interwar period. He was the president of the League of German Architects from 1928 to 1933 (Teut, 68).[48] Between 1910 and 1933, he designed decorative, semi-classicist commercial buildings, including seven department stores, as well as office skyscrapers and factories.[49] Both Kreis and "the Führer himself," however, felt that Weimar had frittered away his talent for monumental architecture (Stephan, 9). Kreis's taste, too, had remained medievalist, as evidenced by his plans for a mongrel Romanesque-Gothic hospital in Frankfurt, the neo-Romanesque Halle Museum of Prehistory, and the neo-Gothic Düsseldorf Planetarium (1925), and by the way he girdled the *Wilhelm-Marx-Haus*, a Düsseldorf skyscraper, with a Gothicizing pointed stone-arch frieze front.[50] His architectural manifesto, *On the Relations between Culture, Civilization and Art* (1927), also reiterated the medievalist commonplace that the organic link between culture and civilization, that characterized the German Middle Ages and found its highest expression in the Gothic cathedral, had been lost. The Weimar Republic he described as a transition period, where artists at most could create "markers on the way to our era's culture."[51]

Between 1928 and 1932 Kreis intermittently worked with the "Association for the Erection of National Monuments." In 1931 he won first prize for a proposed memorial to the German nation (the Berka *Reichehrenmal*) by submitting a hybrid of the Parthenon and Stonehenge. His sketches can be read as representing either a grotesquely oversized monument, or, given that the trees are equally huge, a normal-sized place temporarily occupied by Lilliputians (Stephan, 76-7). But apart from a tiny 1932 memorial to the fallen in the First World War, styled as a Teutonic hut, no actual constructions had ensued. In 1935, however, Hitler chose Kreis as the winner of a competition for a regional political assembly, the Dresden *Gauforum*. He had submitted a neoclassical monstrosity housing 30,000 and adorned with a medievalist tower dedicated to the Hitler Youth

(Stephan, 60-1). Then, in 1938, his good friend Albert Speer commissioned him to design Germania's Army Headquarters, Germanic Museum, World War Museum, and Museum of the Nineteenth Century.[52]

In 1941 Kreis was appointed architectural director for military graveyards. Now, in 1942, on Hitler's commission Kreis and his staff planned war memorials from Norway to north Africa, and all over "the new Eastern territories": Warsaw, Kutno, Witusch, Struma, and Dnieper. For his Nazi memorials, Kreis kept to his Wilhelmian prototypes. Or, as he often described them, his "Nordic, Germanic" models. He was also inspired by Johannes and Walter Krüger's 1924-27 Tannenberg memorial. The huge, eight-towered structure commemorated a 1914 First World War victory, vaguely understood to have overturned the Teutonic Knights' 1410 defeat by the Poles at Tannenberg. The Nazis greatly admired this crouching, sullen monument, modeled on the Knights' Eastern European castles. In 1934, they buried Field Marshal Paul von Hindenburg there. In 1945, rather than leaving it to the Russians, the retreating German army blew it up.

Tannenberg's medievalist megalomania approaches the grandiose plans of the late Enlightenment's visionary architects, who also seem to have inspired Kreis's *Totenburgen*.[53] For example, Kreis's sketch of a *Totenburg* for Noyers Pont Maugis, Bourgogne, like Etienne-Louis Boulée's drawing of a "Cenotaph for a Warrior" (now in the National Library in Paris), is styled as a watchtower, with a giant, enclosed, cubic, and simple body, and miniscule, randomly placed windows (Figure 1). Kreis also underlined its essentially melodramatic character by using a half-frontal view and an exaggerated side shadow, and indeed by the entire manner of presentation, with its far-off view and histrionic clouds. Similar devices are employed in Kreis's 1943 Warsaw *Totenburg* sketch, which takes exceptional pains to dramatize its object (Figure 2).[54] By darkening the drawings' edges, Kreis produced an odd tunneling effect, as if the viewer were a soldier, crouching in a trench, spying from afar through a pair of field glasses.

Hitler had decreed that no memorials were to be built *during* the war. None of Kreis's *Totenburgen* were built. What might they have looked like? The most elaborate *Totenburg* was to be situated along the Dnieper as a "symbol for the defeat of the chaotic forces of the eastern steppes" (Taylor, 191). Kreis planned it as a monstrously large, roughly hewn stone hill (*Hügel*) vaguely modeled on cairns, but topped by an ill-tempered stone eagle, guarded by stone lions, and resting on top of a vaulted room. In the middle of its sunken floor, a stone slate would cover soil gathered from eastern battlegrounds. This pyramid on the Dnieper was Kreis's Teutonic showpiece.[55] The same year he sketched it, he received the Order of Eagle Shield of the German Reich. Kreis's less ambitious *Totenburgen* to some extent varied with their setting: the Egyptian one was a pyramid, the Greek one a Doric temple. But the northern and eastern European ones were mainly designed in a brutalist neo-Romanesque. They would look similar to Annaberg in Upper Silesia, a 1936-38 memorial commissioned by the "People's Association to Care for German War Graves" and commemorating the First World War volunteer corps. Incongruously coupled to a *Thing*, Annaberg emulated the heavily fortified castles of the early Middle Ages (Taylor, 190-91).

But in another sense this squat memorial is far removed from the musings of Kreis. Annaberg was slowly, laboriously executed. Compare it to Kreis's sketched war memorials, published in a booklet at the beginning of 1944, its pages densely packed with exact, small drawings (Figure 3). A full year after the February 1943 annihilation of the German Sixth Army at Stalingrad, most Nazis would have understood that Kreis's sketches would never be built. The *Totenburgen*'s grandiose size only underlined their essential unreality. Lined up side by side in a booklet shrunk and slimmed because of wartime paper rationing, these tiny sketches seem infinitely far away. As they were sent to the printer, the German forces were fleeing the East. They were just one part (and in a sense the most sane, because least concerned with the immediate future) of those imagined new Eastern lands, whose administrative details were busily outlined by German planning agencies, such as the *Reichsstelle für Raumordnung*, *Reichskommissariat für den sozialen Wohnungsbau*, *Reichsheimstätteamt der DAF*, *Reichsministerium für Ernährung und Landwirtschaft*, *Generalgouvernement*, and the SS.[56]

Not only had all building stopped in 1944. The very concept of buildings had become fragile. As the play of two German eight-year-olds in 1945 witnesses,

The toy castle didn't look real because it was completely undamaged. We opened the flap to the back of the main building and stuffed it full with paper. Then we set fire to it. It looked real and alive as the flames leaped out of its Gothic

windows and consumed the frames: Rolf imitated the sounds
of B-17's that circled the castle and dropped more bombs.[57]

In 1942-45 the Germans only completed one building project (to that
they dedicated all their forces): the invisible graves of an entire people
murdered, Europe's Jews. Or, in the words of Paul Celan's *Todesfuge*,
where a German concentration camp guard mocks Jewish prisoners:
"then as smoke you will rise into air / then a grave you will have in
the clouds there / one lies unconfined."[58]
  As a counterpoint to the millions the Germans murdered and left
unburied, Kreis also wrote a field guide on "temporary fields of graves."
A manual for lower Nazi officials having to bury thousands of German
soldiers under field conditions and with a moving frontier, *Soldiers'
Graves and Memorials* (1944) expands on a "Führer order" of 16 March
1941. To better understand Kreis's 1944 manual, one may compare it
to his 1918 design work on La Parriée, a soldiers' cemetery on the
Western front.[59] In World War I, Germans and French cooperated in
burial of the dead. It was self-understood that soldiers from both sides
would be decently buried. Each soldier got an individually designed
grave, with its own flowers, painted or carved decoration, and
inscription—a Bible verse, a short description of the soldier or of his
death, or a line from a poem. The Germans (who undertook the
work) made sure the French soldiers' epitaphs were in French. As in
reflection of the "reconciliatory powers of death," French and Germans
were buried side by side and not in two blocks. On the other hand,
Germans were separated into Prussians, Bavarians, Württembergians,
etc. A huge wooden cross overshadowed the graveyard. The inaugural
memorial service was religious *and* interdenominational. The theme of
its speeches (delivered in French and German) was that the graveyard
and the war were diametric opposites.[60] Such were the wartime burial
rites that Kreis himself had experienced before 1944.
  In *Soldiers' Graves and Memorials*, Kreis issued line drawings of
standardized grave sites, complete with measurements and sample
Gothic alphabets. Christian symbols and Realist statuary, he warned,
were to be avoided. Graves were only to inform about the dead man's
name and rank, and the place and time of death. The idea of burying
Germans side by side with the people they killed, natural twenty-five
years earlier, had become inconceivable. Kreis's pamphlet never hints
at how to treat the Russian dead, let alone the murdered Jews. He
knew already how Germans shoveled the dead and the dying into mass

graves. The soil moved for hours, sometimes days. Or, how they made mass pyramids of naked, freshly killed women and children and then burned them, so that they rose "as smoke in the air." (Their clothes and gold teeth the Germans, always thrifty, saved from fire.)

Instead of anchoring his soldiers' cemeteries to a Christian tradition, Kreis provided a brief historical overview that situated these hasty gravefields in a genealogy stretching to Emperor Theodoric's grave in Ravenna and beyond, into a mythic concoction of mounds and rune stones. He also included, as examples of what the Nazi state would provide after the war for these German men, two small dreamy sketches of his *Totenburgen*.

Kreis's 1944 manual had other Romantic aspects. The setting, he ruled, should ideally combine hills, oak groves, and running water with "Germanic" ruins. Large boulders or clumps of trees should mark the graveyard, and swastikas the graves. Paths should be laid out in stone or grass, not gravel. Only local materials were to be used. Individual grave markers—including nails—should be timber and not metal. Work should be voluntary, collective, and guided by a spirit of sacrifice. When possible, the graves should be dug by German artisan-soldiers. One implication is that Germany's foreign slaves would not be reverent. Kreis might also have attempted to recapitulate a personal experience from the late 1890s, or rather, a fleeting moment of authenticity, that he never forgot. "One [of these Bismarck memorials] that farmers built themselves was really almost made in the same way as, probably, our forefathers built cairns, when everyone worked on it and took on the burden themselves" (quoted in Meissner, 10).

Soldiers' Graves and Memorials is too detailed, or so it seems to a present-day reader, to keep up the fiction of temporariness. The practical orders Kreis lavished on actual, "temporary" fields of graves only underline the unreality of his planned, eternal memorials. They are reminiscent of the mood evoked by one of the Nazis' favorite artists, the Romantic landscape painter Caspar David Friedrich. In *Monastery Graveyard* (1818), Friedrich transformed a well-preserved building, the Jakobskirche in Greifswald, into a ruin. As with Kreis's memorials, we can only know this painting from black-and-white photographs. It was destroyed in the bombing of Berlin. Both Friedrich and Kreis, in portraying sacred buildings, seek to induce the mood expressed in David Mallet's 1726 Gothic poem "The Excursion": "Behind me rises huge an awful Pile / Sole on this blasted Heath, a Place of Tombs, / Waste, desolate, where *Ruin* dreary dwells /

Brooding o'er sightless Sculls, and crumbling Bones."[61] The Germanic ideologue Arthur Möller van den Bruck, author of *The Third Reich* (1922), praised in Kreis's Wilhelmian monuments a similar impulse: "the full unity of nature and monument," or the engaging of nature as expression of history (quoted in Meissner, 16).[62]

Friedrich's paintings might be interpreted as holding out a promise of personal salvation. Kreis's *Totenburgen* are at most a blueprint for a collective dent in the landscape. Kreis expected his monuments to give "an inkling of the greatness of the heroic deeds of our history that we are duty-bound to pass on to the most distant generation" (quoted in Teut, 216). As he also said, "Long after the ages of this great war the memorial sites like testimonials shall always ring with the high song of our people's war for freedom" (*Soldiers' Graves*, 65). The future wanderer would pause in front of Kreis's crumbling *Totenburgen* and gaze as in Mallet's poem upon "the Column grey with Moss, the falling Bust, / the Time-shook Arch, the monumental Stone." He would hear what Kreis called "the Runic song of the stone memorial" (quoted in Teut, 216). It is a vision of an archaic world.[63] Prehistoric cairns and post-historic *Totenburgen* alike enact "the eternal watch." One Nazi in 1943 philosophized about Kreis's war memorials by pondering the moment "when once remote [German] descendants on the plains of the Eastern lands, in Norway's mountain crevices, in the shadow of the Acropolis by Athens, on the banks of the Maas or in the deserts of Africa on foot come across [Kreis's] powerful memorials [executed] in the most penetrating language [and] ponder their forefathers' war of destiny." Stirred by strange emotions, the latter-day German—realizing with a start that once other people lived in Europe—would be overcome "by far-away tones, almost forgotten memories, ancient holy beliefs" (Stephan, 77).[64]

Kreis and his Nazi audience knew, however, that even that hope, however bombastic and pathetic, was only a fantasy, albeit an extraordinarily elaborate one. And it is as fantasy that Kreis's *Totenburgen* reveal themselves as an index to Nazi medievalism. Kreis's diminutive sketches of enormous monuments represent a peevish nostalgia for at once a distant future and a distant past. They seem to hold out a paradoxical hope of being exonerated from the staggering moral responsibilities of the Nazis' war in the east, by envisaging a mythical history of the future where ruined monuments indicate (but never articulate) deeds that in the mists of time have become great—and unspecified—into a merely scintillating inkling. Kreis's *Totenburgen* were thus an amnesiac counterpoint to Nazi history. They functioned not to remember but to forget the past, to erase that terrible history which, at that very moment, was being recorded by Nazi administrators. Kreis sketched his fantastic *Totenburgen*. Meanwhile, the Nazi extermination units, bureaus of deportation, slave labor, and famine, and the whole apparatus of the "final solution," filled out, in carbon copy, monuments to untold cruelty.

Kreis's *Totenburgen* serve as an index to emotions infusing the Nazi medievalism of the 1940s. They also go beyond wartime nostalgia. As their postwar reception in Germany shows, they are still part of the German mental landscape. Perhaps this is not surprising. But as I will now argue, their reception appears in particularly troubling guises. I shall demonstrate this by considering the art of Anselm Kiefer (1945-), one of postwar Germany's most successful artists. A student of Joseph Beuys, in 1980 Kiefer became an overnight sensation at the Venice Biennale.

In Mark Rosenthal's opening words to Kiefer's 1988 US exhibition catalog, "Kiefer's daring, inherently German outlook began to overcome his tentative beginnings in 1969." That year, Kiefer for the first time "assumed the identity of a conquering National Socialist," traveling around Europe photographing himself doing the *Sieg Heil* salute;[65] the resultant series of artworks was titled *Occupations*. He also began reproducing Nazi propaganda images as modern art, as in *You're a Painter*, a photograph of run-of-the-mill Nazi heroic statuary. In the 1970s Kiefer started painting topics such as the Nibelungen Ring and the *Meistersinger* of Nuremberg (he greatly admires Wagner), Scandinavian pagan mythology, and Nazi military operations such as Operation Barbarossa and Operation Winter Storm. In 1974 he created a series of German peasant physiognomies, *Germany's Facial Type*.[66] As Rosenthal comments, "Their features are thoroughly one with the land" (51). Further reflecting that sentiment, in 1975 Kiefer dedicated a book to Heidegger. Kiefer also worked on the perennial German topic of Hermann and Thusnelda's Teutoburg forest massacre of three legions of Roman soldiers (A. D. 9). In 1933 alone, playwrights sent the Berlin State Theatre over five hundred scripts on Hermann and Thusnelda.[67]

Germany's Spiritual Heroes is perhaps the most ambitious of Kiefer's work of the 1970s.[68] It depicts a rough-hewn, early medieval hall, lit by pitch-and-wood torches. Each flame commemorates a medieval mystic, Romantic artist, or military leader, such as Mechthild von Magdeburg, Wagner, and Frederick the Great. Kiefer did not include Enlightenment thinkers or post-Romantic ironists, such as Goethe, Lessing, Mendelssohn, Herder, Heine, Nelly Sachs, or Heinrich Böll. Instead, over the next few years, in the ambitious series *Ways of Worldly Wisdom*, Kiefer celebrated such heroes as "Albert Leo Schlageter (1894-1923), German World War I resistance fighter against the French" and "Horst Wessel (1907-1930), writer of a famed patriotic hymn" (quoted in Rosenthal, 57). Schlageter was a Nazi *Freikorps* terrorist, killed by French occupation forces in the Ruhr region; Wessel was a young Berlin pimp, killed in a street battle over prostitutes' territories. Both were later celebrated as Nazi saints. The modern art world's ignorance of Nazi history of course makes Kiefer's art seem that much more acceptable.[69]

In the early 1980s Kiefer began replicating propaganda photographs of Nazi memorials and public buildings, sometimes by overpainting photographic blowups and sometimes by conventional copying. For example, in *Shulamite*, Kiefer reworked Kreis's 1939 Hall of Soldiers, then baptized the resultant work after the Jewish heroine in Celan's Holocaust poem. In *The Rhine*, Kiefer again reproduces the Hall of Soldiers, placing a facade drawing along the banks of the Rhine. *To the the Unknown Painter,* one of a series, replicates a Norwegian *Totenburg* and romanticizes the wilderness around it.[70] By thus appropriating Kreis's *Totenburg* as the "archetypal tomb of the unknown painter," Kiefer shows how, in Rosenthal's words, "he considers both [soldiers and artists] to be men of action who fight for ideals" (115).

Rosenthal explains that Kiefer's reworkings of Nazi cultural representations are subversive. "Like an alchemist, Kiefer believes in his power as an artist to transmute events, as he had done by turning a Nazi stronghold into a monument for artists" (115). To consider this proposal, compare Kreis's 1939 pen drawing for the Hall of Soldiers in the Berlin Army Headquarters with Kiefer's 1982 watercolor *To the Unknown Painter* (Figures 4, 5). In the place of Kreis's statue of the German soldier, Kiefer has inserted a palette, the painter's tool and signature.

The problem with Kiefer's re-enactments of Nazi propaganda images is not that the rendering of evil is itself evil. Rather, Kiefer's attempts to distance himself from Nazi architecture (those very attempts that are usually considered to legitimize, via a principle of irony, his Nazi-based images), shows him spellbound by its master metaphors. It is an historiographical commonplace that the Nazi movement aestheticized politics. To the Nazis "a Nazi stronghold" *was* "a monument to artists." To Kreis as to Hitler, a self-described "artist-soldier," the Nazi revolution merged the "world of deeds," or the military, and the "world of thought," or artists. Thus Kreis, a volunteer in the First World War and wounded at the Somme in 1918, designated his *Totenburg* staff-artists not by names, but by terms such as "a war wounded," "a young soldier," and *"ein Haupsturmführer der Waffen-SS."*[71]

Kiefer's debased equation of the modern artist and the Nazi soldier as "men of action who fight for ideals" is a belated version of what Saul Friedländer in 1982 termed "a new [artistic] discourse about Nazism." This "Grand Opera approach to the Nazi era," as Friedländer called it (xiii), emerged in the late 1960s and counts among its practitioners Hans-Jürgen Syberberg and Werner Fassbinder. Like Nazis, it takes a sentimental/pornographic delight in juxtaposing Nazi terror to idyllic Nazi propaganda, *Kitsch* to death.

Kiefer might well have understood his faithful rendering of Kreis's vaulted hall as ironic. Yet it inevitably functions on a level less clever, more haunting. Whether one contemplate Kreis's 1939 Hall of Soldiers *or* Kiefer's 1982 *To the Unknown Painter*, the experience is reminiscent of Childe Roland come upon his dark tower. "Burningly it came to me all at once, / This was the place! . . . Dunce, / Fool, to be dozing at the very nonce, / After a life spent training for the sight."[72]

In Robert Browning's poem, the hero of the internalized quest-romance is inevitably defeated by the past, as were those who came before him. His life (the poem turns on this discovery) was a search for his own destruction. Similar to Childe Roland, Kiefer cannot remain detached from the seduction of Kreis's "Tower itself," "blind as the fool's heart / Built of brown stone, without a counterpart / in the whole world." In his attempt to do so, he ignores the fact that it is the distance, whether as time or as irony, that seduces. Fragmenting its wall: declaring it a work of art. Such incantations will not disenchant Kreis's *Soldatenhalle*. They only cast a further spell. For their creator too was overcome by this seduction of the distance. Looking at Kiefer's recapitulation of Kreis's fantasy, a line of V. S. Pritchett comes to mind. "The tower, gray and nasty, is awake again."[73]

Paul de Man has famously characterized Romanticism as the ironization of romance. Precisely Kiefer's postmodernist *pastiche* reveals that he remains part of Nazi sentimentality. It is not surprising that his rendering of Nazi monuments of triumph as weak, and his depictions of German landscapes—such as the moving 1977 *March Sand V* and 1980 *Ways: March Sand*—are artistically strong.[74]   Kiefer's Germany monuments are infused with self-pity.   His German landscapes encounter nature, a force greater than Germans, and therefore more amenable to high art.

Kiefer seems uneasily aware of how his reproductions of Nazi cultural icons parasitize that deep-seated German self-pity that functions as an *ersatz* humanity.   But the unease seems to stem from worries about how he is regarded outside Germany.   Thus, when in a 1990 interview he was asked about his view of America, he immediately answered with a curious observation: "One thing one mustn't forget: 95% of all American collectors that have paintings by me, are Jews. This to be sure is just one part of America, but a very important [one]" (*Dagens Nyheter*, 18 February).   Kiefer's art thus perfectly matches Friedländer's analysis:

> In its more complex examples, the new discourse about Nazism is almost always a mixture of the three following levels of discourse: the language of images and the fascination it creates; strange statements—implicit in the works, explicit in interviews with the authors and directors—about history, modern civilization, superstructure referring to metaphysics, theories of myth, the function of art and literture today, and so on. (xvii)[75]

To summarize my argument, Nazi medievalist architecture began in the early 1930s as a present-oriented and detailed reform program. In the Second World War, it was transformed into a more intense but vaguer nostalgia: for the Middle Ages, to be sure, but increasingly, for any past—including the pasts of the future.   In the postwar era, that nostalgia has been carried over into Kiefer's art and into the public that receives him.

One final comparison may clarify this point.   The Court of Honor in Albert Speer's New Chancellery is rendered, by route of a 1943 propaganda photograph, in Kiefer's 1984 *Athanor*, as well as in the closely related *To the Unknown Painter*.[76]   In effect, Kiefer has Gothicized the building.   "The Time-shook Arch, the monumental Stone" of Mallet's poem are now "Impair'd, effac'd, & hastening into

Dust." Once pompous, the building in Kiefer's hands has become imposing. Kiefer has not only achieved an effect that Speer might have admired. He has fulfilled Speer's architectural program.

For Kiefer's ruin was already Speer's ideal. In the mid-1930s, after chancing on the demolished Nuremberg Streetcar Depot, where "iron reinforcements protruded from concrete debris," Speer formulated a theory of "ruin value." He presented Hitler with a "romantic drawing," which "showed what the reviewing stand on the [Berlin 1936 Olympic] Zeppelin Field would look after generations of neglect, overgrown with ivy, its columns fallen, the walls crumbling . . . ." Delighted, Hitler ordered all important public buildings to be constructed according to Speer's principles. "We should be able to build structures which even in a state of decay, after hundreds or (such were our reckonings) thousands of years would more or less resemble Roman models" (56).[77] Client and architect alike took a sentimental delight in decay. Together they imagined Germania in ruins. It had a grander effect than the prosaic one their politics ensured, Berlin in ruins. Or, as Speer put it, when in early spring 1945 he ghoulishly surveyed Berlin's rubble deserts: "in short, a country thrown back into the Middle Ages" (442).

The German philosopher Hans Blumenberg has argued that the German Romantics' discovery of the Middle Ages around 1800 was an even more momentous event than the Renaissance reception of antiquity. It made possible a historicist reading of history, where each era possessed its own logic and value. A historically grounded personal and cultural identity were thus constituted, which in the nineteenth century "were to stand as the only opponent of natural science."[78] But in Germany, at least, medievalism's force was spent by 1945. Already interwar German medievalism corresponded only to a severely debased version of the Romantic hope expressed already by Friedrich Schlegel, to live, not "in the actual Middle Ages, but only now in the true [wahren] or real ones" (quoted in Blumenberg, 272). During the war, Nazi Romantics' intensifying interest in time and distance collapsed history, by making it too grand and too eternal to study. Towards the end of the war, Nazi "medievalism" and "neoclassicism" thus merged into the same seductive sentimentalism—expressed in the postwar era in Kiefer's art and (in a more artful way, because of its pretended positivism) in Speer's autobiography.[79]

In the spring of 1945, on one of the last days of the War, Speer said a last and obviously not literal *Auf Wiedersehen* to Hitler (sullen and lethargic in his bunker). He then took his leave of the Chancellery he had designed. Importantly, his description of the Court of Honor is one of Kiefer's rendering. "All is dread Silence here, and undisturb'd." For one brief moment or "several seconds," Speer experienced that magic instant that represents the apotheosis of Nazi Romanticism, and that Kreis and Kiefer, German Romantics who "believed themselves to be able to believe" (Blumenberg, 268), placed in the realm of the future.

Time seemed to have collapsed into a far-off moment of the future and the past. Pausing by "the Time-shook Arch, the monumental Stone," the builder was become the halted traveler. In Mallet's words, "The sad Spirit walks with shadowy Foot, / his wonted Round, or lingers o'er this Grave." Or, as Speer put it:

> Since the lights were no longer functioning, I contented myself with a few farewell minutes in the Court of Honor, whose outlines could scarcely be seen against the night sky. I sensed rather than saw the architecture. There was an almost ghostly quiet about everything, like a night in the mountains. The noise of a great city, which in earlier years had penetrated to here even during the night, had totally ceased. (485)

Except of course as Speer, donning his innocuous postwar cloak of the frontline journalist, duly reported: "at rather long intervals, I heard the detonation of Russian shells."

NOTES

This essay is respectfully and affectionately dedicated to Professor Charles S. Maier of Harvard University.

1.   See Fritz Stern, *The Politics of Cultural Despair: A Study in the Rise of the Germanic Ideology* (Berkeley: University of California Press, 1961); George L. Mosse, *The Crisis of German Ideology: Intellectual Origins of the Third Reich* (1964; New York: Schocken, 1981).
2.   On Third Reich architecture in general, see Barbara Miller Lane, *Architecture and Politics in Germany, 1918-1945* (Cambridge: Harvard University Press, 1968); Robert B. Taylor, *The Word in Stone: The Role of Architecture in the*

National Socialist Ideology (Berkeley: University of California Press, 1974); Joachim Petsch, *Baukunst und Stadtplanung im Dritten Reich* (Munich: Carl Hanser, 1976); and the useful collection of primary documents *Architektur im Dritten Reich 1933-1945*, ed. Anna Teut, Bauwelt Fundamente 19 (Frankfurt am Main: Suhrkamp, 1967).

    3.   The German titles are *Kunst und Rasse, Kunst aus Blut und Boden, Krisis der Architektur, Die Brandfackel Moskaus, Rasse und Stil, Verstädterung,* and *Über die Zusammenhang von Kultur, Zivilisation und Kunst.*

    4.   Founded in 1928 by Nazi ideologue and former architecture student Alfred Rosenberg. Paul Schultze-Naumberg frequently lectured for the KfdK. (As Nazi art director in Thuringia from 1930, Schultze-Naumberg fired Bauhaus teachers, including Paul Klee and Wassily Kandinsky.) So did Alexander von Senger. Other activists included the architect Friedrich Nonn, Rosenberg's co-editor of the Nazi Party's daily newspaper, *Völkischer Beobachter,* and head of KfdK's architecture and engineering section; Kondrad Nonn, editor of *Zentralblatt der Bauverwaltung*; and Bettina Feistel-Rohmeder, author of the widely syndicated art column *Deutsche Kunstkorrespondenz* and *Im Terror des Kunstbolschewismus* (1938).

    5.   Founded in 1928 by Schultze-Naumberg, *Bloch* was a response to the most chic, modernist *Ring,* which boasted a select membership of the most innovative architects of the Weimar Republic and was closely linked to CIAM, the International Congresses for Modern Architecture, a prestigious institute which published and exhibited functionalist architecture.

    6.   For example, the distinguished architect Paul Bonatz (1877-1956), a founding member of *Bloch,* often worked in a radically simplified neo-Romanesque as in the the Stuttgart Railway Station (1911-1928). But this German gentile eventually left Nazi Germany for Turkey.

    7.   This was partly a matter of Weimar commissions. But, for example, Schultze-Naumburg was a Biedermeier architect and a medievalist theoretician.

    8.   Martin Heidegger, "The Origin of the Work of Art," *Basic Writings* (New York: Harper and Row, 1977), 168. For a similar argument, see the 1934 inaugural speech of another Nazi party member and university president, Otto Gruber, "Über die Grundlagen einer Erziehung zur deutschen Baukunst," *Aachener Akademische Reden* III. Rektorats-Rede, gehalten am 12. Mai 1934 (Aachen, 1934), especially 1-21; see also Otto Koppel, "Der Baukunstler, ein Trager nationalsozialistischer Weltanschauung," quoted in Teut, 134, which treats the "Aryan spirit" as reincarnated in those two periods; Alfred Rosenberg, *Das politische Tagebuch,* ed. Hans-Günther Seraphim (Berlin, 1936), 22-3; Hans Stephan, *Wilhelm Kreis.* Geleitwort von Reichsminister Albert Speer. Deutsche Kunstler unserer Zeit (Oldenburg: Gerhard Stallings, 1943), 16; and Himmler's 1942 statement that his planned buildings in the occupied East would emulate "die Kirchen in der mittelalterlichen oder das Forum in der antiken Stadt," in Heinrich Himmler, "Richtlinien für die Planung und Gestaltung der Städte in den eingegliederten deutschen Ostgebieten," *Der soziale Wohnungsbau in Deutschland,*

Heft 13 (Berlin, 1942), on the "Allgemeine Anordnung Nr. 13/II vom 30.1.1942," quoted in Teut, 356.

9. Quoted from the title of George Vogel, *Die deutsche Bau-und Bilderkunst des Mittelalters als Ausdruck deutschen Wesens. Ein Weg zur Kunsterziehung der deutschen Jugend.* Schriften zu Deutschlands Erneuerung (Breslau: Heinrich Handel, c. 1933); see also Otto Riedrich, "Die Germanische Seele im Zeitalter der Gotik," *Odal: Monatschrift für Blut und Boden*, 1936, quoted in Taylor, 92.

10. Rudolf Ramlow, "Der deutsche Stil des 20. Jahrhunderts," *Bausteine zum deutschen Nationaltheater*, Organ der NS Kulturgemeinde 3.4, quoted in Taylor, 122.

11. Also see, for one Nazi Gothicist tract, Johannes Eilemann, *Deutsche Seele, deutscher Mensch, deutsche Kultur, und Nationalsozialismus* (Leipzig: Quelle und Meyer, 1933).

12. Quoted from Paul Schultze-Naumberg, *Die Kunst der Deutschen: Ihr Wesen und ihre Werke* (Stuttgart: Deutsche Verlagsanstalt, 1934), 14, also referred to in Taylor, 93. Such claims involved painfully labored arguments about the supposed Germano-Nordic racial purity of the builders of France's Romanesque and Gothic cathedrals. See for example Karl Caesar, "Deutsche Baukunst," *Karlsruher Akademische Reden* 14. Rede gehalten bei der Reichsgründungsfeier der Technischen Hochschule Fridericiana zu Karlsruhe am 18. Januar 1934 (Bühl-Baden: Konkordia, 1935), especially 8-11; Vogel, 7-13; Gruber, 14; and Riedrich, quoted in Taylor, 92.

13. Matties Schmitz, *A Nation Builds* (New York: German Library of Information, 1940), 15.

14. Quotation on "Jesuits" by Alfred Rosenberg from Lane, 97; quotation on Jews from Werner Rittich, *Architektur und Bauplastik der Gegenwart* (Berlin: Rembrandt-Verlag, 1938), 14, "Die Warenhäuser einiger Juden." Probably since outside Augsburg Germany possesses few Renaissance monuments, as opposed to their Italian cousins, the German interwar right rarely discussed Renaissance architecture, while they often celebrated Prussian neoclassicism.

15. The 1927 Weissenhof Siedlung, led by Ludwig Mies van der Rohe, initiated by the Werkbund, partly financed by a new state organ, *Reichsforschungsgesellschaft für Wirtschaftlichkeit im Bau- und Wohnungswesen*, and counting among its contributors Le Corbusier, Walter Gropius, J. P. Oud, Mart Stam, and Max and Bruno Taut, received enthusiastic newspaper reviews, and some 20,000 visitors daily. Patriotism ran high in Germany too, when at the Barcelona Exhibition of 1929 the German Pavilion, a coolly elegant functionalist building designed by Mies van der Rohe, was the exhibition's acknowledged masterpiece.

16. From 1919 to 1926, the school's goal had instead been the left-wing medievalist dream of a "Cathedral of Socialism."

17. "Animal geometrique" is a quotation from the famous functionalist architect Le Corbusier: so is "living machine." Quotation marks around "settlements" (*Siedlungen*) in original.

18. Christopher Isherwood, *The Berlin Stories* (1935; New York: New Directions, 1963), 2:1.

19. See as one representative example Alexander von Senger, "Der Baubolschewismus und seine Verkoppelungen mit Wirtschaft und Politik," *Nationalsozialistische Monatshefte* 5 (1934), 497ff.

20. Better established Weimar circles also celebrated medievalism. For example, in 1928 the parliament president gave foreign visitors a coffee table book on Germany's architectural achievements. Of its eighty images, thirty-one are of medieval buildings. Of the six postwar structures included, three are medievalist, including Wilhelm Kreis's 1925 neo-Gothic Düsseldorf Planetarium and Paul Bonatz's 1911-1928 neo-Romanesque Stuttgart Railway Station. See Dr. Redslob, *Deutsche Bauten als Dokumente Deutscher Geschichte* (Berlin: Deutscher Kunstverlag, 1928). The foreign visitors had come for the twenty-fifth conference of the Interparliamentary Union.

21. "Wenn die verschütteten Quellen des Blutes wider aufgedeckt sein werden, dann wird eine echt nordisch-deutsche Kunst entstehen" (Vogel, 32; see also Gruber, 5, 6).

22. "[E]s war eine wunderbare Zeit, eine Zeit, wie sie Völker in ihrem künstlerischen Schaffen nur ganz selten erleben . . . Wahrlich, eine Blützeit, eine Zeit grossartigen Schaffens! . . . es war auch die Zeit, in der das ganze deutsche Volk in Bewegung war, um sich den notwendigen Lebensraum in Osten zu erobern und altes germanisches Land wieder einzudeutschen. Unvergessliche, unvergängliche Grosstaten unseres Volkes!" "Fühlen doch sogar Amerikaner, die so stolz auf ihre ungeheuren Stein und Betonbauten sind, etwas von unaussprechlichen Zauber einer alten deutschen Stadt, wie die vielen jährlichen Besuche in Nürnberg, Rothenburg und derg. beweisen" (Vogel, x).

23. Bestelmeyer also built in 1914-17 the Busch-Reisinger Museum at Harvard University.

24. "[E]inen Hauch der Reinheit und Grösse des frühen Mittelalters . . . . Wir werden auch wieder Heilige und Könige, Helden und Fabeltier in unseren Hallen malen und in Stein bilden . . . " Quotation from Paul Schmitthenner's "Baukunst im dritten Reich," in *Das Neue Reich*, pub. Deutsche Akademie (Munich: Callwey, 1943), 34, also quoted in Taylor, 246. On these activists' hopes for Nazi Germany, see also Lane, 1-35; Petsch, 39-58.

25. See Jeffrey Herf, *Reactionary Modernism: Technology, Culture, and Politics in Weimar and the Third Reich* (Cambridge: Cambridge University Press, 1984).

26. See also Lothar Suhling, "Deutsche Baukunst. Technologie und Ideologie im Industriebau des 'Dritten Reiches,'" *Naturwissenschaft, Technik und NS-Ideologie. Beiträge zur Wissenschaftsgeschichte des Dritten Reichs*, pub. Herbert Mertens and Steffen Richter (Frankfurt am Main: Suhrkamp, 1980).

27. Todt died in an airplane crash in 1942, and Albert Speer was then appointed Minister of Armaments.

28. Adolf Hitler, *Liberty, Art, Nationhood—Three Addresses Delivered at the Seventh National Socialist Congress, Nürnberg, 1935* (Berlin: Muller und Sohn, 1935), 40.

29. See also Albert Speer, *Inside the Third Reich* (New York: Avon, 1970), 44.

30. Quoted in Ingemar Karlsson and Arne Ruth, *Samhället som teater* (Stockholm: Liber, 1983), 177.

31. Quoted in Sheridan William Allan, ed., *The Infancy of Nazism: The Memoirs of Ex-Gauleiter Albert Krebs 1923-33* (New York: New Viewpoints, 1976), 160.

32. See "Hitler Calls This Living! by a member of the German Freedom Party" (London, 1939); Richard Linneke, "Die Entwicklung der Siedlung in Deutschland," *Das Junge Deutschland*, Heft 12 (1933); Friedrich Kopp, "Der volkpolitische Sinn der Siedlung," *Volk im Werden*, Heft 1 (1933), 56.

33. It reinforced the ban on 29 February 1940.

34. Harald Scholtz, "Die 'NS-Ordensburgen,'" *Vierteljahreshefte für Zeitgeschichte* 15.3 (July 1967), 269-98; Teut, 210-12, 332; Lane, 206-7; Taylor, 206-8. For contemporary propaganda pieces, see "Ordensburgen der Bewegung: Auslesestätten der Besten der Nation," and "Verewigter Glaube: das Erlebnis Nationalsozialistischer Zukunftwillen und neuer deutschen Baukultur, die Ordensburgen Vogelsang, Sonthofen, und Crössinsee," *Völkischer Beobachter* 24 April 1936, Munich edition; E. Bender,"Die Ordensburgen Vogelsang und Crössinsee," *Bauwelt*, Heft 35 (1936); Werner Rittich, *New German Architecture*, ed. Richard Mönnig. Terramare Publications 15/16 (Berlin: Terramare Office, 1941); and Hubert Schräde, *Bauten des Dritten Reiches* (Leipzig: Bibliographisches Institut, 1937), 28.

35. On the *Thing*, see Teut, 228-32, and Lane, 210; for contemporary propaganda pieces see for example Wolf Braunmüller, *Freilicht- und Thingspiel: Rückschau und Forderungen* (Berlin: Volksschaft-Verlag für Buch, Bühne und Film, 1935); Wilhelm von Schramm, *Neubau des deutschen Theaters: Ergebnisse und Förderungen* (Berlin: Schlieffen, 1934); Rainer Schlösser, *Das Volk und seine Bühne: Bemerkungen zum Aufbau des deutschen Theaters* (Berlin: Theater Verlag Albert Langen-Georg Müller, 1935).

36. Ludwig Moshammer, *Die Thingstätte und ihre Bedeutung für das kommende deutsche Theater* (Berlin, 1935), quoted in Teut, 232.

37. On these so-called *Grenzlandsdramen*, which developed out of the Fascist experimental theatre in the late Weimar Republic and dramatized the so-called threat to the German people posed by the Slavic nations, see also "Zur Herausbildung von Formen faschistischer Öffentlichkeit im Theater der Weimarer Republik," *Weimarer Republik*, pub. Kunstamt Kreuzberg and Institut für Theaterwissenschaft der Universität Köln (Berlin, 1977).

38. William E. Dodd and Martha Dodd, eds., *Ambassador Dodd's Diary 1933-1938* (New York: Harcourt, Brace, 1941), entry for 10 June 1934.

39. Quotation from Hans-Georg von Studnitz, *While Berlin Burns. The Diary of Hans-Georg von Studnitz 1943-45* (Englewood Cliffs, NJ: Prentice-Hall, 1963), 259. See also Richard Pfeiffer, "Jagdhaus 'Karinhall,'" *Die völkische Kunst* 1 (1935): 19-24. For life at Karinhall, see Emmy Göring, *An der Seite meines Mannes: Begebenheiten und Bekenntnisse* (Göttingen: Schütze, 1967).

40. Bella Fromm, *Blood and Banquets: A Berlin Social Diary* (New York: Harper, 1942), 239, entry for 7 January 1937. Fromm is reporting the story

second-hand. Even if false, however, it is telling as to what kinds of historicist practices Göring was expected to indulge in.

41. In the well-respected *Monatshefte für Baukunst und Städtebau*, the number of articles on medievalist social planning diminished through the 1930s. In *Moderne Bauformen*, an important German architectural journal, functionalist interiors for private homes had vanished by the later 1930s. Instead, medievalism shifted indoors, to take the form described here.

42. See Teut, 251, 60, 63, 87, 89, 126, and 135. The technocrat Finance Minister Hjalmar Schacht fired Gottfried Feder, leftist head of the Nazi public housing program (*Deutsche Siedlungswerk*); the "old street fighter" (*alte Kämpfer*) and party founder was made a professor. The Green Minister of Agriculture, Walther Darré, author of the medievalist tract *Neuadel aus Blut und Boden* (1934), lost influence. Rosenberg was easily outmaneuvered by Goebbels, a devotee of modern technology and American mass culture. KfdK folded in 1935. Schultze-Naumburg remained head of the Weimar State School for Building, Arts and Crafts; Alexander von Senger was appointed professor in 1936; and Friedrich Nonn in 1935. Those medievalists who already held university chairs, like Schmitthenner, remained there.

43. The Nazi political elite argued that behind heterogeneous Nazi styles lay a fundamental moral and racial unity. See for example Rittich: "Es kann daher für uns keine Frage nach dem Stil der Gegenwart geben, sondern nur die Frage nach der inneren Haltung der Baumeister und nach dem Wesen ihrer Werke" (118).

44. Thomas Nipperdey, "Nationalidee und Nationaldenkmal in Deutschland im 19. Jahrhundert," *Historische Zeitschrift* 1 (Februar 1968), 573; *Deutscher Patriotbund zur Errichtung eines Völkerschachtsdenkmal bei Leipzig*.

45. Begun in Teutoburger Forest Monument (1875) and the Niederwald Germania Monument (1883-), and inspired by Valhalla German Hall of Fame near Regensburg (1830-42). On these earlier monuments, see Taylor, 185, and Nipperdey.

46. Quoted from Kreis in Paul Meissner, *Wilhelm Kreis*, ed. Paul Joseph Cremers. Charakterbilder der neuen Kunst 6 (Essen: Baedeker, 1925), 10.

47. Wilhelm Kreis, "Kriegermale des Ruhmes und der Ehre im Altertum und in unserer Zeit," *Bauwelt* 11/12 (1943).

48. In 1933, as chair of the prestigious governing board (*Vorstand*) of this main German architectural organization, *Bund deutscher Architekten*, Kreis was part of the 21-23 September meeting which introduced the "Aryan clause" and the "Führer principle." BDA was then incorporated into the *Reichskammer der bildenden Künste*. Kreis was the *Reichkammer* president during the war.

49. For one example of these department stores, see Wilhelm Kreis, "Das Warenhaus Tietz in Elberfeld," X. *Sonderheft der Architecktur des XX. Jahrhunderts*, text by Max Creutz-Köln (Berlin: Ernst Wasmuth, 1912); other examples are reproduced in Stephan. For descriptions of Kreis's interwar pre-Nazi work see Stephan, 37-48.

50. The facade drawings of the Frankfurt hospital are reproduced in Stephan, ill. 32; photographs of the "Wilhelm-Marx-Hochhaus" in Düsseldorf are reproduced in Meissner, unpaginated appendix.

51. Wilhelm Kreis, "Übergangszeit," "Marksteine auf dem Wege zur Kultur unseres Zeitalter," *Über die Zusammenhang von Kultur, Zivilisations und Kunst. Neue Werkkunst* (Berlin: Friedrich Ernst Hübsch, 1927), xi.

52. Perspectival drawing reproduced in Stephan, 89; see also Speer, 154. Kreis was a personal friend of Speer: they, as well as the Nazi sculptors Arno Breker and Joseph Thorak and the painter Hermann Kaspar, formed an inner Nazi art circle.

53. Kenneth Frampton, *Modern Architecture: A Critical History* (New York and Toronto: Oxford University Press, 1980), 218.

54. Both drawings are reproduced in Wilhelm Kreis, *Soldatengräber und Gedenkstätten* (Munich: Callwey, 1944), 62, 63.

55. The Germanic tribes Kreis so admired, however, as Tacitus pointed out, "disdain to show honor by laboriously rearing high monuments of stone which would only lie heavily on the dead" (Tacitus, *Germania* [Stuttgart: Reclam, 1962], 24-5).

56. The main plan was to exterminate Slavic people and move Germans there. Terms like *Entpolonisierung* and *Eindeutschung* refer to this. Warsaw and Cracow the Nazis planned to erase from the earth (eighty-five percent of Warsaw was destroyed). See Heinrich Himmler, "Richtlinien für die Planung und Gestaltung der Städte in den eingegliederten deutschen Ostgebieten," *Der soziale Wohnungsbau in Deutschland* 13 (Berlin, 1942), on the "Allgemeine Anordnung Nr. 13/II vom. 30.1.1942."

57. Winfried Weiss, *A Nazi Childhood* (Santa Barbara: Capra, 1983), 174.

58. Paul Celan, *Poems*, trans. Michael Hamburger (New York: Persea Books, 1980), 50-2, originally published in *Mohn und Gedächtnis* (Stuttgart: Deutsche Verlags-Anstalt, 1952): "dann steigt / ihr als Rauch in die Luft / dann habt ihr ein Grab in den Wolken / da liegt man nicht eng."

59. Kreis worked on a number of World War I memorials; see Stephan, 25.

60. Dr. Sames, *Unser Toten. Eine Denkschrift. Der Waldfriedhof von La Parriée*. Architekt Leutn. [Wilhelm] Kreis, Regiments-Adjutant des Landw. Inf. Rgts. [Landwehr Infantry Regiment] No. 81 (n. p., n. d.). The quotations reads, "Der Tod hat eine versöhnende Kraft. Die Gräben unserer Gegner wechseln mit denen unserer Kameraden ab."

61. Quoted in Kenneth Clark, *The Gothic Revival* (New York: Harper and Row, 1962), 30-1.

62. Arthur Möller van den Bruck (1876-1924) was one of the early *völkisch*/Romantic right-wing ideologues; on him, see Stern.

63. Saul Friedländer, *Reflections of Nazism*, trans. Thomas Weyr, expanded and revised English ed. (1982; New York: Avon, 1984), 13.

64. "Und wenn einst späte Geschlechter in den Weiten des Ostens, auf den Felsenrissen Norwegens, im Schatten der Akropolis von Athen, an den Ufern der Maas oder in den Wusten Afrikas am Fusse vor gewaltiger Mahnmale von

eindringlichster Sprache den Schicksalskampf ihrer Ahnen überdenken, so werden sie vor der letzten Krönung des Lebenswerke dieses Mannes stehen." I am grateful to Märit Rausing for translation help.

65. Mark Rosenthal, *Anselm Kiefer* (Philadelphia: Philadephia Art Museum, 1987), 12, 15.

66. *Occupations (Besetzungen)*, *You're a Painter (Du bist maler)*, *Germany's Facial Type (Das deutsche Volksgesicht)*, reproduced in Rosenthal, 15, 12, 51.

67. Geoge L. Mosse, *Nazi Culture* (New York: Schocken, 1981), 186, citing an eyewitness. The total number of submissions that year was around 2400.

68. *Germany's Spiritual Heroes (Deutschlands Geistenhelden)*, oil and charcoal on burlap (private collection), reproduced in Rosenthal, 28-9.

69. *Wege der Weltweisheit*, 1976-77, mixed media on burlap (private collection), reproduced in Rosenthal, 52; *Wege der Weltweisheit—die Hermanns-Schlacht*, 1978-80, woodcut with acrylic and shellac (private collection), reproduced in Rosenthal, 53.

70. *Shulamite (Sulamith)*, 1983, mixed-media canvas (now in the Saatchi collection), reproduced in Rosenthal, 118; *The Rhine (Der Rhein)*, 1980, woodcut with oil (private collection), reproduced in Rosenthal, 106; *To the Unknown Painter (Dem unbekannten maler)*, 1983, mixed media (Museum of Art, Carnegie Institute, Pittsburgh), reproduced in Rosenthal, 115.

71. These quotations are from Kreis's writings in *Bauwelt, passim*.

72. *Poems of Robert Browning* (Oxford: Oxford University Press, 1925), 112.

73. V. S. Pritchett, *London Perceived* (New York: Harcourt, Brace and World, 1962), 48.

74. *Märkischer Sand V*, 1977, twenty-five photographs with sand, oil, and glue, in bound volume (private collection), reproduced in Rosenthal, 44-5; *Wege: märkischer Sand*, 1980, acrylic and sand on photograph (private collection), reproduced in Rosenthal, 78.

75. See also 81, where Friedländer adds, "In this contradictory series, it is not one thing or another that is decisive by itself; it is their coexistence that gives the totality its signficance."

76. *Athanor* (1983-84), mixed media on canvas (private collection), reproduced in Rosenthal, 116; this version of *Dem unbekannten maler*, 1983, mixed media on canvas (private collection), is reproduced in Rosenthal, 117.

77. In practice this meant exterior walls were bearing, so caved-in roofs did not mean their automatic collapse, and reinforced concrete and steel girders were not used.

78. Hans Blumenberg, *Die Lesbarkeit der Welt* (Frankfurt am Main: Suhrkamp, 1981), 267-8.

79. On how Speer presented himself as an innocent bystander, see Mathias Schmidt, *Albert Speer: Das Ende eines Mythos* (Munich: Goldmann Wilhelm Verlag, 1983).

Medievalism as Modernism: Alfred Andersch's Nominalist *Littérature Engagée*

Richard J. Utz

> The past is never dead; it isn't even past.
> William Faulkner

> The "engaged" writer knows that words are action.
> Jean-Paul Sartre

During the last twenty-five years, the importance of medieval nominalist philosophy for interdisciplinary investigations of late-medieval and Renaissance literature has undergone a revolutionary development. Increasing interest in nominalism has led to original reinterpretations of such diverse genres and works as the Chester Cycle and the writings of William Langland, the *Pearl* Poet, John Gower, Chaucer, and John Skelton.[1] Usually these scholarly efforts can be categorized into two groups according to their main objectives: (1) A group of the more philologically-oriented studies tries to demonstrate an author's typically late-medieval mentality as concurrent with or analogous to coeval nominalist trends;[2] (2) Another group examines the tenets of late-medieval nominalism, especially nominalist epistemology, seeking to find them in some way reflecting their own twentieth-century perceptions of art, language, and the world. These studies find something modern, even postmodern, about late-medieval and Renaissance authors, and they attribute their findings to an apparent modern or postmodern quality of nominalist philosophy developing in their work.[3]

Indeed, research in philosophy since the late 1950s has signaled the effects of late medieval nominalist thought on the development of modern science, theology, philosophy, and political theory.[4] Moreover, numerous scholars have established affinities between major modern philosophers such as Gottlob Frege, Bertrand Russell, and Ludwig Wittgenstein and their late-medieval sources and analogues.[5] Finally, Fredric Jameson, in *Postmodernism, or the Cultural Logic of Late Capitalism* (1991), has forthrightly equated "Deconstruction as Nominalism."[6]

As pleased as the guild of ivory tower scholars may be about detecting possible analogies between rather sophisticated late-medieval philosophy and similarly sophisticated contemporary literary theory, writers have so far refrained from responding creatively to the esoteric subject matter of nominalism. There are only two major exceptions to this general trend of abstention: the Italian, Umberto Eco, and the German, Alfred Andersch.[7]

Eco's *The Name of the Rose* is a truly serious piece of creative literary reception of late-medieval nominalism. Eco's William of Baskerville is modeled after the *venerabilis inceptor* of late-medieval nominalism, William of Ockham, and a dominant theme of the book, medieval epistemology and theology in the wake of the recovery of Aristotle, addresses some of the main concerns of fourteenth-century philosophy.[8] However, because *The Name of the Rose* is the work of a medievalist and professor of semiotics at the University of Bologna, the novel is a genial demonstration of Eco's more scholarly investigations on the parallels between the Middle Ages and the twentieth century.[9] Furthermore, if Eco's multi-accented simultaneity of gothic suspense, chronicle, scholarship, and late-medieval philosophy indicates a postmodernist play with the past, Andersch's interplay of short story, poem, novel, and nominalism characterizes him as a traditionalist modernist author.[10]

Unlike Eco, Alfred Andersch did not come to nominalism through scholarly training, so application of nominalist thought in his poetic theory and practice is more unexpected and therefore more difficult to assess. Andersch is generally known as one of the main representatives of Germany's second generation of modern realist writers. The story of his life is a perfect manifestation of what Malcolm Bradbury and James McFarlane have described as the quintessential modern experience:

> those overwhelming dislocations, those cataclysmic upheavals
> of culture, those fundamental convulsions of the creative
> human spirit that seem to topple even the most solid and

substantial of our beliefs and assumptions, leave great areas of
the past in ruins . . . question an entire civilization or culture,
and stimulate frenzied rebuilding.[11]

Born in 1914, Andersch grew up in Munich, one of Europe's
principal centers of modernist culture. As an active member of the
Communist Party, he was arrested in February of 1932, spent three
months in the Dachau concentration camp, and remained under
Gestapo surveillance after his release. In 1940 Andersch was drafted
into the German army, only to desert from it in Italy in 1944. The
Americans took him to an anti-fascist compound in Ruston, Louisiana,
and later made him participate in two programs of cultural and political
re-education before repatriating him to Germany in 1945. Together
with Hans Werner Richter, Andersch co-edited *Der Ruf*, Germany's
first major postwar magazine of literary and cultural criticism. He was
present at the first meetings of the *avant-garde* "Gruppe 47" and thus
among those who, in the words of Ezra Pound, wanted to "make it
new" after the catastrophic dissolution of values, standards, and
institutions on every level of human experience in Europe and
especially in Germany.[12]

Unlike many other postwar German writers, Andersch was not
satisfied with those who gladly concurred with Thornton Wilder's
notion that the world had once more escaped "by the skin of our
teeth" and that reviving the prewar ideals of humanistic education
would suffice to rebuild what had been destroyed. Andersch wanted
to do conscious *Trauerarbeit* and sided with Jean-Paul Sartre, who
demanded fundamental societal changes and believed strongly in the
power of literature to help bring these changes about. Together with
Heinrich Böll and Günther Grass, Andersch became of of the main
representatives of a *littérature engagée* in Germany. Questions arise as
to why and how a modern realist writer of *littérature engagée* would
resort to basing much of his poetic theory and practice on the tenets
of medieval philosophy.

In June 1977, a major German publishing house invited Andersch
to compile an anthology of primary texts based not on scholarly
relevance or assumed objectivity, but on Andersch's own subjective
predilections. Andersch accepted the offer and stated the reasons for
his choice of texts in a short introduction:

> Philosophically I think I am an extreme nominalist. *Universalia sunt nomina.* Down with Plato! I do not even accept the linguistic notion of a universal. Universals are only *flatum vocis*, a voiced aspiration. There are only objects, things. That is why I would like to have lived in the ninth or tenth centuries. The ideas of Roscelin and Abelard as they became visible in Romanesque architecture . . . . Because I am only interested in objects, things—human beings also fall under that rubric—I have used the motto of a Welsh literary critic as the motto for my volume of stories, *My Disappearance in Providence*: "Art is not about abstractions or ultimate issues or infinity or eternity. Art is about buttons."[13]

Without its mention of nominalism, this credo could be accepted as a typical modernist poetic program. As with the Italian neo-realists/neo-verists (e. g., Elio Vittorini and Cesare Pavese) and many of Andersch's American models (Stein, Steinbeck, Hemingway, and Faulkner), his experiences between 1930 and 1950 pressured him to search for a new language. Reacting against the bombastic use and large-scale abuse of language and ideas in fascist Germany and Italy, Andersch joined the postwar cultural movement which aimed at purifying the language of German literature. Hans Werner Richter describes the mood among the writers of the "Gruppe 47" regarding their new means of expression: "What we did not want was a literature of agitation. That seemed to me a 'non-literature' with which the Third Reich . . . had overfed us. . . . What our participants' ears accept are concise clauses of statement. It is as if Gertrude Stein and Ernest Hemingway were with us in the room unnoticed."[14] Andersch does more than establish a clear, concise style oriented after the international or German modernist *avant-garde*, and he arrives at a highly idiosyncratic solution: he connects his own new language and style with what he assumes to be its earliest historical and theoretical precedent, medieval nominalism.

Historically, nominalistic epistemology is the product of an eleventh-century scholarly dispute at the University of Paris.[15] Since antiquity, epistemology had been dominated by Platonic idealism which held that universals were the only true reality and hence the chief prerequisite of any true knowledge. During the early twelfth-century disputes on universals (*Universalienstreit*) this position was challenged for the first time. Deriving from Aristotle's undecided statement on the status of universals as reported by Boethius in his *Commentaries on Porphyry*, two main opinions developed: the nominalists, for example John Roscelin, defined universals as more *voces*, that is to say, mere "voiced air," or as *nomina*, mere names (hence "nominalists") or abstract concepts with only a very low degree of reality; the extreme Platonic realists, for example William of Champeux, held that universals were *res*, or things prior to sensible individual objects, and that they represented the highest degree of epistemological reality. A preliminary synthesis of the problem was reached later by Peter Abelard, a student of both Roscelin and William of Champeaux.[16]

Though Roscelin found himself accused of heresy for employing his theories to undermine the doctrine of the Trinity, this earlier medieval nominalism was on the whole purely academic and triggered few reactions outside institutions of higher learning.[17] The opposite is true of late-medieval nominalism, which shares only a few epistemological details with Roscelin and Abelard. It started as a conservative theological reaction to what nominalists saw as the limitation of God's omnipotence by rationalistic thirteenth-century metaphysics. Thomas Aquinas and others had maintained that human reason could prove even the existence of God. The nominalists, much influenced by their own calamitous fourteenth century, denied the status to human *ratio* of a capability to plumb the mysteries of God. Following William of Ockham, they concentrated on God's absolute power and postulated two strictly separate levels of truth: a religious truth of revelation, which was the only secure truth and gained by faith alone; or a contingent, secular truth gained via human thought. Such separation of truth resulted in a shift of interest from transcendence towards immanence. The secular sphere lost its character as mere *significans* and gained importance as a worthwhile subject of investigation, thereby freeing philosophy and the natural sciences from their position as mere *ancillae theologiae*. Late-medieval nominalism is the main reason why, in the words of David Knowles, we "may well consider the fourteenth century more prolific than the thirteenth in those *idées forces* that were to determine the course of European intellectual life."[18] However, it is necessary to note that this view of the importance of late-medieval nominalism for the development of Western thought is relatively recent. Due to the Thomist orientation of early twentieth-century philosophy and theology, most Roman Catholic scholars have dismissed Ockham and his followers more or less as a negative force which accelerated the breakdown of what they construct as the preferable synthesis arrived at by Thomas Aquinas. Similarly, most Protestant scholars define the late-medieval nominalists as mere forerunners of Luther and the Reformation.[19]

Joseph Quack has linked Andersch's acquaintance with nominalist thought to the author's familiarity with Johan Huizinga's theories on medieval culture and the philosophical background of late-medieval art.[20] At first glance, that may well be true, especially since *The Waning of the Middle Ages* was among the volumes Andersch lost when his mother's Hamburg apartment was bombed in 1943.[21] However, a closer look at the discussion of realism and nominalism in *The Waning of the Middle Ages* reveals that the book can only have given Andersch an initial idea for his idiosyncratic use of nominalist philosophy, for Huizinga writes,

> In pointing out these very strong links between symbolism and realism (in the scholastic sense), we should be careful not to think too much of the quarrel about the universals. We know very well that the realism which declared *universalia ante rem*, and attributed essentiality and pre-existence to general ideas, did not dominate medieval thought without a struggle. Undoubtedly there were also nominalists. But it does not seem too bold to affirm that radical nominalism has never been anything than a reaction, an opposition, a countercurrent vainly disputing the ground with the fundamental tendencies of the medieval spirit. As philosophical formulae, realism and nominalism had early made each other the necessary concessions. The new nominalism of the fourteenth century, that of the Occamites or Moderns, merely removed certain inconveniences of an extreme realism, which it left intact by relegating the domain of faith to a world beyond the philosophical speculations of reason.[22]

It is obvious that although Andersch shared Huizinga's low opinion of realist-symbolist aesthetics, he certainly did not subscribe to the historian's assessment of late-medieval nominalism. Consequently, since Huizinga's underestimation of nominalism reflects the state of research still valid in the 1950s, Andersch's use of medieval philosophy probably represents a conscious poetical/political decision. In contrast to Eco, the expert medievalist, Andersch shows only a rudimentary knowledge of medieval nominalism. He uses Roscelin and Ockham and their respective variants of nominalist thought interchangeably, without attention to fundamental differences between early and late theories. Certain superficial correspondences are more important to him: he strongly believes that universals (as Hegel posits them, *a priori*), bear the danger of dehumanization under the cover of their assumed objectivity, as visible in Hitlerite and Stalinist propaganda. Just as the nominalists criticize the Neoplatonists' careless use of language and want to start from scratch (with the so-called "accidents"), so Andersch postulates their philosophical *universalia sunt nomina* as his poetic *caveat* against the danger inherent in all ideas which are prone to deteriorate into ideologies. Andersch's explanations of the impact of ideology on the development of art is clearly based on his observations during the Third Reich:

> The abstraction is the instinctive or conscious reaction of art to the degeneration of idea into ideology. It is not necessary to delineate the process of this degeneration here; everybody knows that it has taken place. When it became more and obvious on the horizon of thought that the great humanistic and religious ideas were transformed into ideologies, when high models, to which human beings could respond as free individuals, were replaced by all-ensnaring ideological directions of use, when thus all content became questionable, because it related to societal conditions dominated by ideology—at this historical moment which can be singled out in the history of thought, art gave a radical answer by entirely withdrawing from the depiction of content.[23]

The anthology mentioned above, *Mein Lesebuch—oder Lesebuch der Beschreibungen*, gave Andersch a chance to exemplify his political and poetic convictions formed during the 1940s. The book contains exclusively examples of *description*, a genre Andersch believed highly recalcitrant to the ideologically loaded universals:

> A writer's relationship to a thing/object has always interested me more than his ideas, his *Weltanschauung*. The depiction of some houses in Petersburg relates more to me than Raskolnikow's tragedy of conscience. Raskolnikow is a product of the streets of Petrograd, just as the private

investigator would be unthinkable without a special corner in Soho.[24]

Consequently, Andersch added texts to the anthology which speak and influence via their excellence in descriptiveness: Rudolf Borchardt's unrivaled translation of Shelley's "The Cloud," excerpts from Alexander von Humboldt's "Introduction" to his *Ansichten der Natur* (1807), from Friedrich Engels's 1847 description of the workers' situation in capitalist England, from Hermann von Barth's wanderings in the Alps, and from Joseph Conrad's *The Mirror of the Sea*. Andersch also paid tribute to some of his most revered models of style: there is Hemingway's short story "Big Two-Hearted River," a scene from Walter Benjamin's description of Paris, and samples from Ernest Schnabel and Alexander Kluge. The climactic moment of the collection, however, is Hans Magnus Enzensberger's poem "Leuchtfeuer," which, as Andersch saw it, contained *in nuce* the poetic program of his literary nominalism (and modernism), because it states:

> the fire there shines,
> it is nothing but a fire,
> means: there is a fire,
> there is the place where there is the fire,
> there, where the fire is, is the place.[25]

Andersch's deep distrust of idealism and ideology of any kind already informs his earliest theoretical writings. In a short collection of aphorisms entitled "The Antisymbolist," he lashes out against symbolic, parabolic, or allegorical modes of expression which only lead to a degradation of the real, visible world of things.[26] He is convinced that the use of received metaphor only petrifies pre-established clusters and traditional analogies. He likens his own "realism" to "revolution," but parallels "symbolism" with "slavery," since he has experienced symbolism as the perfect tool of fascist political propaganda.

His short story of 1951, "Ein Auftrag für Lord Glouster" ("A Mission for Lord Glouster"), is an excellent example of Andersch's practical application of his literary nominalism.[27] In this story he transposes an English knight from the Hundred Years' War into the 1950s' world of automobiles, Coca-Cola bottles, and industrialization. Strangely enough, Nicolas Glouster, soldier at Agincourt and Orléans, is not surprised by modern technology. He had retired into a

Burgundian monastery at the beginning of the fifteenth century where
he read the works of Duns Scotus, William of Ockham, and Nicholas
of Cusa.

> "That is why I am not too astonished by all this," he added
> and pointed at the landscape of alley trees, high-voltage masts
> and railroad-tracks. "Universalia sunt nomina," he said and
> grinned suddenly. "The ideas are mere words. You know, if
> you get started on this, then you can do with the real things
> whatever you want; then everything falls into place."[28]

His twentieth-century interlocutor, a historian, answers, "Yes, then one
can change the world." And Glouster goes on, "Yes, but those
philosophers could not envisage the reality named Jeanne [d'Arc] . . .
Jeanne was nowhere to be found in their plans, and because I detected
this . . . I was able to believe in her return" (47). He, Lord Glouster,
has been sent on a mission to prepare for Jeanne d'Arc's second
coming.

   This story introduces a second, ethical aspect of Andersch's literary
nominalism. As a result of the concentration on God's absolute power,
late-medieval nominalists believed that God, out of His free will, could
change the current *ordo* at any given moment. Parallel to this axiom,
they fought against prevailing deterministic philosophies and attributed
free will and responsibility to the human individual within an utterly
contingent world. Sheila Delany and I have demonstrated how a
medieval author, Chaucer, seems to represent a coeval literary parallel
to the late-medieval nominalists' anti-determinist cause.[29] Like Chaucer
in his *Troilus and Criseyde*, Andersch believes in a strong subjective
element in human history which he introduces into his short narrative.
Lord Glouster, who—in the eyes of his interlocutor—resembles
Lawrence of Arabia, recognizes in Jeanne d'Arc's appearance to him
irrefutable proof that history is not predetermined by an unchangeable
causality of events. The individual, whether Jeanne d'Arc in the
fourteenth century or Lawrence of Arabia in the twentieth, is evidence
of the individual's potential to change the course of history. Joseph
Quack even interprets Andersch's use of nominalist philosophy as an
attack against the historical determinism prevalent in Communist Party
doctrine. Determinism, dominant in Communist thought as Andersch
sees it, removes the individual's responsibility and thus hinders political
action. Quack further believes that Andersch understands his writing

and all modern art as a healthy, necessary form of objection to the dangerous resignation in face of the seemingly omnipotent "*fatum* of history" (719).

As shown above, Andersch uses medieval nominalist philosophy as historical basis for his modern realist poetics: first, he justifies his skeptical attitude towards symbolic language by making the nominalist "*universalia sunt nomina*" his motto and by choosing the description and the descriptive narratives as his preferred literary genres; and second, he sees in the nominalists' rejection of deterministic theories an apt archetype of his own celebration of the individual's free will and responsibility. In his poem "nominalism" (subtitled "draft for a historical novel"), Andersch comes full circle by using both approaches and by adding a third to his unique nominalist poetics. The poem, which is written in his typically condensed style and in crystal clear, anti-symbolist language, tells the story of a medieval potter who leaves his workshop behind "because he had heard / that in paris a man called / roscelin / taught that / universals were only / flatum vocis / voiced air / and that in reality / there were only / individuals / things."[30]

Andersch's poem is a perfect example of his poetic agenda. Roscelin's epistemological nominalist credo, although not at all influential outside the twelfth-century ivory tower, is presented as engendering an actual political act, when a member of the lower classes, a peasant artisan, is shown following the call of *universalia sunt flatum vocis*. Hearing what a member of the intellectual *avant-garde* has written and said, he is convinced that the general concepts of medieval society and religion, the universals and ideals, have no actual existence, and that nothing will ever remain of his life but his artifacts, the objects he has formed with his hands. Liberated from the propaganda of universals and their inherent determinist premises, the individual leaves his no longer "God-given" but socially defined station to seek his true destiny. The message of Andersch's poem is highly ahistorical and owes more to his strong belief in a *littérature engagée* than to his cognizance of the possible social significance of medieval nominalist theory.[31] Andersch, like Sartre, believed that action begins in the process of reading. The process of conscious interaction between reader and writer consists in naming and thereby uncovering the things.[32] Andersch regarded Faulkner's *Light in August* (1932) as a prime example of how a writer could motivate the reader. The reader would understand Faulkner's novel, taken as a documentary, as an example of lynch law. As a piece of literature, the book presents its events so overwhelmingly that it succeeds in wiping out racial hatred in the hearts of Faulkner's readers. Andersch believes further that the influence of the novel would not even stop there. So well crafted a story would necessarily be retold, becoming known even to people who had never read it: thus, the past would become present for everybody. Social relevance, achieved through narrative intensity, lies in the book's becoming an instrument for doing away with racial hatred, for educating all citizens into their humanity.[33] A similar development seems to occur in Andersch's poem: condensed into the motto *universalia sunt flatum vocis*, Roscelin's nominalism exerts a strong motivational power on the medieval potter prompted to social action on his own behalf. He goes out into the world to tell others about his new insight. The poem thus defines or rather conjures up the social and political responsibility of the writer. It is Andersch's rough draft of his own role in modern society, sketched against a rudimentary foil of historical nominalist thought.

Alfred Andersch, like many other writers after World War II, was faced with a necessity to "make it new." When trying to develop his own modern realist poetics in line with the demands of a *littérature engagée*, he detected a historical supporting structure in medieval nominalist thought. He found his own postwar poetics nicely attuned to some, admittedly simplified, theories of this medieval philosophical superstratum and used those similarities as a basis for his own distinctive voice in the heterogeneity of modern realist voices in post-1945 Germany.[34] Although he grew more and more independent of direct philosophical references, his literary nominalism is discernible in his later as well as in his early work. In his 1974 novel *Winterspelt*, Andersch again implicitly hints at his nominalist/modernist *Leitmotif* in a significant scene where the two protagonists realize their deep mutual sympathy. Major Dincklage, telling Käthe about his life as a soldier, reaches a point where he and his comrades first arrive at the Sahara:

> "That doesn't interest me," she said. "*Describe* the Sahara!"
> He looked at her, and to his own astonishment began *describing* the Sahara.[35]

NOTES

For the completion of this essay I am indebted to the following friends and colleagues: Rüdiger I. Hartmann (Universität Regensburg), William H. Watts (Butler University), and Daniel J. Cahill, Annie Finch, and Noel H. Kaylor (University of Northern Iowa).

1. See Kathleen Ashley, "Chester Cycle and Nominalist Thought," *Journal of the History of Ideas* 40 (1979), 477; Britton J. Harwood, "Langland's '*Kynde Knowyng*' and the Quest for Christ," *Modern Philology* 80 (1983): 242-55; Janet Coleman, *Piers Plowman and the Moderni* (Rome: Edizioni di storia e letteratura, 1981); John F. McNamara, "Responses to Ockhamist Theology in the Poetry of the Pearl-Poet, Langland, and Chaucer," Diss. Louisiana State University 1968; Patrick Gallacher, *Love, The Word and Mercury: A Reading of Gower's Confessio Amantis* (Albuquerque: University of New Mexico Press, 1975), 1-40; Richard J. Utz and William H. Watts, "Nominalist Perspectives on Chaucer's Poetry: A Bibliographical Essay," forthcoming in *Mediaevalia & Humanistica*, n.s. 23 (1993); J. Stephen Russell, "Skelton's *Bowge of Court*: A Nominalist Allegory," *Renaissance Papers* 2 (1980): 1-9.

2. Cf. Lois Roney, *Chaucer's Knight's Tale and the Theories of Scholastic Psychology* (Tampa: University of South Florida Press, 1990); Richard J. Utz, *Literarischer Nominalismus im Spätmittelalter: Eine Untersuchung zu Sprache, Charakterzeichnung und Struktur in Geoffrey Chaucers Troilus and Criseyde* (Frankfurt: Peter Lang, 1990); William H. Watts, "The Interplay of Genres in Chaucer's *Troilus and Criseyde*," Diss. Boston University 1990; Russell A. Peck, "Chaucer and the Nominalist Questions," *Speculum* 53 (1978): 745-60.

3. Cf. Stephen Knight, "Chaucer—A Modern Writer?" *Balcony* 2 (1965): 37-43; Lee Patterson, *Chaucer and the Subject of History* (Madison: University of Wisconsin Press, 1991).

4. Cf. Hans Blumenberg, *Säkularisierung und Selbstbehauptung* (Frankfurt: Suhrkamp, 1985); *Der Prozeß der theoretischen Neugierde* (Frankfurt: Suhrkamp, 1988); "Der kopernikanische Umsturz und die Weltstellung des Menschen," *Studium General* 8 (1955): 637-49. Cf. also Heiko A. Oberman, "Some Notes on the Theology of Nominalism," *Harvard Theological Review* 53 (1960): 47-76, and "Fourteenth-Century Religious Thought: A Premature Profile," *Speculum* 53 (1978): 80-93; and William J. Courtenay, "Nominalism and Late Medieval Religion," in *The Pursuit of Holiness in Late Medieval and Renaissance Religion*, eds. Charles Trinkaus and Heiko A. Oberman, *Medieval and Renaissance Thought* 10 (Leiden: Brill, 1974), 26-59. Cf. also the recent volume *Die Gegenwart Ockhams*, ed. Wilhelm Vossenkuhl (Weinheim: VCH, 1990).

5. Cf. Wilhelm Vossenkuhl, "Wilhelm von Ockham," in *Wilhelm von Ockham: Das Risiko Modern zu Denken*, eds. Otl Aicher, Gabriele Greindl, and Wilhelm Vossenkuhl (München: Münchener Rückversicherungs AG, 1986), 97-

177, and Henry Veatch, *Realism and Nominalism Revisited* (Milwaukee: Marquette University Press, 1954).

6. Fredric Jameson, *Postmodernism, or the Cultural Logic of Late Capitalism* (Durham: Duke University Press, 1990), 217-59. For a short comparison of twentieth-century and late-medieval nominalism, see Claude Panaccio, "Der Nominalismus Ockhams und der zeitgenössische Nominalismus," in *Rekonstruktion und Interpretation: Problemgeschichtliche Studien zur Sprachtheorie von Ockham bis Humboldt*, eds. Klaus D. Dutz and Ludwig Kaczmarek (Tübingen: Narr, 1985), 1-22.

7. Other twentieth-century writers, especially William Carlos Williams, have sporadically been labeled "nominalist." However, no serious claims of a full-fledged literary nominalism have been made. Cf. J. Hillis Miller, *Poets of Reality: Six Twentieth Century Writers* (Cambridge: Harvard University Press, 1965), 307, and Bernard Duffey, *A Poetry of Presence: The Writings of William Carlos Williams* (Madison: University of Wisconsin Press, 1986), 161.

8. The most obvious indication of nominalist influence on Eco is the novel's title, explained toward the end of the book by the Latin quotation *Stat rosa pristina nomine, nomina nuda tenemus*, which mirrors the nominalist axiom of *nomina* as *flatum vocis*. See Umberto Eco, *The Name of the Rose*, trans. William Weaver (San Diego: Harcourt, Brace, Jovanovich, 1983), 502; cf. also Eco's *Postscript to the Name of the Rose*, trans. William Weaver (San Diego: Harcourt, Brace, Jovanovich, 1984), 3, where the author refers to Gertrude Stein's "a rose is a rose is a rose" as well as to the possible, not less scholarly informed, nominalist reading of his title and book.

9. Cf. Jürgen Miethke, "Der Philosophe als Zeichendeuter und Spurensucher, und sein 'alter Freund' Wilhelm von Ockham in Umberto Ecos *Der Name der Rose*," in *"eine finstere und unglaubliche Geschichte?" Mediävistische Notizen zu Umberto Ecos Mönchsroman 'Der Name der Rose,'* ed. Max Kerner (Darmstadt: Wissenschaftliche Buchgesellschaft, 1987), 115-27.

10. For a recent evaluation of the "postmodern" vs. the "modern" attitudes, see the excellent collection of essays *Modernism/Postmodernism*, ed. Peter Brooker (London and New York: Longman, 1992).

11. "The Name and Nature of Modernism," in *Modernism 1890-1930*, eds. Malcolm Bradbury and James McFarlane (Harmondsworth: Penguin, 1978), 19.

12. For a detailed biographical account, see Stephan Reinhardt, *Alfred Andersch: Eine Biographie* (Zürich: Diogenes, 1984); cf. more specifically Karl-Heinz Schoeps, "The 'Golden Cage' and the Re-Education of German Writers in American POW Camps: Hans Werner Richter and Alfred Andersch," in *Amerika! New Images in German Literature*, ed. Heinz D. Osterle (New York: Peter Lang, 1989), 29-42.

13. "Im philosophischen Sinne fühle ich mich als extremer Nominalist. *Universalia sunt nomina.* Down with Plato! Nicht einmal den Begriff eines Begriffes laß ich gelten, der Begriff ist für mich nichts als *flatum vocis*, ein stimmlicher Hauch. Es gibt nur Dinge, Sachen. Das ist einer der Gründe, warum ich am liebsten im 9. oder 10. Jahrhundert gelebt hätte. Die Ideen von Roscellin

und Abälard, sich entfaltend in romanischer Architektur. . . . Weil mich eigentlich nichts interresiert als Sachen, Dinge—, im weitesten Sinne natürlich, auch der Mensch ist ein Ding—, habe ich meinem Erzählband *Mein Verschwinden in Providence* zwei Sätze ein walisischen Literaturgelehrten also Motto vorangestellt: 'Art is not about abstractions or ultimate issues or infinity or eternity. Art is about buttons.'" *Mein Lesebuch—oder Lesebuch der Beschreibungen*, ed. Alfred Andersch (Frankfurt: Fischer, 1978), 8. All translations of German quotations are mine.

14. "Doch was wir nicht wollten, war eine Agitationsliteratur. Sie erschien uns als Un-Literatur, als Propaganda, mit der uns das Dritte Reich und vorher die Parteien überfüttert hatten. . . . Was Bestand hat vor den Ohren der Teilnehmer sind die knappen Ausgesätze. Gertrude Stein und Ernest Hemingway sind gleichsam unbemerkt im Raum." Hans Werner Richter, "*Der Ruf.* Sein Entstehen und sein Untergang," in *Hans Werner Richter und die Gruppe 47*, ed. Hans A. Neunzig (München: Nymphenburger, 1979), 62ff.

15. For concise surveys of early medieval nominalism, cf. Julius R. Weinberg, *A Short History of Medieval Philosophy* (Princeton: Princeton University Press, 1964), 58-91, and Hans Joachim Störig, *Kleine Weltgeschichte der Philosophie* (Frankfurt: Fischer, 1984), 1:238-45.

16. For a concise description of Abelard's solution, see Kurt Flasch, *Das Philosophische Denken im Mittelalter. Von Augustin zu Machiavelli* (Stuttgart: Reclam, 1986), 211-25.

17. Cf. James W. Earl, "Nominalism and Sex," *Hellas* 3.1 (Spring 1991): 60-92: "The immediate relevance of the debate [about universals], which might be mistaken as being quaintly medieval, is demonstrated by Wittgenstein—and also in Eco's *Name of the Rose*: Sherlock Holmes' deductive reasoning—i. e., science—as well as poststructural semiotics, are only possible, it turns out, in a nominalist world. You can only follow a trail of clues through the labyrinth of the world if you keep reminding yourself that the objects and people you are tracing are individuals, and not just ephemeral manifestations of Platonic ideas or general principles" (84).

18. David Knowles, *The Evolution of Medieval Thought* (Baltimore: Helicon, 1962), 333f.

19. Most scholars followed the expert conclusions in Etienne Gilson's classical investigation *La philosophie au moyen-âge de Scot Erigène à Guilleaume d'Occam* (Paris: Payot, 1922). For a concise history and a bibliography of the reception of nominalist thought see Utz, *Literarischer Nominalismus*, 22-41.

20. Joseph Quack, "Alfred Andersch, ein literarischer Nominalist," *Neue Deutsche Hefte* 32/4 (1985): 731.

21. See Volker Wehdeking, *Alfred Andersch* (Stuttgart: Metzler, 1983), 161-5.

22. Johan Huizinga, *The Waning of the Middle Ages* (Garden City, New York: Doubleday, 1954), 204.

23. "Die Abstraktion ist die instinktive oder bewußte Reaktion der Kunst auf die Entartung der Idee zur Idologie. Es ist unnötig, den Prozeß dieser Entartung hier nachzuzeichnen; jedermann weiß, daß er stattgefunden hat. Als es sich immer

deutlicher am Horizont des Geistes abzuzeichnen begann, daß die großen humanen und religiösen Ideen von den jeweils herrschenden Mächten zu Ideologien umgeformt wurden, als an die Stelle hoher Leitbilder, auf die der Mensch individuell und in Freiheit antworten konnte, die ideologische Gebrauchsanweisung trat, die den Menschen total umgriff, als so alle Inhalte fragwürdig wurden, weil sie sich auf gesellschaftliche Verfassungen bezogen, die von der Ideologie regiert wurden—in diesem historischen Augenblick, der geistesgeschichtlich exakt bezeichnet werden kann, gab die Kunst eine radikale Antwort, indem sie sich vom Inhalt überhaupt zurückzog." Alfred Andersch, "Die Blindheit des Kunstwerks," in *Die Blindheit der Kunstwerks und andere Aufsätze* (Frankfurt: Suhrkamp, 1965), 26.

   24. "Die Beziehung eines Schriftstellers zu einer Sache hat mich stets stärker interessiert als seine Ideen, seine Weltanschauung. Die Schilderung einiger Häuser in St. Petersburg geht mich mehr an als Raskolnikows Gewissenstragödie. Raskolnikow ist ein Geschöpf aus den Straßen von Petrograd, wie der Geheimagent undenkbar wäre ohne einen bestimmten Winkel in Soho" ("Art Is about Buttons," 8f.).

   25. "das feuer dort leuchtet / ist nichts als ein feuer, / bedeutet: dort ist ein feuer, / dort ist der ort, wo das feuer ist, / dort, wo das feuer ist, ist der ort" ("Art Is about Buttons," 15).

   26. "Der Antisymbolist," *Frankfurter Hefte* 3/10 (1948): 1145.

   27. "Ein Auftrag für Lord Glouster," first published in Alfred Andersch, *Geister und Leute* (Olten: Walter, 1958), republished in *Alfred Andersch: Gesammelte Erzählungen* (Zürich: Diogenes, 1974), 43-9; all references are to the later edition.

   28. "Deswegen erstaunt mich das hier nicht allzusehr", fügte er hinzu und deutete auf die Landschaft aus Alleebäumen, Tankstellen, Hochspannungsmasten und Eisenbahnschienen. "Universalia sunt nomina", grinste er plötzlich. "Die Ideen sind nichts als Worte, verstehen Sie, wenn man damit mal anfängt, dann kann man mit den Realien machen was man will—dann ergibt sich alles andere von selbst" (47f.).

   29. See especially Delany's essay "Undoing Substantial Connection: The Late Medieval Attack on Analogical Thought," *Mosaic* 5 (1972): 33-52, and Utz, *Literarischer Nominalismus*, 109-92.

   30. "weil er gehört hatte / daß in Paris ein mann namens / Roscellin / lehrte / die begriffe seien nichts als / flatum vocis / ein stimmlicher hauch / und in wirklichkeit / gäbe es nur dies / einzeldinge / sachen." "nominalismus. skizze für einen historischen roman, " in Alfred Andersch, *Empört Euch der Himmel ist Blau* (Zürich: Diogenes, 1977), 90-1.

   31. Ironically enough, the best essay on this topic, written by Paul Honigsheim, might have been easily available to Andersch: "Zur Soziologie der mittelalterlichen Scholastik. Die soziale Bedeutung der nominalistischen Philosophie," in *Hauptprobleme der Soziologie. Erinnerungsgabe für Max Weber*, ed. Melchior Palyi (München and Leipzig: Duncker & Humblot, 1923), 174-213.

32. Cf. Jean-Paul Sartre, *What Is Literature?*, trans. Bernard Frechtman (New York: Philosophical Library, 1949), especially 7-37.

33. Cf. Alfred Andersch, "Böse Träume," *Tintenfaß* 2 (1981): 43ff.

34. Cf. "Art Is about Buttons," 9, where he sees clear correspondences between the twelfth- and fourteenth-century nominalist revolt against scholasticism and the nineteenth-century revolt of materialism against idealism.

35. "'Das interessiert mich nicht', sagte sie. 'Beschreiben Sie die Sahara!' Er sah sie an und begann zu seinem eigenen Erstaunen, die Sahara zu beschreiben." English translation from Alfred Andersch, *Winterspelt*, trans. Richard and Clara Winston (Garden City, New York: Doubleday, 1978), 195.

The Economic Decline
and Reinfeudation
of the State of Milan
in the Seventeenth Century

Thomas Barbiero

The seventeenth century remains one of the most perplexing periods of Italian economic history. During that century the economy of the peninsula endured one of the steepest declines ever seen in the annals of economic history. From being the most vibrant economy during the Renaissance, Italy had become, by the end of the seventeenth century, along with Spain, Europe's economic backwater.

This study focuses on the State of Milan,[1] which concurrently declined in the course of the seventeenth century and underwent a "refeudalization" of sorts. While it is difficult to determine the direction of the causal links between these two phenomena, the evidence suggests that they reinforced each other. By the end of the century, Lombardy's economy resembled what it had been in the medieval period, with agriculture by far the most important activity, rather than the nascent industrial economies of northern Europe on the threshhold of the modern industrial era.

Why industry and commerce declined, while at the same time investments in infeudated lands increased, has been the focus of numerous studies. Carlo Cipolla maintains that the reasons for Italy's economic decline in the seventeenth century can be divided into three categories: (a) excessive control by guilds that continued to insist on outdated methods of production and organization; (b) excessive taxation by governments; (c) and relatively high labor costs which made Italy's goods less competitive on international markets.[2] Thus, with lower profits in industry and commerce, investments were attracted to agriculture, which included infeudated lands.

While there is no doubt that rigid guilds, high taxes, and wages were contributing factors to the economic decline of the State of Milan, I propose an alternative hypothesis to explain the renewed interest in agricultural investments in general and infeudated land in particular. It can be argued that during the period of economic crisis which began around 1620 those with the economic means in Lombardy looked to the past for answers, and the "medieval model" of social and economic organization, which had effectively worked for so long, had compelling appeal. This may explain why a significant proportion of the industrial and commercial class decided during the course of the crisis to cease its vocational activity and purchase its way into the noble class by acquiring infeudated lands. It may also explain why the guild system became even more rigid during the seventeenth century rather than giving way to a more flexible economic institution.

That the State of Milan experienced a severe economic decline during the first half of the seventeenth century is abundantly clear from the available information. The most dramatic evidence is the almost complete collapse of textile production, the State of Milan's most important industry. In the city of Milan at the beginning of the century there were seventy firms producing woolen cloths with a total annual output of approximately 15,000 cloths. By 1650 the number of firms had dropped to fifteen with an annual production of only three thousand cloths. The silk sector experienced a similar decline: the number of firms producing silk cloth dropped from more than five hundred at the end of the sixteenth century to only thirty-two by the early eighteenth century (Cipolla, 119, 197). A report by the Guild Association in 1662 on the State of Milan's industries brought the following information to light: the number of loom operators belonging to guilds dropped from five thousand in 1640 to a mere two hundred in 1662; the number of teaselers from forty to eight; dyers from twenty-four to four; embroidery firms from forty to ten. The dyeing guild reported that the volume of fabric its members worked had dropped from 200,000 *libbra* to only eight thousand annually.[3]

Evidence from smaller urban centers in the State of Milan also demonstrates a precipitous economic decline. In Como there were sixty firms producing woolen cloth at the start of the 1600s with an annual production of about ten thousand cloths. By 1650 only four firms remained, producing a total of only four hundred cloths.[4] In

Monza, of the twenty firms producing woolen cloths in 1620, none remained in 1640.[5] Its hat industry also declined during this period. The silk sector fared no better: of the fifty silk masters registered in Pavia in 1630, only ten were left in 1650. In Como the local guild had thirty silk spinners registered in 1630, but only two by 1650. The cotton textile industry in Cremona was completely destroyed in the first half of the century (Cipolla and Aleati, 394, 396).

If the city of Milan and other smaller urban centers declined, there are indications that industrial activity in small villages and rural areas picked up partly to offset the dramatic fall of overall manufacturing production in Lombardy. For example, after 1620 both the textile and silk industries flourished on a small scale in Tremezzo, Menaggio, and Bellaggio (Cipolla and Aleati, 396). Although the silk industry disappeared from Cremona, it sprang up in Monticelli, Busseto, and Parma. Records show that a woolen factory was established in Busto Arsizio and a hat factory in Corbetta. After 1650 the production of mixed cotton fabrics and silk yard expanded in the Gallarate district.[6] As Cipolla points out, however, it appears highly unlikely that the industrial revival in rural areas compensated the economic decline of the city of Milan and other urban centers in Lombardy (202). The result was that the Lombard economy transformed from one well entrenched in international commerce to one largely preoccupied with meeting local needs. By 1650 agriculture was by far the largest sector in the economy.[7]

The decline of industry and commerce had far-reaching social and economic implications. The entrepreneurial class increasingly sought out land investments, particularly infeudated lands sold by the government. With the purchase of the latter came a feudal title and rights to levy certain taxes on the peasant families living on them. Also, the buyer received powers of jurisdiction, both civil and criminal notary prerogatives.[8] One of the attractions of purchasing infeudated lands was the automatic entry to the ranks of the nobility, which brought prestige to the owner as well as the usual privileges accorded to members of the noble class. The purchase of a parcel of land with fifty hearths came with the title of Count, and with one hundred hearths the title of Marquis (Vismara, 167).[9] As the economic crisis deepened, the government's tax base eroded—for example, the excise tax yield dropped fifty percent between 1620 and 1650 (Sella, "Two Faces," 11)—and, as a consequence, the State put up more infeudated lands for sale. While their sale provided instant cash for the government treasury, such actions further undermined its long-run fiscal position because of the taxing privileges it gave away with these lands. As can be seen from Table 1, the decline of industry and commerce was accompanied by a large increase in the sale of infeudated lands in the State of Milan. Between 1646 and 1700 the number sold was almost double that in the previous 145 years. The entrepreneurial class dwindled as many of its members rose to the ranks of nobility with the acquisition of infeudated lands. Thus, in a general sense the social and economic structures of Lombardy came to resemble those of the medieval period. The feudal lords once again became a powerful class even if the military aspects of feudalism were not present because of of the existence of a central government with an army of its own.

Table 1

SUMMARY OF INFEUDATED LANDS
STATE OF MILAN 1500-1700[10]

Period	Number of Infeudated Lands
1500-1599	68
1600-1645	43
1646-1700	207

The economic crisis of the seventeenth century appears to have greatly augmented an existing desire by many members of the merchant class to enter the ranks of the nobility. As Ferdinand Braudel points out, in the sixteenth and seventeenth centuries "the rich bourgeois of every origin were irresistibly drawn towards the aristocracy as towards the sun."[11] Indeed, in the first half of the sixteenth century the number of rich merchants purchasing their way into the aristocracy had so alarmed the existing nobility that the latter required its members to abstain from any form of commercial activities (Vismara, 162). This restriction, however, did nothing to dissuade merchants and industrialists from their burning desire to become nobles.

A case in point is provided by the Orombelli family. Giovanni Antonio Orombelli was one of the most successful textile merchants in Milan in the third and fourth decades of the sixteenth century. He died in 1553, leaving a sizable fortune to his wife and three sons. Surprisingly, none of the sons continued in his father's business, even though it was a lucrative one. The family fortune was invested in

land.[12]   In the sixteenth century the chronicler Bandello wrote of a
similar story.   A noblewoman who married a merchant of
undistinguished ancestry forced her son on her husband's death to
withdraw from his father's business, thereby removing him from the
world of commerce so that he could be reinstated to noble rank (cited
in Braudel, 729-30). Examples of other Milanese merchant families who
entered the ranks of nobility by acquiring infeudated lands include the
Barromeos, the Littis, the Durinis, and the Cusanis (Caizzi, 339).

As the table shows, as the economic crisis deepened more
infeudated lands were purchased, many by the merchant class. Was the
increased interest in land, however, simply a rational economic
response to the crisis of industry and commerce?   One could argue,
with some credibility, that since Lombardy's industrialists and
merchants could not longer effectively compete either at home or
abroad they turned to land investments, which were presumably more
lucrative in comparison to those in industry and commerce.[13]

While this is a compelling argument, it is not totally persuasive for
three reasons. First, it is far from certain that land investments yielded
relatively high returns when compared to other forms of investments.
For example, Aldo de Maddalena has shown that in the case of one
large landowner, Ambroggio d'Adda, return on rural land investments
amounted to an average of only 1.5 percent *per annum* between 1600
and 1647.[14] This was much lower than the four or five percent that
could be had from public bonds.[15] Secondly, investments in infeudated
lands appear to have been motivated primarily by the accessibility to
the noble class such purchases made possible, rather than by potential
profits.[16] As already noted, once part of the noble class, ex-merchants
were pressured to cease commercial activities.   Thirdly, one would
expect that as more investments flowed into agriculture, at one point
they would be so large that returns to land investments would begin to
fall, and owners of capital would shift it to more profitable activities,
presumably industry and commerce. Such a movement does not appear
to have taken place for almost two centuries; only late in the
nineteenth century do we witness the beginning of the industrialization
of Lombardy, and to a lesser extent the rest of Italy.

This brings us back to the hypothesis put forth earlier, that the
reinfeudation of the State of Milan as a response to the economic crisis
can be interpreted as a desire on the part of the merchant class to
return to the "medieval model" of social and economic organization
which had functioned so well for so long. The keen observer will no

doubt object and point out that had the government not put up infeudated lands for sale the reinfeudation of the State of Milan could not have occurred. The story would then be interpreted as follows: the economic crisis caused a fiscal crisis, which led the government to put the infeudated lands for sale; therefore, the State of Milan became reinfeudated. While part of this interpretation is undeniable, it does not explain the demand factor: what caused the commercial and industrial class to be so willing to purchase more infeudated lands[17]—certainly much more than in the past—or indeed, did the larger government supply of infeudated lands come forth as a result of an increased demand for such lands? Needless to say, the cause and effect here is difficult to disentangle and it is the reason my argument must be presented as a tentative hypothesis.

The notion of looking to the past for answers at a time of crisis can also explain the intransigence of the guilds in the State of Milan to any form of change that might have endangered their members' livelihood. Guilds were not a new institution to seventeenth-century Lombardy, having been in existence since the latter part of the medieval period. The guilds had not always been as conservative as during the economic crisis of the seventeenth century. During the prosperous times of the fifteenth and sixteenth centuries they had often conceded special licenses to private individuals to work in their own home. Giovanni Orombelli, the Milanese textile merchant discussed above, often had nuns in the convent of Santa Maria and Sant'Orsola weave silk for him without any opposition from the weavers' guild (Maddelena, "Excolere," 351). Verri recounts that in the first half of the sixteenth century foreign artisans were welcomed to Milan and allowed to practice their trade without opposition from the guilds (351). It was only after 1630 that guilds refused entry to new members or merchants who wanted to establish firms with new technologies. For example, they were successful in stopping John Hauford in 1663 from establishing a shoe factory that used machines to cut down on labor costs. They also stopped a certain Gariboldi from manufacturing textiles along the same lines as in England, and another merchant, Boisset, from setting up a shop to shine jewelry as practiced in Venice (Caizzi, 356). Today we know that such action was not only economically detrimental to society at large but indeed to the guilds themselves, since it resulted in higher prices than imported goods and thus falling demand for the guilds' own production. However, the guilds' actions are quite understandable in the face of a crisis that threatened to wipe out their members' jobs. They naturally enforced rules and regulations which had worked so well since the Middle Ages. Their intransigent behavior was an effort to impede impersonal market forces from taking control of their lives, what Karl Polanyi calls embedding economic relations in social relations.[18] As in the case of the *bourgeoisie* acquiring infeudated lands during the economic crisis, the actions of the guilds in the seventeenth century suggest that they too looked to the past, particularly to the medieval period during which they came to existence, to search for solutions to the crisis.

It was thus that the economy of the State of Milan once again came to resemble, in a general way, that which had existed in the Middle Ages. From today's perspective the economy of Lombardy regressed, but then such a judgment is a normative one, since "progress" implies more abundant material wealth: a notion that arguably was not a dominating drive in the medieval era. One could argue, in fact, that the economic events of the seventeenth century were a blessing in disguise, for they allowed Italy to avoid for almost two centuries the trauma England went through during the Industrial Revolution, accompanied as it was with severe dislocation of labor, exploitation of child labor, and the creation of an urban industrial proletariat grudgingly drawn to the factory work. Italy, as a latecomer to the ranks of industrial powers, was able at least partially to avoid some of the more negative aspects of its own Industrial Revolution late in the nineteenth century. But even as Italy began to industrialize, the economic events of the seventeenth century continued to influence the nature of industrial development. "Feudal residues,"[19] particularly in the South, continued to exist well into the nineteenth century as still politically powerful landlords resisted being drawn to the modern age, no doubt longingly looking to the past when society's social and economic organization seemed to function, at least in their view, so well.

NOTES

1. The State of Milan encompassed almost the whole of Lombardy. It was made up of nine major urban centers and their surrounding countryside: Milan, Cremona, Pavia, Como, Lodi, Novara, Alessadria, Tortona, and Vigevano. In this article "the State of Milan" and "Lombardy" are used interchangeably.

2. Carlo Cipolla, "The Economic Decline of Italy," in *The Economic Decline of Empires*, ed. Cipolla (London: Methuen, 1970), 205, 207-8.

3. Pietro Verri, "Memorie Storiche Sulla Economia Pubblica dello Stato di Milano," in *Scrittori Classici Italiani di Economia Politica*, ed. Verri (Rome: Edizioni Bizzarri, 1966), 17:28.

4. Carlo Cipolla and G. Aleati, "Aspetti e Problemi Nell'Economia Milanese e Lombarda nei Secoli XVI e XVII," in *Storia di Milano* (Milan, 1958), 11:394.

5. Sergio Zaninelli, *Storia di Monza e della Brianza* (Milan: Edizioni Il Polifilio, 1969), 43.

6. Domenico Sella, "The Two Faces of the Lombard Economy in the Seventeenth Century," in *Failed Transition to Modern Industrial Society*, eds. F. Krantz and M. Hohenberg (Montreal: International University Center for European Studies, 1974), 13. Sella does not believe the economic crisis of the seventeenth century was as bad as some claim because decline in the urban center was partially offset by a revival in smaller urban centers and the countryside. See Sella's "Industrial Production in Seventeenth-Century Italy: A Reappraisal," *Explorations in Entrepreneurial History*, Series 2, 6 (1968-9): 235-53.

7. Even before the economic crisis, agriculture was still the largest sector in the Lombard economy, but as the crisis deepened and industry and commerce stagnated, the importance of agriculture became more pronounced.

8. Bruno Caizzi, "Le Classi Sociali nella Vita Milanese," *Storia di Milano* (Milan, 1958), 11:40. The purchase of infeudated lands was the first step in becoming part of the nobility. As of 1531, being a member of the nobility required one hundred years' residency in the State of Milan with a noble title. See Giulio Vismara, "Il Patriziato Milanese nel Cinque e Seicento," in E. F. Guarini, ed., *Potere e Societa Negli Stati Regionali Italiani* (Bologna: Il Mulino, 1978), 158.

9. It should be noted that the word "infeudation" is partly misleading. In the European medieval period a lord would give his vassal a parcel of land over which the latter had taxing and powers of jurisdiction. In return, the vassal provided military service for the feudal lord. In seventeenth-century Italy the military obligation associated with holding infeudated lands had disappeared.

10. The table is from F. Arese, "Feudi e Titoli nello Stato di Milano alla Morte di Carlo II," *Storia di Milano*, 11:xix.

11. Ferdinand Braudel, *The Mediterranean and the Mediterranean World in the Age of Philip II* (London: Collins, 1973), 2:729.

12. Aldo de Maddalena, "*Excolere Vitam Per Artes*: Giovanni Antonio Orombelli, Mercante Auroserico Milanese del Cinquecento," *Fatti e Idee di Storia Economica nei Secoli XII-XX* (Milan: Il Mulino, 1977), 363.

13. This would be the standard economic explanation for the renewed interest in land investments. Ruggiero Romano has suggested that in Italy it was a preference for rents that led to land investments on a larger scale in the seventeenth century (see his "Italy in the Crisis of the Seventeenth Century," in *Essays in European Economic History*, ed. Peter Earle (Oxford: Clarendon Press, 1974), 193.

14. Aldo de Maddalena, "I Bilanci dal 1600 al 1647 di una Azienda Fondiaria Lombarda," in *Storia dell'Economia Italiana*, ed. Carlo Cipolla (Torino: Boringhieri, 1959), 603. It should be noted that returns on investments were three percent *per annum* from 1600 to 1620, but between the latter date and 1647 they fell to about one percent.

15. However, it should be noted that there was a risk involved in lending money to the government, since there had been cases where it refused to honor its obligations. See Federico Chabod, "Usi e Abusi nello stato di Milano a mezzo il 500," in Guarini, 115.

16. This remains a hypothesis. Since becoming part of the nobility included many privileges, including in some instances the ability to avoid paying any taxes at all, it could very well be, once more evidence is brought forth, that acquiring infeudated lands was indeed a purely economic decision.

17. The standard economic response would be that since industry and commerce were in decline, infeudated lands must have been more profitable. As noted above, the profitability of infeudated lands compared to other investments is still uncertain.

18. For an exposition of the Polanyi thesis, see S. C. Humphreys, "History, Economics and Anthropology: The Works of Karl Polanyi," *History and Theory* 3.2 (1969).

19. The notion of "feudal residues" was originally introduced by Antonio Gramsci to explain the incomplete bourgeois revolution in nineteenth-century Italy. For a detailed discussion of the implications of feudal residues, see Emilio Sereni, *Capitalismo Nelle Campagne (1860-1900)* (Torino: Einaudi, 1947), 30-1.

Medievalism and Science in the Tuscany of the Last Medici

Michael Lavin

In the preface to his collection of essays *Pour un autre moyen âge*, Jacques Le Goff presented the idea of a medieval period which began in the second or third century after Christ and died slowly, under the blows of the Industrial Revolution, somewhere between the nineteenth century and the present day.[1] In the context of the Grand Duchy of Tuscany of the late seventeenth and early eighteenth centuries, this notion of the *longue durée* of history—the notion of history living and acting in the present—is of central importance. As I shall suggest, the presence of the medieval *Weltanschuung* was not only forcefully felt but indeed fundamental to the Tuscan culture of the period. The University of Pisa—the most important center of learning in the contemporary Grand Duchy—was in fact the arena of a struggle between an institutionally established world view which was essentially medieval (the philosophy of Aristotle as interpreted by the Scholastics), and a classical philosophy, *atomism*, which found its roots in the thought of Democritus and in the writings of Epicurus and Lucretius. We shall see also that both groups benefited from the ability to appeal, in the pleading of their respective causes, to extra-philosophical discourses: in the case of the atomists to the myth of Galileo, and in the case of the Aristotelians to God and to the public good.

Medievalism in late seventeenth and early eighteenth-century Tuscany is thus a very different notion from medievalism in the modern western world. In the Tuscany of the period, the culture of the Middle Ages was still very much alive, both in literature—in the form of the cults of Petrarch and Dante—and in philosophy and science, in the shape of Aristotelianism.[2] In the halls of the various Florentine academies—the *Accademia Fiorentina*, the *Accademia degli Apatisti*, the *Accademia della Crusca*—men of letters vied with each other to demonstrate their erudition in matters concerning the poetry of Dante and Petrarch, the fathers of the Tuscan language, and authors whose work constituted the methodological support of the *Crusca*'s *Vocabolario*, the first dictionary of what would later officially become the Italian language.[3] Dante, regarded as the "theological poet,"[4] was presented in the academies as a source of moral inspiration for Florentine and Tuscan youth, while Petrarch was lauded for the sweetness of his style and enthusiastically recommended to the numerous aspiring poets among the Grand Duchy's wealthier classes. While it was by no means rare for other authors to be discussed in Florence's literary institutions, the prestige of the Tuscan poets of the fourteenth century was unassailable.

But in the world of philosophy and science the presence of the Middle Ages was less benign. In the University of Pisa, the curriculum was still based on the works of Aristotle.[5] Despite the fact that Magnen, a scholar working at the university in the 1640s, had published a work on atomism entitled *Democritus revivscens*,[6] aspiring natural scientists were still obliged to base their view of the world on Aristotle's *Physics* and *De Caelo*. Since the Council of Constance and the condemnation of John Wycliff for his nominalist views on the Eucharist in the fifteenth century, materialist philosophy of all kinds had been relegated to the sidelines in all Catholic institutions of higher learning. Thus Thomas Aquinas's medieval tome the *Summa theologicae*, which had explained the miracle of transubstantiation in terms of a process he named *hylomorphism*—to which we shall be returning—was influential in the field of science, as well as that of philosophy.

In terms of science, however, Tuscany was something of a distinct society. The Aristotelians, whose position in the University of Pisa was strong, did not represent the only respectable tradition of scientific thought. For the ambiguous figure of Galileo was always lurking in the background, gnawing away at Peripatetic hegemony. As Paolo Galuzzi explains in his article on Medici patronage of the sciences, under Cosimo II, in the early decades of the seventeenth century, Galileo had been reclaimed from the *Studio padovano*, the major university of the Republic of Venice, largely for reasons of cultural prestige, after having used a peculiar Dutch instrument to make a tremendous astronomical discovery, the moons of Jupiter. When he had been in Tuscany, however, the Pisan had been shunned by the court: on his return to Florence he exacted a certain revenge by having himself called the philosopher and mathematician of the Grand Duke.[7]

For reasons beyond the control of the Medici, Galileo's time under their patronage was not without its problems. The attentions of Cardinal Bellarmine in 1616 and the inquisitorial trial of 1633 were good neither for the dynasty nor for its philosopher. However, the myth of Galileo remained useful within the context of the Medici's cultural policy, and under Grand Duke Ferdinand II and his brother Prince Leopold, it was given new institutional life in the 1650s and 1660s in the form of the *Accademia del Cimento*. The *Cimento* was a loose association of a number of the leading scholars of the Tuscany of the time, many of whom worked at the University of Pisa. It included students of Galileo himself, such as the Florentine Vincenzo Vivano and the Calabrian Alfonso Borelli, as well as leading provincial Tuscan intellectuals like Francesco Redi and Alessandro Marchetti. The academy, founded in 1657, was unofficially wound up ten years later with the publication of the *Saggi di naturali espirenze* (*Essays on Natural Experiments*), a collection of scientific experiments which was presented to the Royal Academy in London by the diplomat and secretary of the *Cimento*, Lorenzo Magalotti.[8] Despite the undoubted scientific value of the *Saggi*, it is interesting to note that copies of the book were sent by the academy's patron, Prince Leopold de Medici, exclusively to noblemen rather than to scientists (see Galluzzi, "L'Accademia del Cimento").

At the *Cimento*, the myth of Galileo was celebrated not in terms of his discovery of the *stelle medicee*—the moons of Jupiter—as had been the case some sixty years earlier during the reign of Cosimo II, nor in terms of his propagation of the Copernican theory of heliocentrism (which had been condemned during the trial of 1633), but rather within the framework of an experimental approach to natural philosophy consonant with a self-image of Tuscan culture in general which highlighted the supposedly down-to-earth, practical nature of the Tuscans themselves. But the methodology informing the activities of the academy was not, as the Medici princes themselves might have preferred, entirely neutral in the political sense. Pietro Redondi has suggested that the origins of Galileo's troubles with the Vatican lay not in his espousal of the Copernican theory of the structure of the universe but rather in the atomist approach he employed in *Il Saggiatore* (*The Essayer*).[9] And the *cimentisti* themselves were, for the most part, atomists. Alessandro Marchetti, for example, had produced a Tuscan—that is, an Italian—translation of Lucretius's *De rerum natura*, the most complete ancient espousal of corpuscularist philosophy.[10]

Alfonso Borelli's work on the vacuum depended on atomist premises, while Francesco Redi's scientific works, while not quite as open in their support of the atomist methodology, were nevertheless notable for their sometimes rather sharp attacks on Aristotelians such as Anastasio Kircher. These scholars were, in short, moving away from the medieval world view.

The *Cimento*, however, was a private institution and thus had a certain ideological freedom unavailable in the public domain of the *Studio pisano*—the University of Pisa. In Pisa, the academicians of the *Cimento* were hard pressed to carry their research work into the classroom. Here, the Aristotelians found themselves on firmer ground; rather than being obliged to argue in strictly scientific terms with their "Galileian" adversaries, they could instead begin to talk of the public good. In 1669 Giovanni Maffei, in his capacity as spokesman for a committee especially devised to investigate the polemics raging between atomists and Aristotelians at the university, accused the Galileians of propagating a philosophy unsuitable for impressionable young students. His Machiavellian style of reasoning led him to value the rigors of a system which inculcated a healthy respect for authority rather than one which placed an undue emphasis on intellectual individuality. For Maffei, regardless of the relative philosophical merits of Democritus and Aristotle, the doctrine of the latter should always hold the upper hand, since it was "appropriate to the tranquility of the states, to the orderliness of peoples, to good political and civil government." His opinions were succinctly summarized in the statement "useful things, even if they are damaging, are to be preferred to things which are not useful, even it they are true."[11]

Alessandro Marchetti himself responded on behalf of the Galileians. His 1671 letter to Prince Leopold pleaded the cause of *libertas philosophandi* in terms of a freedom to employ a synthetic approach to philosophy which relegated Aristotle from his status of unquestioned master to that of a philosopher among others.[12] To be sure, Lucretius, as well as his atomist forebears Democritus and Epicurus, made more than honorable appearances in the pamphlet, but Marchetti's rhetorical approach was to draw attention as far as possible away from the major point of antagonism shared by the two parties.

This point of antagonism was not purely political in nature. Although the Aristotelians were doubtless concerned about the palpable threat posed by the corpuscularists to their intellectual hegemony at the unversity and despite the fact that the experimental method proposed so wholeheartedly in the *Cimento's Saggi di naturali espirienze* did nothing to further the habit of submission to authority which men such as Giovanni Maffei would like to have seen encouraged in the student body, the dispute was, at least in the immediate sense, theological. In fact, the Democrito-Epicurean tradition, so vital to the members of the *Accademia del Cimento*, was accused in no uncertain terms by its Aristotelian adversaries of the basest impiety. Since Democritus conceived that the universe was composed from an infinite number of inestimably small particles of matter called atoms which had come together in their present configuration entirely by chance, those who followed him necessarily denied a physical first cause in the creation of the universe and were thus—as well as being anti-Aristotelians—in fact atheists.

Marchetti's letter to Prince Leopold has been seen variously as a manifesto on behalf of the atomists at the University of Pisa and as a desperate plea launched to his former patron—shortly after the *Cimento* ceased to function Leopold became a cardinal—by a scholar painfully aware that his life was going to become gradually more difficult as the position of his adversaries grew inexorably stronger.[13] As will become apparent, the latter thesis is the more convincing of the two: the position of the Tuscan atomists at the University of Pisa and, indeed, in the Grand Duchy in general, deteriorated dramatically during the course of the second half of the seventeenth century. The charge of impiety, continually leveled at them by their adversaries, was their most troublesome obstacle. Nor were they helped by the fact that Cosimo III, who had become Grand Duke in 1670, shared none of the enthusiasm for research into natural philosophy displayed by his father Ferdinand II, or his uncle Leopold, preferring instead to spend his time, and the state's money, on ostentatious acts of piety.[14]

But the task of presenting Democritus as a religiously sanctioned alternative to a fundamentally medieval version of Aristotle was not abandoned. Canon Donato Rossetti, a lowly professor of philosophy at Pisa, took upon himself the task of attempting, in a manuscript of 1673 addressed to Francesco Redi entitled *Two Propositions . . . Demonstrating How the Aristotelian Can Agree with the Democritan in the Explanation of the Eucharist*, to solve the most central theological problem confronting the Tuscan atomists: the Eucharist.[15]

The problem was of the greatest importance. The mystery of transubstantiation was at the heart of Catholic theology and, in a very real sense, at the heart of Catholic science. Transubstantiation raised two fundamental problems. First, how was the host turned into the body of Christ and into His blood? Did the bread and wine disappear entirely, or did they subsist in some material way? Secondly, how could it be that the senses still registered the presence of bread and wine? The word "miracle" offered one sort of explanation, but the longing for a more rational solution was impossible to assuage.

The solution was found in Thomas Aquinas's *Summa theologicae* and was termed *hylomorphism*. Hylomorphism posited that a physical body is composed of two metaphysical principles: matter and form. Matter provides the body with extension, while the qualitative principle of form provides the body with its specific properties. These two metaphysical principles combine to constitute a substance. As far as transubstantiation is concerned, the body of Christ coincides with neither the extension nor with the physical properties of the consecrated host. We are thus left with a situation in which the substance (the body of Christ), is different from its extension (the host). Hylomorphism is thus economical and rational: transubstantiation consists in the miraculous separation of a body from its extension. What remains, of course, are the accidents of the host, its color, smell, taste, weight, and so on (Redondi, 267-8). In his letter to Redi, Rossetti set himself the task of reconciling atomism with hylomorphism while at the same time using the Aristotelian terminology familiar to theologians. He managed to reconcile the scholastic dichotomy between substance and accident with atomism simply by stating that there was indeed a difference between an object's being a substance and its being a substance with mobility or extension. In this case he would be able to accept the Thomist interpretation of transubstantiation with no difficulty whatsoever. A small problem arose, however, over the diverging explanations of taste, color, and smell. For Rossetti, these sensations were caused by the interaction of minute particles of matter with the sensory organs; thus, during the process of transubstantiation, the substance of each single particle was separated from its accidents. The miracle took place, in other words, at the atomic level.[16]

Since the attraction of Thomas Aquinas's solution had been its economy, and since that solution had been considered dogma by the likes of Bellarmine and Francisco Suarez,[17] a corpuscularist alternative which posited a seemingly infinite number of separations of substances and accidents every time a priest offered up a host was unlikely to have been accepted with Christian resignation by the Peripatetics. Francesco Redi, the recipient of the treatise, not surprisingly thought better of having it published. Rossetti eventually left the Grand Duchy to work in Turin, apparently leaving much ill will behind him.[18] Despite the fact that he had managed to publish a number of overtly atomist works in Livorno, he never managed to enter the mainstream of Tuscan intellectual life. His theoretical audacity was perhaps not entirely to his advantage.

The career of another Tuscan atomist, Giuseppe Del Papa, took a different turn from those of his atomist colleagues at the University of Pisa. His political skills were finer than theirs and he was able to publish numerous atomist works during a career in which he was held in high esteem by certain members of the Medici family—most notably Prince Francesco Mattia—if not by the Grand Duke himself. In 1674 Del Papa produced *A Letter Concerning the Nature of Heat and Cold*[19] in which he maintained, against the Aristotelians, that coldness was not a quality in itself, but merely a lack of movement in the atoms which composed all bodies. This line of reasoning was continued and developed in his *Letter Discussing Whether Fire and Light Are One and the Same Thing* of 1675 and in *On the Nature of Humidity and Dryness* of 1661.[20] All of these treatises were addresses to Francesco Redi, the Grand Duke's personal physician and author of the dithyramb *Bacco in Toscana*,[21] the most popular work of literature of the period and quoted on the labels of numerous bottles of Tuscan wine to this day. It is interesting to note, however, that when Del Papa himself succeeded Redi as the Grand Duchy's leading medic, many of Redi's Galileian colleagues took a dim view of the affair, considering that the atomist newcomer's success was due more to his skills as a courtier rather than to any solidarity with their philosophical cause.[22]

Nevertheless, not even the diplomatically correct Del Papa could escape the institutional traps laid by the Church. After surviving the criticisms of the Jesuit Giovanni Vanni who had considered it scandalous that anyone should propagate a philosophy so evidently incompatible with Catholic dogma, he and his fellow Tuscan atomists were faced with a far greater obstacle.[23] In 1691, Cosimo III, mindful of the growing preoccupations of the Holy See and of the anti-atomist events on Naples which were soon to become known, significantly, as the "Atheist trials," issued the following decree:

> It is the will of the Grand Duke that none of the professors of the University of Pisa should read or teach, either publicly or privately, in writing or by voice, the Democritan or

atomist philosophy, but only the Aristotelian, and that anyone who should in any way contravene the will of His Highness be *ipso facto* relieved of the post he holds.[24]

Just as Marchetti's letter to Leopold had been a reaction to pressure imposed by Giovanni Maffei and others at the University of Pisa, Cosimo's decree can be legitimately considered a reaction to the more radical position take by certain atomists whose stated aim was to modernize the medieval foundations of science. In 1681, Lorenzo Magalotti, former secretary of the *Cimento*, had himself, in his infamous *Lettere familiari contro l'ateismo* (*Letters against Atheism*) produced a defense of Democritanism against Aristotelianism. Included in one of the letters was a passage which could not have failed to raise the hackles of the Aristotelians:

> You should know that a very great and erudite personage who lived not many years ago in Rome told me once that he had been involved in this reform [to rehabilitate Democritan atomism] and to have promised—having removed the wolf's skin covering the philosophy of Democritus—, to make it either appear to be or to become a sheep. One is persuaded of the truth of this not only by the fact that it had been asserted by such a man, but by the knowledge that the Church knows and tolerates it, a certain sign that it does not judge it a bad thing in itself and understands it very well.[25]

The letters, which circulated widely in manuscript form during the reign of Cosimo III but like Marchetti's Lucretian translation were never published during their author's lifetime, were written from a viewpoint that was apparently of the strictest Catholic orthodoxy. Like Rossetti in his treatise on physics, the *Antignome*,[26] he found no difficulty in reconciling atomism with the Creation. In one letter, for example, he argued against the theory of the chaotic coming into being of the universe by presenting the idea of the creation of Rome by chance as an obvious absurdity (2:38-41). But there were others, outside as well as inside Tuscany, who were not convinced.

Among them was Giovanni Battista De Benedictis, a Neapolitan Jesuit who in his *Lettere apologetiche in difesa teologia scolastica e della filosofia peripatetica* (*Apologetical Letters in Defense of Scholastic Theology and Peripatetic Philosophy*), published in 1694 under the pseudonym of

Benedetto Alentino, called into question the intellectual integrity of those atomists who claimed that their philosophy was reconcilable with the tenets of Catholic theology. He claimed in no uncertain terms that there existed "a very strict relationship or link . . . not obvious to everyone, between atoms and atheism." Either, he argued, Democritus and Epicurus were to be taken seriously as philosophers, in which case their notion of chance as the creator of the universe, supported by the doctrine of atomism, had to be taken at face value as an atheist philosophy, or they were merely to be discarded. Furthermore, even if a theological rehabilitation of atomism were possible at the theoretical level, such a rehabilitation would be dangerous for the masses since "it is vain, amongst so many, to hope for the virtue and knowledge necessary to resist the attractions of such a malevolent error, which unleashes the vices and renders lawful every wrongdoing." For De Benedictis, the philosophy of Aristotle, with its concentration on the first cause as a means of explanation for natural phenomena, was one of the "bulwarks of religion" which rendered a move to Democritan atomism unthinkable.[27]

In this atmosphere of distrust, the atomists were forced to carry their battle outside the halls of the University of Pisa. Interestingly enough, however, the obstacles they faced did not prove insuperable. Just as the *Accademia del Cimento* had enjoyed a certain amount of academic freedom, unaffected by the public and political concerns of the University of Pisa, certain of the Galileian party enjoyed similar freedom in terms of the publication of anti-Aristotelian works. In 1710, Guido Grandi, professor of mathematics at Pisa, in conjunction with Giovanni Bottari, vice-director of the Medici's official publishing house, and Lorenzo Ciccarelli, a Neapolitan publisher specializing in works which had been placed on the Index, produced an edition of Galileo's *Dialogue on the Two World Systems*, which included the notorious *Letter to the Grand Duchess of Tuscany* in which the Pisan had pleaded for a separation of science from theology. 1715 saw the publication of Evangelista Torricelli's *Lezioni accademiche*, and in the following year Francis Hauksbee's *Physico-Mechanical Experiments* were translated into Italian.[28] And in 1718 Grandi, Bottari, and others produced an edition of the *Works of Galileo Galilei* which, while not including the *Dialogue*, offered a "Universal Preface" by Tommaso Buonaventura in which *libertas philosophandi* was exalted at the expense of the Aristotelians.[29]

As the century wore on, the Aristotelians lost ground. After the publication—carried out under the aegis of the Grand Duke's official publishing house in 1717—of the complete works of Pierre Gassendi,[30] the atomists found themselves in a far stronger position *vis-à-vis* the institutional authorities. True, the old guard did not remain entirely silent: Tommaso Ceva's Latin poem *Philosophia novo-antiqua* which, informed by a distinctly medieval Christian spirit, leveled charges of impiety at Democritus, Epicurus, Lucretius, Gassendi, and Descartes, was republished in Florence in 1724 (it had originally seen the light of day in Milan in 1704). But it was soon answered by the *Diacrisis* of the prestigious Guido Grandi, a poem which ridiculed the anachronism of the followers of Aristotle.[31]

The succession of the last Medici Grand Duke, Giangastone, was another blow to the Aristotelians. According to all reliable historical sources,[32] Cosimo III's son shared little of his father's religious bigotry and saw fit to undermine the once powerful position of the Jesuits in the Medici court. Apparently more interested in sexual gratification than in the ostentation of piety—he is reported to have spent the last eight years of his reign in bed surrounded by hired ribalds—the ailing Giangastone survived to see the body of Galileo exhumed and reburied in Santa Croce, the historical mausoleum of the Italian *intellighentsia*, a highly symbolic maneuver which could only have been perceived as an affront by those uneasy at seeing such an honor accorded an individual who had been tried by the Inquisition.

While it would not be entirely accurate to speak of a complete defeat of the Aristotelian faction, at least in the reign of the last two Medici Grand Dukes—Carlo Tagliarini complained of the *plebe di filosofianti* (Rodolico, 6), or rabble of pseudo-philosophers, at the University of Pisa as late as 1729—there was certainly a shift in the level of influence enjoyed by the opposing groups. The medieval world view of the Aristotelians which had been so vociferously defended at the University of Pisa and elsewhere in Italy during the later part of the seventeenth century began to give way to a view, based largely on the philosophy of the ancients, which had been reproposed by the likes of Galileo—especially in *Il Saggiatore*—and Pierre Gassendi in his laborious rehabilitation of Epicurus, some decades before.

The Aristotelians, in other words, were fighting a political, rather than an epistemological battle. Their appeals to theological arguments, while no doubt in many cases informed by a genuine concern as to the possible consequences of a move away from Aquinas and towards a rehabilitated Democritus, were based in a belief in the superiority of speculation over experiment.[33]   That belief, in the context of the direction being taken by contemporary European science, in which the experimental approach of Newton had rendered obsolete even Descartes—one of the *bêtes noires* of De Benedictis and Ceva—was increasingly difficult to sustain. Finally, what rendered most onerous the situation of the Aristotelians at the University of Pisa was the Tuscan myth of Galileo himself. If Cosimo II had fully realized the political possibilities of making the discoverer of the Medici Planets his personal philosopher and mathematician, and Ferdinand II and Prince Leopold, for reasons of prestige, had erected the *Accademia del Cimento* to his memory, then it was unlikely that even such a pious figure as Cosimo III would be entirely insensitive to the extra-scientific significance of the figure of Galileo.

Perhaps the final word should be left to a contemporary. Quoted by Niccolo Rodolico in his influential study of Tuscan Church-State relations in the eighteenth century, Giulio Rucellai, member of an aristocratic Florentine family and Secretary of Jurisprudence under both Giangastone and Grand Duke Stefano of the house of Lorraine, the successor to the by now defunct Medici dynasty, had this to say of the University of Pisa: "The University of Pisa has been the only obstacle to the reduction of Tuscany to the state of ignorance in which almost all of the rest of Italy has suffocated" (19).

Such a sentiment could only have been expressed by an individual who had seen that even during the course of the *siècle des lumières*, the medieval view of the world was still very much alive.

NOTES

1. Jacques Le Goff, *Pour une autre moyen âge. Temps, travail et culture en Occident* (Paris: Gallimard, 1977), 10.

2. On the literary taste in the Tuscany of the late seventeenth and early eighteenth centuries, see Domenico Pietropaolo, *Dante Studies in the Age of Vico* (Ottawa: Dovehouse Editions, 1989), 243-377, as well as his article "Literary Taste at the Court of the Last Medici," *The Spirit of the Court: Selected Proceedings of the Fourth Congress of the International Courtly Literature Society*, eds. Glyn S. Burgess and Robert A. Taylor (Manchester: D. S. Brewer, 1984), 264-72.

3. For the author of the preface to the third edition of the *Accademia della Crusca*'s *Vocabolario* (Florence, 1691), Dante and Petrarch, together with Boccaccio, were the finest authors of the *buon secolo*—the fourteenth

century—during the course of which "one spoke and wrote with uncorrupted frankness and without the variety and barbarism which was afterwards induced by the admixture of other dialects and the efforts employed in studying the Latin language which thus occasioned a neglect of the mother tongue" (13). As can be seen from this quotation, a healthy respect for the aesthetics of the Middle Ages was institutionally sanctioned in the Tuscany of the last Medici.

4. In the *Divine Comedy* Dante expresses his orthodox views on atomism in *Inf.* 10, in which he places the Epicurean Cavalcante Cavalcanti in the circle of the heretics. Cavalcante's son Guido, to whom Dante dedicated his *Vita Nuova*, was a follower of Averroës and reputed to have been an atheist.

5. On the contemporary curriculum at the University of Pisa see Stefano De Rosa, *Una biblioteca universitaria del secondo '600: la libraria della sapienza dello Studio pisano, 1666-1700* (Florence: Olschki, 1983).

6. Jo. Chrysostomi Magnen, *Democritus reviviscens, sive de Atomis . . . Addita est Democriti vita* (1646). For a modern commentary on the work, see Ugo Baldini, "Il corpuscolarismo del Seicento, Problemi di metodo e prospettive di ricerca," *Ricerche sull'atomismo del Seicento: Atti del Convegno di Studio di Santa Margherita Ligure* (Florence: La Nova Italia, 1977), 3-74.

7. Paolo Galluzzi, "Il mecenatismo medice o e le scienze," *Idee, istituzione, scienze ed arti nella Firenze dei Medici* (Florence: Giunti-Martello, 1980), 189-215; Paolo Galluzzi, "*L'Accademia del Cimento*: 'giusti' del principe, filosofia e ideologia dell'esperimento," *Quaderni storici* 48, fasc. 111 (1981), 188-91.

8. For an English translation of the *Saggi*, see A. E. Knowles Middleton, *The Experimenters. A Study of the "Accademia del Cimento"* (Baltimore: Johns Hopkins University Press, 1971).

9. Pietro Redondi, *Galileo eretico* (Turin: Einaudi, 1983). Redondi's thesis is in large part based on a document discovered in the Vatican library. This document, which Redondi attributes to the Jesuit Orazio Grassi (attacked by Galileo in *Il Saggiatore*), is an official complaint lodged with the Congregation for the Holy Faith, in which the atomism theorized in *Il Saggiatore* is accused of incompatibility with the doctrine of the Eucharist.

10. Marchetti's translation of Lucretius, *Della natura dell cose*, was eventually published, after the author's death, in London in 1717. On the work's troubled publishing history and on the accusations of impiety endured by its author, see Mario Saccenti, *Lucrezio in Toscano. Studio su Alessandro Marchetti* (Florence: Olschki, 1966), 44-100.

11. Quoted in Paolo Galluzzi, "Libertá scientifica, educazione e ragion di stato in una polemica universitaria pisana del 1670," *Atti del XXIV Congresso Nazionale di Filosofia* (Rome, 1974), 2:406-7.

12. Marchetti's letter to Leopold, "Risposta de' filosofi ingenui e spassionati, falsamente detti democritici, alle obiezioni e calunnie de' peripatetici," is found in Francesco Marchetti, *Risposta apologetica dell'avvocato Francesco del nobile Alessandro Marchetti da Pistoia . . .* (London, 1762), 19-34.

13. See Teresa Poggi Salani, "Introduzione," *Saggi di naturali esperienze*, ed. Salani (Milan: Longanelli, 1974), 15, and Maurizio Torrini, *Dopo Galileo. Una polemica scientifica (1684-1711)* (Florence: Olschki, 1979), 16.

14. As Pietropaolo points out in *Dante Studies in the Age of Vico*, piety and politics were not separate entities in Cosimo III's Tuscany. "Retribution for transgressions of the laws of the Church and of the State was frequently exacted in the public squares with sadistic cruelty, and the suppression of potential currents of thought contrasting with the position of the Church was zealously pursued, while incessant homilies repeated to satiety messages of salvation" (243). For a somewhat romanticized but nevertheless highly informative account of the Tuscany of the time, see Harold Acton's *The Last Medici* (London: Faber and Faber, 1932).

15. On the problem of the Eucharist, see Redondi, 257-87.

16. Donato Rossetti, "Due proposizione di disinganno . . . ," *Zibaldone di Francesco Redi*, Ms Palatino 1099, VII (Biblioteca Nazionale di Firenze), ff. 45r-45v.

17. On the orthodox Catholic position concerning the problems of transubstantiation—*accidentia sine subjecto*—see the *Dictionnaire de théologie catholique* (Paris: Letouzey et Ané, 1911), 1368-1452.

18. For an example of Rossetti's torrid relations with Geminiano Montanari, Professor of Mathematics at Bologna and a fellow atomist, see the former's open letter, "Aviso del Canonico Donato Rossetti Matematico di S. A. R. a'suoi amici," dated Turin, 1 March 1678. A copy is held in the Bibliothèque Nationale de Paris, K. 5030.

19. Giuseppi Del Papa, *Lettera intorno all natura del caldo e del freddo . . .* (Florence, 1674, 1690).

20. Giuseppi Del Papa, *Lettere nella quale si discorre se il fuoco e la luce sone una cosa medesima . . .* (Florence, 1675, 1690); Giuseppe Del Papa, *Della natura del caldo e del freddo . . .* (Florence, 1681).

21. Francesco Redi, *Bacco in Toscano, ditirambo di Francesco Redi . . . con le annotazioni* (Florence, 1685).

22. On the career and character of Del Papa, see Ugo Baldini's entry, *ad vocem*, in the *Dizionario biografico degli italiani*.

23. On Vanni's attacks on Del Papa, see Torrini, 21-7.

24. Grand Duke Cosimo III's anti-atomist decree of 10 October 1691 marks the low point of the fortunes of the Tuscan atomists. It is a text of central importance in the cultural history of the period. The handwritten decree is conserved in a packet of documents in the Archivio di Stato di Firenze, Ms Miscellanea Medicea 87:14.

25. *Delle lettere familiari del conte Lorenzo Magalotti contro l'ateismo* (Milan, 1825), 1:214. For a survey of efforts made in contemporary Rome to replace Aristotelianism with Democratanism, see Jean-Michel Gardair, *Le "Giornale de' Letterati" de Rome (1668-1681)* (Florence: Olschki, 1984), 206-20.

26. *Antignome fisico-matematiche con il nuovo orbe e sistema terrestre del Dottore Donato Rossetti* (Livorno, 1669).

27. Benedetto Aletino [Giovanni Battista De Benedictis], *Lettere apologetiche in difesa della teologia scolastica e dell filosofia peripatetica* . . . (Naples, 1694), 280-1, 285.

28. *Lezioni accademiche d'Evangelista Torricelli* (Florence, 1715); Francis Hauksbee, *Physico-mechanical experiments on various subjects* . . . (London, 1709 [original ed.]).

29. Tommaso Buonaventuri, "Prefazione universale," to *Opere di Galileo Galilei* . . . (Florence, 1718), viii-lvi. It is interesting to note that even in Buonaventuri's anti-Aristotelian preface, references to Dante abound.

30. *Petri Gassendi Diniensis ecclesiae praeposti* . . . (Florence, 1727).

31. Niccolo Rodolico, *Stato e chiesa in Toscano durante la reggenza lorenese (1737-1765)* (Florence: Le Monnier, 1910; diplomatic reprint 1972), 16-18.

32. The fundamental text for historians working in the period is Riguccio Galluzzi, *Istoria del Granducato di Toscano sotto il Governo della Casa Medici* (Florence, 1781). Eric W. Cochrane's *Enlightenment and Tradition in the Tuscan Academies* (Rome: La Nuova Italia, 1961) and *Florence in the Forgotten Centuries* (Chicago: University of Chicago Press, 1973) are also of great interest.

33. De Benedictis/Aletino's comments on the subject of experiments left his readers in no doubt of his views. All speculation prevails over experimentation, he argued, since if speculation "is the form and those [experiments] only the matter of philosophy, putting experiment before speculation is to judge the labourer superior to the architect and the hod-carrier superior to the engineer. Furthermore, a peasant can think up a new experiment; a new speculation can occur only to the mind of a philosopher" (301).

Celluloid Criticism:
Pasolini's Contribution to
a Chaucerian Debate

Carol L. Robinson

While it may be obvious that every film based upon a novel or other literary text is an interpretation of that text, the role of film as a form of literary criticism is less widely recognized. Pier Paolo Pasolini's *I racconti di Canterbury* (1972) is one such case in point. Martin Green argues that considering Pasolini's diverse literary and cinematic interests, "any adaptation he does is as much an exercise in literary criticism as it is an exercise in film-making."[1] Both elliptical and oversimplified, emphasizing (perhaps even exaggerating) the sexual earthiness in Chaucer's work, his film is less a demonstration of how Chaucer might have imagined *I racconti di Canterbury* on the screen than a display of how Pasolini imagines *The Canterbury Tales* from the printed page. Pasolini's film may be seen as a series of critical "essays" that thus cannot be viewed as components of a faithful adaptation of *The Canterbury Tales*. One such "essay" is an interpretation of Geoffrey Chaucer's Wife of Bath.

This century has seen the accumulation of a relatively large mishmash of ideas about who or what the Wife of Bath is. George Lyman Kittredge's ground-breaking article, from the beginning of the century, essentially interprets her as a good-natured heretic.[2] In the second half of the century, interpretations became more and more tendentious. As Barrie Ruth Straus correctly observes, Alisoun's "critics have not only been polarized, but have occasionally lost the measured tone of professional response."[3] Traditionalists (coming out of the post-World War II era) have hated and laughed at her, reading her as a "wys womman," a "stock figure for the avaricious Woman," an irrational "creature" who "thinks" she is rational and who, "in her 'ludicrous' attempt to subvert the 'natural' order, is immoral," a non-constructive Dionysian character.[4] She is "'a bad lot,' 'a battered personality,' 'a hardened sinner,' a 'bossy woman who longs to be mastered in the bedroom,' or 'a chip off old Dipsas's block.'"[5] She is a murderer, a psychopath, or some other sort of "deviate" (Straus, 527). Others do not hate or laugh at her, but love and laugh with her. She is a "'high and gallant symbol of humanity in which weakness and fortitude are inextricably mixed,' a 'subtle charmer,' a fun-loving woman or even a religious one" (Rowland, 137-8). She is a "private" feminist.[6] She is "an old hand at waging war against authority and authorities."[7] She is a "great comic" who challenges the "external trappings of order."[8] Walter C. Long comments that the Wife of Bath may be seen as a "master rhetorician" who "displays extraordinary argumentative ability" and is "aware of the bind in which she has placed herself, being outside of moral convention: that if she were to present her argument in straightforward fashion, she would immediately be censured as immoral by her audience (by everyone save, perhaps, Chaucer Pilgrim)" (273, 282). Finally, Straus concludes that all this paperwork has been a waste of time, that Alisoun cannot be interpreted:

> The Wife is the uncontrollable voice that eludes interpretative truth. The ultimate secret she reveals is that all who think they can control, penetrate and master such texts as she represents are deluded. . . . The Wife's discourse threatens the loss of our professional tool, and this jeopardizes the life of literary criticism. (550)

Straus's idea that the Wife of Bath is so elusive that she is as complex as a real human being is a great compliment to Chaucer's creative genius. Straus seems to be proudly singing the rap song "U Can't Touch This" while also affronting us with the realistic threat to the means of our very livelihoods.

But it is *just* a threat. James Joyce made a similar threat when he challenged scholars with his *Finnegan's Wake*, and no one seems to have paid much attention; indeed, attempting to "control, penetrate, and master such texts" (without necessarily succeeding) seems to be the very drive that keeps most critics going. Pasolini (1922-1975) is a member of this league—a poet, film-maker, film theorist, and literary critic who once told Ezra Pound (in perhaps the American poet's last public interview):

> Instead of imagining you spread across an enormous linguistic territory, I see you as if down a well, in which you have reduced the world to only a few elements, and that is, to a group of quotations that are always the same, to a group of friends that are always the same, x, y, and so on. As if you worked at the bottom of a very narrow well, where you constantly recollect and reflect on your life.[9]

Four years after this interview, Pasolini completed the second film of his "Trilogy of Life," *I racconti di Canterbury*.[10] In making this film, this Marxist and misogynistic thinker seems himself also to be "at the bottom of a very narrow well." From there, he may have intended to address the masses but was doing so through the process of constantly recollecting and reflecting on his personal life, while attempting to "control, penetrate, and master" parts of Chaucer's text, such as the Wife of Bath's Prologue. By rewriting Alisoun's life story-oration into a third-person narrative, Pasolini provides us with an image of what he understands her to be telling the reader about herself. Pasolini debates with other Chaucerian critics on how to read her Prologue politically. However, because he is stuck in the bottom of his own Marxist-Utopian well, where very few women are allowed to exist, Pasolini reads the Wife as a rebellious heretic who is yet a sexual and clownish bully; he celebrates her heresy while laughing at her anti-antifeminist antics.[11] Thus, he generates a critique that is both a blending of medieval and modern ideologies and a contrast to his personal misogyny and Marxist politics. In so doing, like any critic, he rewrites Alisoun's reality into his own.

In order to understand Pasolini's celluloid criticism of the Wife of Bath, it is first important to understand his approach to literature, film, and the relation between them. Martin Green observes in Pasolini's films a circular process running between reality and cinema, between the real world and the screened fictional world, where cinema not only translates reality into the sacred, mythic epic, but conversely translates the sacred, mythic epic into reality (47). Two questions may arise from this: (1) where does literature and its adaptation fit into this schema (a semiotics question), and (2) which reality is being translated into (or from) the sacred, mythic epic (a psychosociological and metaphysical question).

Pasolini could not have intended anyone to view *I racconti di Canterbury* as a literal adaptation. In his essay "The Nonverbal as Another Verbality" he argues extensively that language and cinema are in binary opposition to each other: written-spoken languages evoke reality, while audio-visual languages reproduce reality.[12] However they do it, by evoking or reproducing, both mediums translate reality. Therefore, cinema and literature share the same translated reality, though not the same translation. When Pasolini translated one medium into another, he is translating one translation of reality into another, which is not the same thing as a literal adaptation.[13]

One signficant structural difference between Chaucer's text and Pasolini's film is the movie's omission of the (though incomplete) dramatic-narrative links between the tales. Except for the film's beginning, where the viewer gets to meet several of Chaucer's pilgrims as they converge at the tavern before the trip, the viewer never sees them actually playing the Host's storytelling game. According to Naomi Greene, Pasolini believed that "the presence of several narrators would . . . have proven 'mechanical and awkward' in the film." Instead, there is one infrequently seen narrator: Chaucer, played by Pasolini. And, suggests Greene, it is this fictional character "who clearly bears, as Pasolini said, the 'meta-linguistic meaning of the film'" (188).

That no causal connection exists between his version of a part of the Wife's Prologue and the other surrounding excerpts from the *Tales* indicates that this is an art film, not a Hollywood-style production. That this is an art film reinforces the idea that Pasolini is commenting on the text, interpreting it and its characterization of Alisoun. David Bordwell says that an art film's strength is in its parallelism, just as its weakness is in its causality: "The films sharpen character delineation by impelling us to compare agents, attitudes, and situations."[14]

Pasolini, like Jean-Luc Godard, rejected both the traditional and (after 1968) "liberated" cinema. "For Pasolini," Ben Lawton explains, "art is valid only when it is 'revolutionary,' that is, when the artist is on the 'firing line,' breaking the laws of the system within which he operates."[15] In an interview with Gideon Bachmann, Pasolini stated that all three films in his "Trilogy of Life" constituted a study of narration and the process of making a film that outwardly lacks ideology.[16]

I racconti di Canterbury successfully blends both modern and medieval ideologies internally. Gilles Deleuze argues that this is because film, the visual image, is working from the pre-verbal (pre-historical) into the present. "Not that we are taken back to prehistory," he explains,

> (there is an archaeology of the present), but to the deserted layers of our time which bury our own phantoms; to the lacunary layers which we juxtaposed according to variable orientations and connections. . . . These are the deserts of Pasolini, which make prehistory the abstract poetic element, the "essence" co-present with our history, the archaen base which reveals an interminable history beneath our own.[17]

Furthermore, Teresa de Lauretis suggests that Pasolini is "keenly aware . . . that cinema's writing, its representation of human action, institutes 'cultural consciousness' of that encounter with reality."[18]

This is emphasized by Pasolini's use of what he argues in *Heretical Empiricism* to be free indirect discourse—though it is only hypothetical in film. What really exists is a form of free indirect discourse: free indirect subjectivity.[19] Free indirect discourse, in literature, is the means by which the storyteller explains a character's thoughts, feelings, or speech in his or her own words, rather than either quoting or paraphrasing the words of that character. In cinema, Pasolini says that free indirect discourse is (hypothetically) "the immersion of the filmmaker in the mind of his character and then the adoption on the part of the filmmaker not only of the psychology of his character but also of his language" (175). Deleuze is quick to point out that this idea resembles Mikhail Bakhtin's. Drawing from Bakhtin's *Marxism and the Philosophy of Language*, Deleuze interprets Bakhtin as stating that

> there is not a simple combination of two fully constituted subjects of enunciation, one of which would be reporter, the other reported. It is rather a case of an assemblage of enunciation, carrying out two inseparable acts of subjectivation simultaneously, one of which constitutes a character in the first person, but the other of which is present at his birth and brings him on the scene.[20]

Free indirect subjectivity occurs, Deleuze says, when objective and subjective images become indistinguishable: "the distinction between what the character saw subjectively and what the camera saw objectively vanished, not in favor of one or the other, but because the camera assumed a subjective presence, acquired an internal vision, which entered into a relation of simulation ('mimesis') with the character's way of seeing" (*Cinema II*, 148). The camera is not imitating the characters' gaze, not representing it, but sharing that view. I think this is what Pasolini is emphasizing when he plays the role of Chaucer the narrator in the film: he claims to be sharing the medieval poet's point of view.

However, Pasolini's films, poetry, and criticism usually seem to suffer from a contradiction between his personal experience and his politics: each constantly modifies the other. As Lawton points out, Pasolini's pieces are full of seeming contradictions: favoring sexual liberation, yet condemning sexual permissiveness; fighting for the sub-proletariat, yet offended when the fight is successful. "These paradoxes," explains Lawton, "reflect the film-maker's inner conflicts, his fluid reactions to specific events, and his deliberately polemical stance *vis à vis* his audience." These paradoxes also reflect an outer conflict, between Pasolini and his society. Though he was an influential Marxist, he was often in conflict with his peers and party; furthermore, his sexual preferences (and lack of shame over them) made him an outcast of his own society. His unusual death illustrates this point—to this day, many still believe he was murdered under conspiracy. At the time of making his "Trilogy of Life," Lawton believes, Pasolini was searching for a utopia in which his homosexuality and social condition would be acceptable, "a world free of prejudgments, a world in which one could *be*, that is, one could exist in a state of Edenic grace, a condition somewhere between that of animals and angels: the condition, presumably, of children, subproletarians, inhabitants of the third world, and of the mythical past" ("Rejection," 167-8). The Wife of Bath fits into this third category, "of the mythical past," but Pasolini is not looking to her as part of his utopian idealism.

Pasolini was known generally to praise man over woman. As James Roy Mac Bean notes, for instance, he once commented that few women (his mother being one exception) even had souls. Mac Bean observes further that Pasolini's films also tend "to privilege the celebration of male sexuality, whether hetero or homo" over female sexuality.[21] This is certainly true of most of the films before Saló (1975). The viewer would therefore not expect Pasolini to choose to film a female protagonist who portrays herself and her sexuality in the positive light proposed by some Chaucerians. But, while he may not be celebrating her *female* sexuality, he is at least celebrating her sexuality. He therefore addresses both sides of an argument of how to view the Wife of Bath in her Prologue: as an anti-antifeminist orator and as a narrative example for antifeminism.

Realizing how little Pasolini thinks of women, the viewer should fear what his contribution could be to this debate in literary criticism, what underlying ideology exists in Pasolini's fragment of the Wife of Bath's Prologue. But, as de Lauretis points out, there is value in "some of his views on the relation of cinema to reality and to what he called human action."[22] If Pasolini claims to be translating reality, he is claiming that his depiction of women, originally fictional or not, is a reflection of what is at least a cultural reality. Indeed, Pasolini said he read each of the adapted texts for his trilogy as "a premature and prophetic image of what a society would be like," and for him "*The Canterbury Tales* already contains Shakespeare and the modern English world" (quoted in Naomi Greene, 184, from a 1974 interview with Michel Mangois).

Judith Mayne sees a close link between women represented in film and women represented in culture, a spectacle/spectator relationship: "Since women are spectacles in their everyday lives, there's something about coming to terms with film from the perspective of what it means to be the object of a spectacle and what it means to be a spectator that is really a coming to terms with how that relationship exists both upon the screen and in everyday life."[23] We cannot, of course, directly correlate the image of the medieval wife to modern wives. But Pasolini, like the traditionalists discussed above, seems sincerely to believe (and so reinforces) the mythic Alisoun's boast that "'For half so boldely kan ther no man / Swere and lyen, as a womman kan'" (lines 227-8).[25]

Pasolini does not show her telling her fellow pilgrims the story of when she met and married her fifth husband, much less give the rhetoric that surrounds it; the viewer does not even have the context from which this narrative part of her oration comes. The scenario opens with a shot of Alisoun's fourth husband on top of her, performing his manly deed, while she nags him to hurry up and finish.[24] The old man collapses, she squirms out from under him, quickly dresses, leaves the house, and dodges into a friend's house to peep lustily on her future husband examining himself while bathing. Her fourth husband's death is hilarious: about to die, he looks down at Alisoun kneeling at the foot of their bed and gestures to her that he wants to screw her one more time. Alisoun's response is crude laughter hidden in wails. She proposes marriage to the Oxford student, Jankyn, while giving him a hand job at a spring festival. She attends her fourth husband's funeral, changes hats, crosses to another side of the church, and marries Jankyn. When Jankyn reads to her from his antifeminist book, there follows a malicious fight that recalls slapstick comedy, and this episode ends with a close-up of her fiercely biting him on the nose.

Clearly this is not an oration. But neither is it a narrative in the Hollywood sense of the word. Pasolini conducts an interpretation of Alisoun through the "free indirect discourse" defined above; as Deleuze states, "Pasolini discovered how to go beyond the two elements of the traditional story, the objective, indirect story from the camera's point of view and the subjective, direct story from the character's point of view, to achieve the very special form of 'free indirect discourse,' of a 'free, indirect subjective'" (*Cinema II*, 148). In *I racconti di Canterbury*, Pasolini is speaking as/through Chaucer and subsequentially as/through the Wife of Bath. In his essay "Comments on Free Indirect Discourse," Pasolini writes, "It is certain that every time one has Free Indirect this implies a *sociological consciousness* clear or otherwise, in the author, which seems to [him] the fundamental and constant characteristic of the Free Indirect" (*Heretical Empiricism*, 82). Instead of dramatizing this part of the Wife's Prologue in an oratorical fashion, where she would be telling her fellow pilgrims her story (as in Chaucer's text), Pasolini provides the viewer with an idea of how one pilgrim, Chaucer, might have conceived her tale.

Pasolini states this by playing Chaucer the Pilgrim himself. He further emphasizes this point of view by altering the text. For example, as stated above, a level of Chaucer's *Canterbury Tales* has been removed: instead of Chaucer the Pilgrim telling the reader/viewer what the Wife of Bath tells everyone on the trip, Pasolino shows what Chaucer the Pilgrim might have imagined as he listened to and then recounted the Wife's Prologue. For another example, Chaucer the Pilgrim's wife appears at one point in this film. Chaucer, as played by Pasolini, dozes off at his desk, where he is writing *The Canterbury Tales*—that is, remembering the journey we saw him initially partake in at the beginning of the film. His nagging wife looks down at him from her (powerful) position at the top of the stairs and frowns at his snoring. "Geoffrey Chaucer!" she shrieks, and he jumps in his chair to reply meekly, "Yes, my love," as he goes back to his work. Since Chaucer's "love" is a slavedriving hag, how else could this Pilgrim perceive the Wife of Bath? Furthermore, there is not a single likable female character in the entire film. Finally, while Alisoun implies in Chaucer's text that she wishes always to have the upper hand in marriage, she says so in response to the Christian doctrine that wives should submit to their husbands. In the movie, the viewer sees her fight with Jankyn when he begins to read from his book called (in the text) "Valerie and Theofraste" (line 671). The fight is so farcical that she comes off as a bully beating up her boyish husband. Indeed, in speaking of the lighter, comical *Il Decamerone*, Pasolini told writer Dario Bellezza, "I do not claim to express reality with reality (or men with men or things with things) in order to create a work of art, but simply in order to 'play' with a reality that jokes with itself" (quoted in Greene, 185). The jokes in *I racconti*, as Naomi Greene points out, are "crueler and coarser" than in *Il Decamerone* (191). Pasolini portrays Alisoun as an aging *femme fatale* who has mellowed: she no longer needs money, so her exploitative drives turn toward sex. Pasolini's film interprets Alisoun's recounting of meeting and marrying her fifth husband as a "wys womman" speech, which is emphasized when she subverts it with a personal story that she is exactly what antifeminists dread and preach against. In this way, Pasolini takes sides with the antifeminists against this seemingly stupid, nagging whore.

Yet, as Martin Green suggests, Pasolini's presenting the Wife meeting (and crudely proposing to) her fifth husband at a spring festival "brings out the pagan vitality underlying medieval Christian culture and folkways" (46). While Pasolini attacks Alisoun personally and socially as a woman, he also celebrates her heresy. He seems also to take seriously Alisoun's statement that she will speak of the "wo that is in mariage" (line 3). Naomi Greene argues that in each film of the Trilogy, "*like a film beneath a film, Pasolini's bleak and disabused view of human nature—and especially of sexuality—continually subverts the supposedly 'joyful' Eros of the trilogy's many tales*" (189, italics Greene's). While Pasolini's portrayals of the Wife's ending fourth and beginning fifth marriages are comical, they are also awful.[26] The only good marriage is an ended marriage. The Christian doctrine of marriage, we infer, is sexual exploitation; Alisoun is sexually exploited by her first four husbands (in exchange for their wealth), and she sexually exploits Jankyn (in exchange for her kindness). When he rebukes her, she bites him on the nose.

Pasolini argues that "a film-maker working today not only knows how to, but wants at all costs to frustrate the expectations of the viewer, and he does this through his editing." Two categories of spectators result: "category A enjoyed the sado-masochistic freedom of film-makers, almost participating in the orgy of transgressions, while category B (the overwhelming majority) was scandalized, withheld itself, laughed, screamed, in short, covered the authors with shame that they were explicitly demanding (self-punishment for the transgressions against linguistic fraternity)" (*Heretical Empiricism*, 270-1). Clearly, the presentation of the Wife of Bath's Prologue is not an adaptation of any kind but a commentary upon the text. Martin Green sees the whole of Pasolini's film in this manner: "whatever the limitations of Pasolini's films are, the idea of *The Canterbury Tales* as cinema is a powerful insight into the inner dynamic of Chaucer's work" (53). It is also a powerful insight into the inner dynamics of Chaucerian criticism. The devout Marxist Pasolini demonstrates his characteristic anti-Christian Marxism, but he also shows a traditionally misogynistic blind spot. Like most critics and poets, Pasolini is stuck down at the bottom of a well, fiercely trying to "control, penetrate, and master" the object of his obsession.

NOTES

1. Martin Green, "The Dialectic Adaptation: *The Canterbury Tales* of Pier Paolo Pasolini," *Literature/Film Quarterly* 4.1 (1976), 47. Millicent Marcus, in "The *Decameron*: Pasolini as a Reader of Boccaccio" (*Italian Quarterly* 82-3 [Fall 1980-Winter 1981]), takes a similar approach, arguing that the very word "adaptation" implies a "hierarchical bias, and we should do well to replace it with a term less prejudicial" (175). For Marcus, Pasolini is justifiably making an unfaithful adaptation in order to create a kind of circular dialogue of criticism between the literary original and the cinematic copy.

2. George Lyman Kittredge, "Chaucer's Discussion of Marriage," *Modern Philology* 9 (1911-12): 435.

3. Barrie Ruth Straus, "The Subversive Discourse of the Wife of Bath: Phallocentric Discourse and the Imprisonment of Criticism," *ELH* 55 (1988), 527.

4.   Walter C. Long, "The Wife as Moral Revolutionary," *The Chaucer Review* 20 (1986): 273-5.

5.   Beryl Rowland, "Chaucer's Working Wyf: The Unraveling of a Yarn-Spinner," *Chaucer in the Eighties*, eds. Julian N. Wasserman and Robert J. Blanch (Syracuse: Syracuse University Press, 1986), 138.

6.   H. Marshall Leicester, Jr., "Of a Fire in the Dark: Public and Private Feminism in the Wife of Bath's Tale," *Women's Studies* 11 (1989), 157.

7.   Peggy A. Knapp, "Alisoun of Bathe and the Reappropriation of Tradition," *The Chaucer Review* 24 (1989), 45.

8.   Laurie A. Finke, "Falstaff, the Wife of Bath, and the Sweet Smoke of Rhetoric," *Chaucerian Shakespeare: Adaptation and Transformation*, eds. E. Talbot Donaldson and Judith J. Kollmann (Detroit: Fifteenth Century Symposium, 1983), 9.

9.   Quoted in David Anderson, "Breaking the Silence: The Interview of Vanni Rosisvalle and Pier Paolo Pasolini with Ezra Pound in 1968," *Paideuma* 10 (1981), 338.

10.   The other two films are *Il Decamerone* (1971) and *Il fiore delle mille e una notte* (*Tales of a Thousand and One Nights*) (1972).   Some of the other tales addressed in *I racconti di Canterbury* include the Miller's Tale, the Reeve's Tale, and the Pardoner's Tale, and Pasolini suggests a wonderful ending to the Cook's Tale.

11.   It is perhaps only fair to recognize that Pasolini might not have criticized the Wife of Bath's Prologue the same way later.   Ben Lawton shows Pasolini changing his views after he created his Trilogy of Life.   Lawton refers to Pasolini's last essay, "Abiura dalla 'Trilogia della vita'" ("Disavowal of the Trilogy of Life," Lawton's translation), translating from this essay Pasolini's statement, "I disavow the 'Trilogy of Life,' even though I don't regret having made it" and suggests, "For Pasolini of the Trilogy of Life the only hope lay in culture, in the possibility of communication between individuals, between the film-maker and the single viewer."   By the time Pasolini filmed *Salò*, his last film, "this faith was moribund" ("The Evolving Rejection of Homosexuality, the Sub-Proletariat, and the Third World in the Films of Pier Paolo Pasolini," *Italian Quarterly* 82/83 [Fall 1980-Winter 1981], 173, 171).   Furthermore, *I racconti* is the gloomiest film in the trilogy, and Naomi Greene observes, "Forced to acknowledge the film's disturbing undertow, Pasolini remarked that this second film might be seen as a kind of 'hiatus' in the trilogy, which, he confessed, reflected a moment of deep [personal] unhappiness on his part" (*Pier Paolo Pasolini* [Princeton: Princeton University Press, 1990], 191).

12.   Pier Paolo Pasolini, *Heretical Empiricism* (*Empirismo eretico*, 1972), ed. Louise K. Barnett, trans. Ben Lawton and Louise K. Barnett (Bloomington: Indiana University Press, 1988), 263.

13.   Umberto Eco, Christian Metz, and other critics generally scoffed at concepts such as this.   For these semiologists, the poet/film-maker's theories were too "unscientific," too subjective.   "Considered threatening to the legitimation of 'scientific' semiotics," writes Giuliana Bruno, "his work was looked at as if

through a screen, one that did not enable critics to accept the importance of critical 'dissemination,' the fascination of 'intertextual' cultural theory, and the nuances of theoretical 'pastiche,' nor to see beyond that notorious question of reality" ("Heresies: The Body of Pasolini's Semiotics," *Cinema Journal* 30.3 [Spring 1991], 31). Pasolini seems to have brought a sense of aesthetics into semiotics, something that critics have only recently begun to accept.

14.   David Bordwell, *Narration in the Fiction Film* (Madison: University of Wisconsin Press, 1985), 207. Bordwell cites Pasolini's *Pigpen* as an example of parallelism at its limit, when "it can form the explicit basis of the film" (207).

15.   Ben Lawton, "Theory and Praxis in Pasolini's Trilogy of Life: *Decameron*," *Quarterly Review of Film Studies* (2 (1977), 397.

16.   Gideon Bachmann, "Pasolini Today: The Interview," *Take One* 4 (1973), 21.

17.   Gilles Deleuze, *Cinema II: The Time Image*, trans. Hugh Tomlinson and Robert Galeta (Minneapolis: University of Minnesota Press, 1989), 243-4.

18.   Teresa de Lauretis, *Alice Doesn't: Feminism, Semiotics, Cinema* (Bloomington: Indiana University Press, 1984), 51.

19.   In the translation of *Heretical Empiricism*, it is worded as "free indirect point-of-view shot," but neither Deleuze (in his original French) nor Greene (who is working with Pasolini in the original Italian) call it this. They both translate the term as "free indirect subjectivity."

20.   Gilles Deleuze, *Cinema One: Movement-Image*, trans. Hugh Tomlinson and Barbara Habberjam (Minneapolis: University of Minnesota Press, 1986), 73.

21.   James Roy Mac Bean, "Between Kitsch and Fascism: Notes on Fassbinder, Pasolini, (Homo) Sexual Politics, the Exotic, the Erotic, & Other Consuming Passions," *Cineaste* 13.14 (1984), 14, 15.

22.   Teresa de Lauretis, "Language, Representation, Practice: Re-reading Pasolini's Essays on Cinema," *Italian Quarterly* 82/83 (Fall 1980-Winter 1981), 159.

23.   Judith Mayne, "Women and Film: A Discussion of Feminist Aesthetics," *New German Critique* 13 (Winter 1978), 86.

24.   I am assuming, perhaps incorrectly, that this is the fourth husband—but he acts more like one of the earlier, aged husbands. It is even possible that Pasolini is trying to suggest that all her husbands, before Jankyn, were alike: sexually driven beings she contended with until their dying days.

25.   *The Riverside Chaucer*, ed. Larry D. Benson, 3rd ed. (Boston: Houghton, Mifflin, 1987).

26.   He doesn't even show the conclusion to Alisoun's story. Chaucer's Alisoun says, "And whan that I hadde geten unto me, / By maistrie, al the soveraynetee, / And that he seyde, 'Myn owene trewe wyf, / Do as thee lust the terme of al thy lyf; / Keep thyn honour, and keep eek myn estaat'— / After that day we hadden never debaat" (lines 817-22). By eliminating this part of her story, Pasolini effectively eliminates the crux of her anti-antifeminist (and thus anti-Christian) argument: that not only should men not have sovereignty over women, but women should have sovereignty over men.

Eco on Medievalism

Domenico Pietropaolo

If there is a single contemporary author who needs no introduction to students of medievalism, that author is surely Umberto Eco. His name, however, is more likely than not to raise the expectation that every paper in whose title it is mentioned is about *The Name of the Rose*, and so I hasten to explain that I do not intend here to analyze that celebrated novel but rather to discuss his shorter essays and incidental remarks on medievalism in his *Travels in Hyperreality*.[1] Furthermore, since this book is also fairly well known and is crystal clear in every detail, my discussion will not assume the form of an exegetical exercise but that of a critique, focused on the critical consequences of the chief inferences that can be drawn from his perspective on the phenomenon of medievalism throughout history, that is to say on the implications, both methodological and theoretical, that Eco's work has for us today.

The principal defining features of Eco's perspective are (1) an acknowledgment of the categorical autonomy of the study of medievalism from adjacent fields of scholarship, such as the study of the Middle Ages and the study of Romanticism; (2) a recognition of the fact that in the postmodern compositive outlook on culture there is a special affinity with the medieval *Weltanschauung*; (3) the distinction of a total of ten different models of the Middle Ages operative behind all the varieties of medievalism identifiable in western culture; and (4) the postulate that history periodically attempts the partial recovery of a medieval model as an alternative mode of understanding or constructing the world.

The empirical base from which this perspective is extrapolated is, in the first place, interdisciplinary, including as it does movements in philosophy, opera, and literature as well as architecture and the visual arts. In the second place and with respect to the non-philosophical side of the phenomenon, we can further say that Eco's empirical material is non-hierarchical, since it includes great works of art, such as the poetry of Ariosto and Tasso, alongside mass-produced mediocrities by writers whose only cultural value consists in the fact that they figure among both the causes and the manifestations of the spreading market for "pseudo-medieval pulp in paperbacks, midway between Nazi nostalgia and occultism" (62). However, we must add that while he does not intentionally exclude from his purview any relevant material, Eco does maintain that there is a hierarchy of forms of medievalism, some of which he does not consider worthy of serious scholarly examination: next to "responsible examination" of the Middle Ages, "fantastic neomedievalism" has little significance for Eco (63). In the third place we might say that Eco's empirical data are also international, since the phenomena that he considers are not restricted to any national culture and are further grouped into ten categories, eight of which transcend all geographical and historical boundaries: the Middle Ages as a narrative pretext, as the site of an ironical revisitation, as a period of barbarism, as the locus of romantic projection, as the foundation of scholasticism, as the originary world of occultism, as the product of responsible philological reconstruction, as the origin of national identities, and as the dream world of decadence. Only the last two models in this list have found specific roles to play in national histories, since they have occasionally stimulated the "celebration of past grandeur" or become part of a "project of nationalistic restoration" (70), especially in Italy. But even here Eco's view is not really concerned with the uniqueness of national cultures, since the category of decadent medievalism includes for him the Pre-Raphaelite Brotherhood, Ruskin, Huysmans, Giosué Carducci, Gabriele D'Annunzio, and "a lot of fakes" in the visual arts and architecture (70). It seems that for Eco medievalism is medievalism—that is to say, a form of culture consciously shaped to resemble in some measure one of his ten models of the medieval world view; national and historical qualifiers are neither contemplated nor excluded.

Eco states that he was prompted to carry out his analysis of medievalism not only by the magnitude of the phenomenon itself in the twentieth century but also by the symposia that had then already been devoted to its examination (63). Because the essays in *Travels in Hyperreality* were written over several years, from the late Sixties on, but were revised throughout the Seventies and early Eighties, by which time *Studies in Medievalism* had sponsored a number of conference sessions on the subject at the annual International Congress on

Medieval Studies at Kalamazoo, it would be interesting to know if these were familiar to Eco. In his book there is no evidence one way or another, but it is certain that if he was at all aware of them, he did not suspect that they were the result of a systematic effort to define the parameters of the study of medievalism as a new discipline of scholarship and, simultaneously, gain acceptance for it in the academic establishment. This could not have been familiar to Eco quite simply because it became clear only over a long period of time, as the sessions began to proliferate and their scope to become wider, finally enabling *Studies in Medievalism* to venture out of the Medieval Congress and confidently to begin to organize annual international conferences of its own. And it is also likely that these conferences were then organized in total independence of Eco's effort to elucidate the concept of medievalism. There was no crossover.

If Eco had known of this effort, he would surely have mentioned it, since in many respects it was parallel to his own and was furthermore the only one of its kind in North America, to whose culture and cultural industry he was gravitating with increasing rapidity. And, of course, if Eco's essays had enjoyed then a fraction of the popularity they they enjoy now, they would surely have had a significant catalyzing effect on the development of the North American reflection on medievalism prompted by these conferences, offering it a conceptual apparatus and a methodology well rehearsed in imaginative scholarship. At that time, when Eco's own work of literary medievalism *The Name of the Rose* existed only in secret gestation, and when his essays on the concept of medievalism were largely unknown to scholars in the field, the thing to do would have been to gloss his paradigms and to seek their acceptance or their critical revision by the scholarly community. But that is surely not what is called for now, when the study of medievalism in North America has registered considerable progress and shaped an impressive consensus around some ideas that are also basic to Eco's work.

The scholarly setting of the study of medievalism has indeed changed in the past fifteen years or so. To those of us who have been watching from the margins, it is clear that at least in North America the study of medievalism has come of age as a discipline in its own right, that it has reached that level of professional maturity which is a prerequisite for membership in the scholarly establishment, needing now only institutional existence as the focal point of a research and teaching center in order to enjoy the status of full adulthood in

Academia. That so much has been achieved in so short a period of time and despite the natural hostility of some disciplines (such as medieval studies and the study of Romanticism, which now had to face the prospect of losing dominance over nebulously perceived areas of their traditional territories) is a powerful testimonial to the vision and endurance of a small community of scholars who, under the leadership of Leslie Workman, have preferred the precariousness of an uncharted territory to the security of the received tradition.

These were difficult years, but the results have been gratifying. The study of medievalism no longer needs to defend the legitimacy of its candidacy to status as a scholarly discipline. It has successfully gone through the required polemical exercise of demarcating its domain, principally against the claims of English and German scholarship on Romanticism, and in the process it has achieved sufficient internal clarity and coherence to reduce to an acceptable degree the level of uncertainty that inevitably clouds the self-understanding of any new discipline. The front has been mostly academic and organizational, focused, as it has had to be, on self-definition, self-justification, and proselytism. Henceforth it needs to be chiefly political, delimited by the more forbidding doors of the administrative and financial officers with the power to bestow institutional legitimacy on intellectual labor.

In the context of this changed American situation and in light of Eco's status as a luminary of contemporary medievalism himself, his essays on medievalism can no longer have the impact of a fresh discovery. But it makes perfectly good sense to ask what implications his view of medievalism as a field of study has for us today. Leaving aside the principle of the conceptual autonomy of the discipline, which is no longer seriously or even frequently challenged in North America, and any criticism of the medievalistic tenfold division of medievalism (which shows how even in his essays Eco is able to contribute to the practice of contemporary medievalism and to shed critical light on it at the same time), we can begin by observing that the first significant inference to be drawn from his considerations is that the study of medievalism in art and literature should be as independent as is logically possible from pre-established notions of aesthetic and intellectual excellence, since its material expressions must include works representative of the entire hierarchy of culture, from the trivialization of the medieval world in amusement parks to its sublimation in the recondite allusiveness of higher art forms available in their fullness only to an aristocracy of readers. Of course, Eco's own contribution to the practice of literary medievalism needs no justification as an object of serious study, since it enjoys the quasi-universal approbation of a great classic. But none of the phenomena that he mentions in his essays can ever hope to achieve a fraction of that degree of recognition.

The task of the discipline in the future will be chiefly to encourage the study of these allegedly less important cultural phenomena in a quantitatively significant manner, so as to enable later scholars to sketch a sociological profile of the medievalism of each postmedieval age. It should not be so, but it is nonetheless a fact of academic life that young scholars working on authors who do not appear to exhibit a minimum of intellectual and aesthetic excellence, as these values are defined by the received critical tradition of each individual discipline, are generally regarded as wasting their talent if they limit themselves to a strictly textual analysis of artistic and philosophical issues. But a sociology of medievalism would be interested in such things as the statistics of taste and ideology, the market conditions of translations, adaptations, and vulgarizations, the instrumentalization of infrastructures for the dissemination of culture by the producers of medievalistic goods, the social and cultural backgrounds of its consumers, and so on for a score of other factors, each conceived with sufficient precision to make possible its mapping onto a chart and yet with sufficient latitudinarianism to make the numerical base of such a mapping statistically significant.

Such a sociological profile is surely the first step to take if we are to discover the parameters of medievalism in the real world of history, wherein not infrequently it figures as a significant agent of change or preservation. A key consequence of such a sociology would be a deeper and more precise awareness of the utility of medievalism to the culture of a given group. Contemporary North American students of medievalism do not seem to be acquainted with the idea of utility as a historiographic category, but Eco is, and he makes the point very clearly. "This is where modern western man came to maturity," he says of the Middle Ages, "and it is in this sense that a model of the Middle Ages can help us understand what is happening in our own day" (75). Eco's observation can be easily and legitimately generalized to refer not only to the modern sociological base of medievalism but to that of every age.

There are two ways in which we can understand the utility of medievalism and of the study of medievalism. In the first place the medieval world model can be said to have a direct explanatory power for us because a good part of our reality is historically grounded in it, having originated in the Middle Ages and having come down to us in a form or with a function recognizably close to those with which it first came into being. In the second place the medieval model may be said to constitute for us a good base for conjectural thinking, since in that part of our reality which is not historically rooted in the Middle Ages there are events and social experiences which manifest patterns of occurrence and internal structures strikingly similar to those of parallel phenomena in the medieval world. With respect to the first of these two theses on utility it is sufficient to recall that such things as eyeglasses, checks, universities, and cathedrals, all of which were invented in the Middle Ages, necessarily retain the medieval world view of their origin as their innermost layer of historical memory, which is to say as the logical and chronological foundation of their essence. We cannot fully grasp that essence unless we take cognizance of the fact that it represents the modern entelechy of a medieval seed, which however could contain it only in latency; nor, we can add, is it possible for us fully to grasp the nature of that seed as historical latency if we do not take into account its later developments.

On this argument, it would seem that in our experience of the contemporary world a dose of medievalism and a scholarly analysis of it are not only cognitively useful, as Eco observes, but also logically necessary. Mainstream students of medievalism working in North American universities may well find such a hermeneutical principle inimical to their scholarly practice, which is generally concerned either with the isolated study of a text in relation to its own historical context or else with the supposed secrets that it yields when observed through the prism of contemporary theories of literature, but the fact is that American historiography offers us one of its strongest justifications and one of its finest practical applications, next to which Eco's proposal loses much of its originality. In his address to the Medieval Academy at its Princeton meeting on 26 April 1941, entitled "Medieval Institutions in the Modern World," Charles Howard McIlwain, eminent medievalist and Pulitzer Prize historian of the American Revolution, defended the view that from the perspective of constitutional history, the most medieval of modern ideas is the notion of limited government, understood as a synonym for constitutionalism, which cornerstone of the modern world, therefore, historians cannot fully understand unless they seek hermeneutical orientation from the Middle Ages. And he did so by adopting the general methodological principle that historians should not be afraid to allow their perceptions of the medieval presence in the modern world—that is, the cultural events and phenomena of today which may be regarded as a legacy of the Middle Ages—to affect their understanding of the Middle Ages; and conversely, that they should let their understanding of the Middle Ages guide them in their interpretation of the modern world.[2] The methodological implications of this proposition for the study of medievalism, with respect to that part of it which is related to the medieval world by uninterrupted continuity, are very clear, and, despite the fact that McIlwain's address is now more than half a century old, its chief lesson could not be more timely.

As for the second thesis on the utility of medievalism, concerning phenomena which cannot be regarded as historical developments of medieval ideas, the sense of medieval *déjà vu* that we experience when we try to unravel some aspects of our world is based on our ability to recall good medieval analogues. Eco gives us several illustrations: the crisis of central authority in both periods, the slow decay of *Pax Americana* as a parallel to the decay of *Pax Romana*, the sense of an impending cosmic doom, which in our own day may be military or ecological (79) but is in any case no less apocalyptic or punitive than the cataclysmic end that colored medieval theology, and so on. This analogical procedure, which is warranted only by the psychology of associationism, lends itself to two objections. The first of these, of lesser moment, is that the less obvious parallels are visible only to someone who, like Eco, is a "medievalist in hibernation" and hence accustomed to seeing the Middle Ages everywhere.[3]

The second, of much greater import, is that in the explanation of similarity we are naturally brought to seek for a concrete link and to postulate or tacitly presuppose the existence of a common root even when there is none—if A and B are similar, we tend to assume that there is a C from which they can both claim filiation. The human mind, as Karl Popper once suggested, seems unable to explain resemblance other than genetically.[4] In the case at hand, unless we guard our thinking very closely, this sort of associationism may translate into the risk of silently postulating as the agent of history a sort of Hegelian Absolute Spirit capable of materializating in distinct but recognizably parallel forms in different periods (the Middle Ages and the age under scrutiny) and for different social groups. That would take us perilously close to the historical reification of suprahistorical causes and would quickly lead us out of the province of history into the domain of mysticism and metaphysics.

One way to avoid this mystification of historically unconnected parallelism and yet explain the disquieting sense of medieval *déjà vu* in our experience of the world is to postulate that the medieval model of reality incorporates some ontological factor also found in all other models, with the difference that whereas in the medieval world view that factor is explicitly affirmed, in other models it remains as a rule implicit, manifesting its presence only in special circumstances. This distillation of the Middle Ages down to an ontological essence, which is not the reification of a suprahistorical spirit but a real aspect of the being of man and hence is confined to history and remains imperishable as long as there is history, represents the existential approach to the study of the Middle Ages and of medievalism favored by the contemporary Italian medievalist Ovidio Capitani. When it is stripped of all of its accidental features, the medieval experience of being is recognizable in its fullness in other periods of history, in phenomena that we would call episodes of medievalism. In that sense, says Capitani, we can correctly speak of the eternal *actualité* of the Middle Ages, or, better still, of the Middle Ages as *Erlebnis*, that is to say, the Middle Ages as authentic experience of being as such. Wherever modern man, prompted by the failure of human history to deliver the sense of existence and burdened by the feeling of cosmic pessimism that inevitably follows the discovery of that fact, responds to the call of reason to seek a meaningful realization of being, there the medieval *Erlebnis* emerges from the darkness of consciousness to color his self-understanding and his perception of the scheme of things.[5] The conclusion to which Capitani's premise leads is that authentic medievalism represents the more or less successful cultural textualization of the medieval *Erlebnis* in postmedieval times. Its original core of medievalness may not be conspicuous; it is the task of scholarship to bring it out.

Neither McIlwain nor Capitani is mentioned by Eco. To be sure, neither one of them is directly excluded by his premises, although they both go well beyond them. The hermeneutical principle of the reciprocal illumination of past and present is common to both, but whereas McIlwain focuses on the continuity of past and present as manifested in the philological material of the evolution of ideas, Capitani focuses on the philosophical similarity in the predicament of modern and medieval man in their search for the authentic understanding of existence. North American scholarship on medievalism—which, as far as I can tell, is located somewhere between the two but is unaware of either—can considerably profit from both as it seeks to define its own methodological identity. But it cannot accept either McIlwain or Capitani without applying to them the corrective measures suggested by a sociology of the materials of medievalism, since these, as Eco makes abundantly clear, are heterogeneous with respect to both quality and content.

Therefore, if ideas such as constitutionalism develop in the history of a given national group, it must be because the internal structure of their material existence and the form of their relationship to the larger ideological context of society are based on tension rather than equilibrium, since the latter would necessarily mean the end of all change. Similarly, no effort to overcome the inauthenticity of existence in the present can logically occur in total isolation from the rest of reality, as if it had no external motivation, but rather must be understood as the result of the subject's inability to dominate his sense of alienation from history and to escape his imprisonment in the finitude of material being. In tempering the perspectives of McIlwain and Capitani, the task of students of medievalism must clearly include identification of the dialectical tensions of change within the culture of medievalism and the material causes of man's spiritual alienation from the ontological authenticity of history, of which the most sombre medieval ethos is perceived as a concrete expression by various forms of medievalism.

Precisely which forms of medievalism regard the medieval ethos as grounded in an authentic understanding of being, by virtue of which it can re-emerge throughout history because it is generated by something presumed to be more basic than history, and which forms consider instead that ethos to be the product of a vacuous philosophy that in postmedieval times can have only a mythological appeal, much like the appeal that the tales of the pagan gods had for Christian classicism—these issues are concerned more with the nature of the texts themselves than with the larger purviews of the total history of medievalism in which they occur or with the function that they serve in the total configuration of contemporary culture. But it is clear that outside of such purviews, a revival of the medieval ethos, whatever the degree of its philosophical purport, loses much of its meaning. An expression of medievalism may or may not be part of an inherited tradition of medievalism and always presupposes that in contemporary culture there is a need that it can meet. It is as indispensable to establish these facts—historical the first, sociological the second—as it is to determine the context of a word in a real sentence before deciding on its meaning. The literary cult of Dante in Florence at the turn of the seventeenth century, when compared to the virtual absence of such an idealization in the culture of other cities in contemporary Italy, exemplifies a phenomenon that cannot be understood in isolation from the traditional ideological bias of Tuscan philology with respect to its medieval authors and from the fact that some familiarity with Dantesque motifs and quotations was presupposed in Tuscan readers of cultural texts, from works of biology to works of philosophy.[6]

As we have already seen, the history of medievalism is not subdivided by Eco according to national cultures, or, before the age of nations in the proper sense of the term, to regional cultures, and that is definitely a weakness of his method: but there can be no question as to his perception of the importance of the vertical span of the purview in which each expression of medievalism should be examined. For Eco the whole of western history, from the early Renaissance on, is characterized by a continuous *return to* or *rediscovery of* the Middle Ages (66-7), expressions which for him encapsulate the formative role played by the medieval model in a succession of postmedieval periods. But the terms *return to* and *rediscovery of* have at least two other logical implications, both of which are left unexplored by Eco. The first of these is that the Middle Ages and its later recollections are separated by a distinct ontological hiatus: one returns to something only after one has severed all links with it, and one can discover anew something previously familiar only after one has somehow lost touch with it. In this view the Middle Ages and medievalism are related by discontinuity in their substance and intended similarity in their form. The second implication is that the origin of that will-to-resemblance—which must be regarded as the very foundation of all forms of medievalism conceived as nostalgia—is, of course, entirely due to the postmedieval period in question and not to the Middle Ages. It constitutes an effort to grasp some aspect of the Middle Ages through the salvaging operation of recollection. The presence of the medieval world in medievalism seems to be nothing more than a recollected presence, and recollection, we would do well to remind ourselves, is only the epistemological mode assumed by the mind when it turns to the past.

Now it is precisely these implications that reveal the shortcomings of theories such as Eco's, since the assumptions of an ontology of discontinuity and an epistemology of recollection logically imply looking at history backwards—or, more precisely, looking backwards into history. Such theories remain alien to all forms of medievalism based on uninterrupted continuity. Recollection is the past-oriented structure of the present; it is not the present aspect of the past. History understood as and through recollection fails to see the present as a futural dimension of the objective past or as an evolutionary consequence of the past. And although it speaks of the Middle Ages as of the infancy of modern man and points out the medievalistic origin of part of our cultural reality (65), such a history has in fact an insufficient grasp of the continuity of forms in time. McIlwain is a good corrective in this case. When the morphology of an intellectual apparatus for the production of order and sense in men's lives is caught in the contest of competing forces of historical dominance, it is reshaped, sometimes in a radical manner, but it does not altogether lose its original character, which is still found in the present as a trace or, in periods of chronological proximity, as a fully functional hermeneutical key. This presence of the Middle Ages in the present is not the fruit of recollection; it is, rather, independent of the subject's will-to-resemblance, warranted by a historical ontology of material continuity, and fully intelligible to an epistemology of objectivity. As McIlwain would say (279), adapting Aristotle, the present oak is the medieval acorn.

These considerations are not meant to deny the obvious fact that even in the most scholarly of contexts, we *also* look at history backwards; or indeed to suggest that contstructive recollection has no role to play in the narrativization of history. We do in fact stand in the historicity of our own time, as indeed we must, in order to look intelligently at and into the past, which we are naturally drawn to textualize in narrative forms consonant with the ideologies that we serve. A non-Hegelian, sociological, and materialist perspective, such as the one that I have been trying to sketch in this critique of Eco, does not presuppose anything different. The self-preserving thrust of the ideology of change, oriented towards the past as a configurative structure of consciousness, is only one of what must be reckoned as the two chief shaping principles of historical discourse. The other is the inimical self-preserving thrust of the ideology of conservation, oriented towards the future as the purported logical implication of present reality. As Eco teaches in every page of his essays, ideology cannot logically be avoided, since the truth of things is always the truth of the ideology which cuaes the mind to see them as such.

As far as the practice of medievalism is concerned, it is also rhetorically and logically necessary, since the intelligent narratation of history is hardly possible without a set of assumptions from which to call it forth into coherent structures. The student of medievalism has therefore the primary task of identifying the ideological forces at play in its configuration. In the late twentieth century, Eco says, we dream of the Middle Ages. If the content of the dream is the business of exegetical criticism and the manner of dreaming is the subject of rhetorical criticism, the why of the dream is the responsibility of ideological analysis. But in performing this analysis, we as students of medievalism cannot ever cease to remind ourselves that we too are caught in the tension of history, and that our appraisal of the different modes assumed by medievalism is not without the bias of the ideology that we serve. Our only claim to validity consists in not concealing this fact from ourselves and from others and in making every effort to respond to the corrective import of contrasting perspectives. Beyond that, scholarship cannot go.

NOTES

A shorter version of this article was read at the Seventh Annual General Conference on Medievalism, University of South Florida, October 1992.

1. Umberto Eco, *Travels in Hyperreality*, trans. William Weaver (San Diego: Harcourt Brace Jovanovich, 1986).
2. Charles Howard McIlwain, "Medieval Institutions in the Modern World," *Speculum* 16 (1941): 275-83 (see especially 277-9).
3. Quoted from Eco's "Postscript to *The Name of the Rose*," trans. William Weaver (San Diego: Harcourt Brace Jovanovich, 1984), in *Naming the Rose*, ed. Teresa Colletti (Ithaca: Cornell University Press, 1988), 27.
4. Karl Popper, *Objective Knowledge*, rev. ed. (Oxford: Clarendon, 1981), 196.
5. Ovidio Capitani, *Medioevo passato prossimo* (Bologna: Il Mulino, 1979), 275.
6. For details, see Domenico Pietropaolo, *Dante Studies in the Age of Vico* (Ottawa: Dovehouse Editions, 1988), Ch. 4-5.

Medieval Nostalgia
in France, 1750-1789:
The Gothic Imaginary
at the End of the Old Regime

Roland Bonnel

To research the Gothic imaginary current in France at the time of the Enlightenment no longer constitutes an attempt of the impossible. Modern research shows, for example, that a literary Gothic did in fact exist during the second generation of the French Enlightenment.[1] Rousseau and Diderot, as well as many novelists, developed in their work a world of "sensibility" partially influenced by Locke's psychology and Richardson's novels, a "sensibility" which would eventually contribute to the rediscovery of architectural Gothic in nineteenth-century France. It is imperative to define here the exact connotation of the term "sensibility" and to establish for the reader its precise significance in the language of the eighteenth century. In the latter context, the word "sensibility" (*la sensibilité*) denoted the human capacity to feel compassion, to be sensitive and to be capable of affection. It referred to a type of *process* of knowledge which developed on the basis of emotion and which thus differed significantly from intelligence and will. This "sensibility" was the real energy of the medieval imaginary and thus one of the sources of the Gothic revival.

Modern critics, however, must exercise caution in their assessment of this eighteenth-century French "Gothic," for in actual fact it does not appear adequate to speak of a Gothic revival during that particular period. To be certain, no attempt was ever made to rehabilitate the Middle Ages in either philosophical or artistic discourse, but only at the level of the imaginary. The aim of the present study is to show and assess a few examples of the latter, thereby documenting the existence of a medieval nostalgia on the eve of the French Revolution and facilitating a more general inquiry into Gothic imaginary in eighteenth-century France. Despite the fact that most examples selected have been drawn from the field of literature, the multidisciplinary approach has been used whenever possible and examples given from the realm of fine arts, architecture, and nonliterary texts. As far as the scope of this research is concerned, it must be noted that this study is neither a systematic analysis of the medieval themes at the end of the Old Regime nor a review of the assessment of the Middle Ages by the Enlightenment. However, since both approaches provide concepts which will prove useful, they must also be taken into consideration. The former approach underscores the manner in which the Gothic imaginary could have been shaped into a discourse, while the latter reveals a paradox which helps explain why eighteenth-century Gothic took the form of a nostalgia rather than that of a reasoned discourse.

The study of early indications of the rediscovery of the Middle Ages frequently results in a tendency to stress either the negative assessment of the Middle Ages made by the Encyclopedists in the name of reason or the aesthetic debate about the Gothic taste. With regard to the latter, it is widely recognized that Gothic taste was more developed in eighteenth-century England than on the Continent. This, however, does not imply that a certain Gothic taste did not exist in France as well. As early as 1709, the drawings of various items of garden architecture made by Antoine-Joseph Dézallier d'Argenville in *La Théorie et la pratique du jardinage* shows that the abstract representation of nature contained a potential impetus for the revival of the Gothic vault. In 1753, in his *Essai sur l'architecture*, Abbé Marc-Antoine Laugier underlines the grandeur of religious Gothic architecture. Furthermore, in 1776, the rustic cabins drawn by Georges-Louis Le Rouge in his *Jardins anglo-chinois* convey a pattern comparable to the Gothic ornaments of Joseph Halfpenny (*Rural Decorative Architecture in the Augustine, Gothic, and Chinese Taste* [1753]) and Charles Over (*Ornamental Architecture in the Gothic, Chinese and Modern Taste* [1758]). Although Gothic taste in garden architecture was not as tangible in France as it was in England, its significance must not be ignored or underestimated. The Parc Monceau designed by Carmontelle in 1773, for example, depicts a few Gothic *fabriques*; and the Méréville gardens painted by Hubert Robert (now in the Nationalmuseum in Stockholm) show several Gothic artifacts, among which is a Gothic castle on top of a hill. Although the number of such examples could be multiplied, the presence of Gothic *fabriques* in a garden is not a sufficient factor to prove the existence of a Gothic revival in France. These *fabriques* were mainly intended to create a microcosm, a type of living encyclopedia providing the visitor with a pictorial summary of history and geography. As such, the medieval theme was not utilized for the specific purpose of stressing its medievalness, but because it was one element within the wider range of human history.

On the other hand, the negative assessment of medieval times which was made by the Encyclopedists had far deeper consequences. In a time when liberty was invented, to use the terminology of Jean Starobinski,[2] and rationality proposed as a model, the word "Gothic" meant aesthetic tastelessness and obscurity. This negative judgment did not focus only on the arts but also on the wider spectrum of society as a whole: according to the *Encyclopédie méthodique*, "the word *Gothic* designates all that which in the arts and society is a reminder of times of ignorance." Politically, the Middle Ages meant no less than feudal despotism. Moreover, medieval values were challenged. For example, the value of *gloire* is no longer linked by the Encyclopedists to the military honor of medieval warlords but to the principle of utility. Sully is given as an example of the implementation of such a principle and thus presented as the first to sever the relationship with medieval times.[3]

Despite this negative assessment, an assessment which spread well beyond the limits of enlightened circles, the consequences which economic changes had on the foundations of aristocratic power could have led to the development of a neo-feudal theory. The debate on the identity of the nobility, i. e., a nobility devoted to the military versus a nobility involved in commerce, shows that the feudal pattern was still alive, as in Henri de Boulainvilliers' *Essai sur la noblesse de France* (1732) and the Chevalier d'Arcq's *La noblesse militaire ou le patriote français* (1756). The military reforms carried out in France during the eighteenth century (in 1718 by the regent, in 1727 by Louis XV, in 1776 by Saint-Germain and in 1781 by Ségur) tended to favor the old aristocracy to the detriment of the *bourgeoisie* and the most recent nobility. This tendency must be seen as an element of a more general movement traditionally called the *réaction nobiliaire*, the reaction of the nobility against the political consequences of the Enlightenment. This trend, nevertheless, cannot be considered ideologically as a Gothic revival but rather as one of the last attempts of the aristocracy to fight for its privileges at the end of the Old Regime. As will be demonstrated below, this discourse of reaction against modernity conveyed themes with medieval characteristics insofar as it opposed the abstract principles of the Enlightenment. However, it is also representative of a modern conception of aristocratic power which emerged during the seventeenth-century *fronde* in the fight against royal absolutism. In his speech to the National Assembly on the 28th of July, 1789, Stanislas Clermont-Tonnerre shows that he is conscious of these two tendencies within the eighteenth-century nobility:

> Nos commettants, Messieurs, sont tous d'accord sur un point: ils veulent la régéneration de l'état; mais les uns l'ont attendue de la simple réforme des abus et du rétablissement d'une constitution existant depuis quatorze siècles . . . d'autres ont regardé le régime social existant comme tellement vicié, qu'ils ont demandé une constitution nouvelle.[4]

The most traditionalist segment of the nobility agreed that primitive liberties had been destroyed by the institution of absolute monarchy and that it was time to return to the natural authority of the lords over their subjects, an authority which had its legitimacy in the conquest of the country by the Frank warlords. Such was the argument of Boulainvilliers in his *Etat de la France* (1727). However, the issue is not as simple as it may first appear. Medieval references did not exist only among the most conservative nobility. Most of the enlightened nobles who disagreed with the Boulainvilliers hypothesis would base the legitimacy of the nobility on familial ancestral traditions and possession of lands: as the Comte de Montlosier wrote, "[les paysans] admettaient entre eux une sorte de noblesse, laquelle se tirait, comme partout, de l'ancienneté de la famille dans le même lieu et sur la même propriété."[5] Simultaneously, the nobility was conscious that this nostalgia for feudal times could no longer serve as an ideology and that another basis for the superiority of the nobility had to be proposed. From this awareness there emerged a complex pattern where sensibility took an ideological connotation, mixing the medieval imaginary with the duty of *bienfaisance* toward the people. As will be shown below, this revival of disguised medieval values would eventually lead to the fostering of an aristocratic legitimacy paradoxically based on the common people, the target of aristocratic *bienfaisance*.[6]

It is important to note that this revival of medieval values did not occur among the most conservative aristocrats. If there existed a real revival of medieval values—although, as already stressed, it took the form of a nostalgia for a mythical period of history rather than the form of a discourse—it must be sought in only a few circles of the Enlightenment, more precisely in those circles which at the beginning of the Revolution constituted the enlightened or "liberal" monarchists, i. e., the *monarchiens* of Clermont-Tonnerre and Tromphime-Gérard Lally-Tollendal. The religious factor also must be accounted for, insofar as this too depends ultimately on a form of nostalgia. An example may be found in the speech on Christianity delivered by Turgot at the Sorbonne in July 3, 1750: "O que j'aime mieux ces édifices gothiques où le pauvre et l'orphelin trouvent un asile! Monuments respectables de la piété des princes chrétiens et de l'esprit de la religion! Si votre architecture grossière blesse la délicatesse de nos yeux, vous serez toujours chers aux coeurs sensibles!"[7] Turgot's words reveal that both the aesthetic and the religious factors are in effect secondary to an imaginary—not only individual but also collective—which has survived beyond the rational and aesthetic discourse. Here the Gothic taste appears to be linked to the principle of protection, which in this case is symbolized by the sheltering offered by the Gothic building to the poor and the orphan. It seems also to be linked closely to sensibility. The appraisal of the deeds of the enlightened ancestors shows that on the one hand they fought, in Voltaire's wake, against the survival of feudal laws such as the *mainmorte*. Furthermore, it shows simultaneously that these nobles sought to implement in their estates a new order based on the value of *bienfaisance* which it was hoped would regenerate society. In so doing, they were unconsciously giving shape and reality to an imaginary which ultimately would justify the very existence of the Second Order.

The ideological usage of the medieval imaginary by the enlightened nobility was fostered by an intellectual movement which took the form of a practice rather than a systematic theory. In the second part of the eighteenth century, France experienced a movement related to the development of the idea of nature in the wake of Rousseau's *La Nouvelle Héloïse* and related also to an increasing interest in agriculture dating back to the first part of the century. This movement, more often presented as a trend rather than a school of thought, is traditionally called *le retour à la campagne*, the return to the country. If it can be considered as an expression of a spiritual and moral consciousness which developed thanks to a new approach to nature, it should also be considered in its specificity as a school of thought promoting the idea of a new order based on paternalistic values and involving the return to a Golden Age shaped along mythical medieval values. By the end of the eighteenth century, the countryside was no longer the mere urban way of life transported into the fields; it had rather evolved into a philosophical means of questioning contemporary institutions. The pastoral discourse had become a moral discourse in which the medieval imaginary would develop. The castle becomes again the center of life in the country; it was viewed, as in the poem *Les Quatres Saisons* by the Cardinal de Bernis, as the shelter of ancient values giving way to a patriarchal style of life.[9] Even the utopian communities envisaged by a few enlightened *philosophes* were indebted to the medieval pattern of the duty of protection owed by the lord to his subjects.

The *Généralif* of Joseph d'Hupay de Fuvéa is the description of a utopian community, *une maison patriarcale et champêtre* as the title states.[8] In a romantic landscape—Hupay uses the word *romantique* (7)—there is located the community, an autarkical society (18) where relationships among community members are based on the familial and sentimental model of authority (8-9) and where the hierarchy between masters and servants is founded in the feudal principle of protection and in the duty of *bienfaisance* (25-7). This may well have been a dream, as was remarked by the American Governeur Morris, a very observant witness of the time, when he visited the Petit Trianon: "La royauté a fait ici des frais énormes pour se cacher à ses propres yeux, mais sans y réussir. Une laiterie remplie de porcelaines de Sèvres ne ressemble pas suffisamment à la vie rustique." The dream would eventually give way to a nightmare, the French Revolution, when the sheep decided to eat the shepherds: "La révolution qui a lieu actuellement dans ce pays est étrange. Les quelques personnes qui l'ont mise en branle sont étonnées de leur propre ouvrage."[10] This astonishment is in effect found in all the letters and memoirs of the few liberal nobles who had developed the duty of *bienfaisance* to its extreme limits when protection had become no longer necessary. The medieval imaginary and the traditional ideology of the nobility had fostered a type of conservative socialism in reaction to the growing power of gold and its corollary, luxury, linked with the ascension of the bourgeoisie. However, the characteristics of this medieval imaginary need to be analyzed further to understand its full significance.

Many enlightened gentlemen who had read Rousseau returned to their estates not only to discover the virtue of innocence but also to implement new agricultural methods and to improve the living conditions of the peasants. In so doing they were in keeping with the traditional ideology of the nobility, which had always emphasized the value of the land.[11] Simultaneously, they were also giving proof of modernism in a time when the Encylopedists, the Physiocrats, and the Agronomists agreed that agriculture, and thus the management of the land as well as the implementation of modern methods of culture, was the main productive factor contributing to the wealth of the country. However, the ethics governing this return to the country were not these of modern individualism but those of the aristocratic principle. While the philosophy of Voltaire or Mandeville emphasized the individual characteristics of happiness, the philosophy of the return to the country was founded in a community spirit, in the aristocratic idea of society, according to which the duty of the lord is to protect his subjects. Thus, the rediscovery of the land and the rehabilitation of agriculture, as well as the revival of land-related values, eventually fostered a nostalgia for the medieval pattern of the productive village or community nestled around and sheltered by the castle and its lord, symbols of a paternalist form of authority. An important rediscovery was made in the middle of the century: there still existed a few *communautés tacites*, rural communities composed of one large family created in the thirteenth and fourteenth centuries. The *Journal Oeconomique* was the first to mention their existence, in 1755 and 1756,[12] and its findings would be developed further by Joachim Faiguet de Villeneuve in the *Encyclopédie*.[13] These communities appealed to the Enlightenment because of their utopian characteristics; they appealed to the enlightened nobility because they provided a model of moral regeneration based on a patriarchal and harmonious government. In such communities, the authority was founded on familial values and institutions, and thus on a type of personal and effusive relationship between the ruler and his subjects. The practice of the return of the nobles to the country followed the same pattern. The somewhat impersonal authority of the absolute king or of any type of institution was to be replaced by a personal contract binding the subjects to their local lord. Paternalism, agricultural autarchy, and authoritarian management constitute the principles of a new "quasi-feudal" ideology.[14]

Hence, this school of "the return to the country" did not limit itself to agricultural improvements; it found its way into all domains of thought and life and generated a way of life as well as a *Weltanschauung* bearing proof of the existence of a medieval imaginary. An example of such a nostalgia for medieval times is found in Claude-Nicolas Ledoux's architectural project of a hunting lodge for the Prince de Bauffremont in Franche-Comté.[15] A few decorative items recall the times of Roman antiquity, but the general impression given by the engravings is that the lodge is a stronghold, a fortress, massively rebuilt and designed for resisting attacks by invaders. The interior plan reflects the medieval custom of very large multipurpose rooms. Another example of medieval imaginary is the agricultural and military community imagined by Goyon de la Plombanie.[16] This fortress, designed on the model of Vauban's military citadels and built around a church, was meant to hold 250,000 inhabitants segregated according to their social status, i. e., nobles or commoners. This architectural project is the perfect graphic transcription of the medieval dialectic of protection and surveillance, which is very different from the enlightened dialectic of guidance and surveillance, an example of which is found in Ledoux's Saline de Chaux at Ar et Senans (1773-78).

While the rediscovery of nature did not limit itself to a social category or a specific milieu and should rather be considered as an intellectual movement or a *mentalité*, the school of "the return to the country" had an ideological signification. It was intended specifically for the nobles, who were given a series of instructions so that they might enjoy happiness with their family in an Edenic environment while being involved in the duty of improving living conditions of the poor. Thus they were provided with a new legitimacy replacing the medieval legitimacy based on military duty.

A good example of this rhetoric may be found in *Le Bonheur rural* by Pierre Etienne, the full title of which is *Lettres de M. de*** à M. le marquis de***, qui déterminé à quitter Paris et la Cour pour vivre habituellement dans ses terres, lui demande des conseils pour trouver le bonheur dans ce nouveau séjour*. The Preface stresses the importance of the ancestors who were living on their estates, taking care of the lands and providing their subjects with military protection. The writer recognizes that the military component has shifted to a social one, but he explains simultaneously that the duty of protection remains identical in its spirit:

> Mais que les grands propriétaires se fixent au milieu de leurs
> domaines. Le touchant spectacle de la nature disposera au

moins leur coeur à la pitié pour leurs malheureux vassaux . .
. . Ils fixeront malgré eux leurs regards sur le tableau des
travaux champêtres . . . . Témoins assidus des travaux
pénibles du malheureux cultivateur, ils verront ce qu'il en
coûte à ces êtres laborieux pour leur procurer l'abondance . .
. . Ce spectacle, nouveau pour eux, ouvrira leur coeur à la
bienfaisance; ils chercheront naturellement les moyens de
soulager les malheurs de l'indigence.[17]

In Etienne's letters, the living conditions of the peasants and the rule
of the lords are depicted as respectively inhuman and despotic because
they have been corrupted by the lure of wealth which has emerged
with the development of commerce. Therefore, Etienne recommends
that the old order be reinstated, an order based on friendship and
personal relationship as it was when "the towers" and "the crenels"
would signify "security" and "trust" for the subjects and when the lord
was "the father" and "the protector" (2:48-9).

A similar example of this type of neo-feudal discourse at the end
of the eighteenth century may be found in *Le Bonheur dans les
campagnes* by the Marquis de Lezay-Marnésia (1785 edition). The new
order may be summarized in the following description of the family of
the lord:

Quel tableau! . . . une famille toujours occupée d'objets utiles,
où l'ordre fait régner l'abondance, que la gaieté n'abandonne
jamais, et que la piété, la bienfaisance animent toujours! De
ce château que le bonheur habite, il le répand sur les villages
qui l'environnent. Secondé par les dignes pasteurs que la
religion a donnés pour guides depuis longtemps à ses vassaux,
il en a banni les vices; ils les a remplacés par l'activité,
l'industrie et la sagesse. Juge, médecin et père, par l'autorité
de l'amour et du respect, il arrange les procès et visite les
malades.[18]

Lezay-Marnésia's book is interesting in several ways: first, because it is
one of the rare works where medieval nostalgia takes the form of
reasoned discourse, and secondly, because of the personality of the
author. On the one hand, as an enlightened aristocrat, Lezay-Marnésia
abolished labor service and *mainmorte* in his estates and started a
campaign in Franche-Comté to abolish a few seigneurial taxes and to

achieve equal liability to taxation. In 1789, he was one of the forty-seven members of the minority of the nobility to join the Third Estate and become one of the *monarchiens*. On the other hand, despite this enlightened outlook and a real encouragement to merit, the regeneration of society he proposed ended up by reinforcing the aristocratic principle. He never supported the abolition of privileges and was always opposed to the division of lands. Moreover, the real level of public life is not, in his eyes, that of institutions based on abstract principles but the local autonomous community with its type of patriarchal authority. In effect, the main feature of the Golden Age given as a model for regeneration is one of paternalism. The gentry remains a benefactor and benevolent class and, as such, the center of social life.

In a literary analysis of this text, I have shown that the terminology used by Lezay-Marnésia constitutes a neo-feudal vocabulary and that *bienfaisance* can in no way be considered a step towards the abstract notion of justice.[19] Furthermore, there is no occurrence of the word "citizen" in the text. The notion of citizen has even no real existence outside the act of obedience and respect. On the contrary, the noble, defined as the friend of the king, has very clear functions: he is a model for the people, a protector of the poor, and the intermediary between the people and the king (16, 19). The rights and duties of the government are themselves defined in terms of protection (128). Each aspect of this society revolves around the lord. The *état de nature* itself is ultimately a variation of the Rousseauist theory: it is replaced by a world where the country loses its innocence when the nobles do not get involved, when they no longer reside on their lands and when they remain remote from the peasantry. The model is one of a mythic feudal society: as has been stressed above, authority is based on a personal relationship between master and servant which is viewed as sentimental. It is a world where the Arcadian shepherds of the Pastoral genre have given way to the mythic model of the good-willed nobles as the only way to effective happiness.

The 1788 edition of *Le Bonheur dans les campagnes* is even more radical in its aristocratic outlook. There, Lezay-Marnésia recommends a complete separation between the nobility and the Third Estate and opposes what he calls "these false pretenses to liberty and equality" (115-16) aimed only at abolishing all privileges. In his eyes, each social category has its own function: the people must obey, the Third Estate (the *bourgeoisie*) is to be responsible for commerce, and the nobility is to be "the decoration of the throne and its support, the gates of the Empire and one of its necessary Orders" (88). Thus, the crisis of identity experienced by the nobility is solved. The function of the nobles is one of "sacrifice" as in the *Patriote français* of the Chevalier d'Arcq. Their reward is the trust of the monarch; their salary is the respect of the subjects; their principle is honor (89).

This type of discourse is heavily indebted to the principles of the ideology of the medieval nobility. It would not be fully understandable, however, without taking into account the background which favored its development: the Gothic imaginary which had existed, along with the theme of return to the country, in the *mentalités* of the time and among the enlightened nobility. In order to assess this Gothic imaginary, I have selected a corpus of texts as examples because of the well defined specificities contained therein: the final analysis relies on a few texts representative of a poetic school traditionally called Descriptive Poetry (*poésie descriptive*) which in France was written mainly by gentry and intended for their peers.

French Descriptive Poetry—a label potentially misleading for modern critics—is a literary movement corresponding to a well defined period and milieu. The milieu is the nobility, and the period that preceding the Revolution, when traditional values were jeopardized and the nobility experienced a legitimacy crisis. It may be considered as the poetry of the well-intentioned gentlemen returning to their country estates. It offers a representation of the countryside indebted to various traditions. Its main reference is the poetry of Virgil and Hesiod; as such it may be called (and has been called by the poets themselves) Georgic Poetry. It is also indebted to Rousseau's representation of nature in *La Nouvelle Héloïse*, although to a lesser extent, since Rousseau did not really innovate but rather reflected a concern of the time. French Descriptive Poetry was more influenced by his utopian model of Clarens, the expression of a sensitivity spread in post-1761 aristocratic circles.[20] The qualification of "descriptive" was given to this type of poetry by Jean-François de Saint-Lambert after the English school and the Thomson model.[21] It refers to a poetic style which does not yet qualify as romantic but which is an important step towards a picturesque description of nature. However, when referring to the rhetoric of these poems, Didactic Poetry proves a better name. Nature in French Didactic Poetry, as in Virgil's work, is not meant to convey a type of melancholy. Nature is rather described as an inhabited and cultivated landscape. The genre is in effect the poetic expression of the ideology of the return to the country. In his poem, the author instructs his readers on how to improve conditions of life and agriculture in the country. The poem is also a lesson on how to live in the country according to the seasons. Many poems are called *Les Saisons* and most Didactic Poetry is a description, month after month, of the deeds of the nobles who have settled on their lands.

The technique is that of presenting various *tableaux*, which are more than mere descriptions. The poet does not describe the country as it is but as it should be. Each *tableau* resembles a scale model designed for the scenery of a play or an opera. Such a technique, Saint-Lambert says, is intended to evoke specific feelings in the reader, who is considered a spectator (4, 6, 10). Furthermore, this Didactic Poetry breaks away from the pastoral tradition. The traditional shepherds are replaced by gentry (xx-xxi), a change which carries not only a literary value but an ideological signification. The didactic poem of the return to the country is an aristocratic one, intended for the use of the country gentry, as Saint-Lambert explains:

> J'ai fait des Géorgiques pour les hommes chargés de protéger les campagnes et non pour ceux qui les cultivent. . . . Peut-être la noblesse pensera-t-elle enfin que dans les moments où elle n'est pas nécessaire à nos armées, elle peut employer son temps à éclairer ses vassaux, à perfectionner l'agriculture et à s'enrichir par des moyens qui enrichissent l'état. (xxiv-xxv)

The values stressed are only apparently those of the Enlightenment and the Physiocrats; in effect the modern principles retained are those compatible with an aristocratic society, for they reflect a nostalgia for an aristocratic order with many medieval characteristics. The poet does not directly mention medieval society; he suggests rather that modern society should be regenerated by the return to a Golden Age which ultimately reveals itself as a representation of a mythic feudal society. Thus, the return to the country is, in its poetic expression as well as in its discourse, the expression of a nostalgia for a bygone period which is not historically defined but depicts medieval characteristics. This is further illustrated by the analysis of the treatment of two selected themes. First, at a more general level, the ideological background shows that, next to a few principles of the Enlightenment, this poetry is the heir of the ideology of the medieval nobility. Secondly, and more specifically, the theme of the nobles and their deeds reveals a true medieval nostalgia.

To present the various components of the medieval imaginary in Descriptive Poetry is no easy task insofar as all of these components are highly intertwined, and any attempt at characterization must remain somewhat arbitrary. The general background of such Descriptive Poetry is the traditional ideology of the nobility, i. e., the importance of the land and the fight against luxury. The importance attached to the land is related not only to the restoration of the power of the local lords but also to the prosperity of the country and its people, along the lines set by the Physiocrats and the Enlightenment:

> J'admirais tes bienfaits, divine agriculture,
> Tu sais multiplier les dons de la nature;
> Toi seule à l'enricher forces les éléments:
> Elle doit à tes soins ses plus beaux ornements.
> Sans toi, ces végétaux que tu sais reproduire,
> Périssent en naissent, ou naissant pour se nuire.
>   (Saint-Lambert, 49)

The importance of the cultivation of the land for the prosperity of the country is of such magnitude that agriculture is even considered as the new war, replacing the older military wars:

> Laisse aux Rois belliqueux étendre leurs domaines,
> Viens féconder le sein de nos terrains ingrats;
> Tout l'art d'agrandir les écarts
> Est d'en fertiliser les plaines.[22]

Thus, land and agriculture are considered the major and most useful values in the country and are constantly opposed to commerce. Hence, Fresnais de Beaumont stresses in *La Noblesse cultivatrice* (1778) that land and agriculture should be the only values next to military duty to be taken into consideration for ennoblement.

The condemnation of luxury is closely linked to the revival of agricultural values, for luxury was regarded as caused by the development of commerce. The fight against the influence of luxury on social life should not be considered as the opposition of a life of leisure in the cities to the simplicity of country life, for such is only the literary transcription of a deeper ideological insight. The criticism of luxury has been a constant theme of the ideology of the nobility (Galliani, 63-72). Luxury was equated with the growing power of new social categories whose wealth was not based on possession of land. It was therefore perceived as a means of leveling the hierarchy of orders and eventually undermining the power of the rural lords.

Saint-Lambert wrote an *Essai sur le luxe*, reprinted in the *Encyclopédie*, in which he recommends that a general rule be applied when dealing with luxury: human passions which lead to luxury must be subordinated to concepts of honor and glory. They must also be subordinated to the spirit of community, for this is the sole way to avoid corruption of morals.[23] In *Les Saisons*, the theme of luxury is examined as a literary form. Saint Lambert emphasizes the potential for happiness offered by the countryside as opposed to urban boredom:

> Je sens renaître en moi la joie et l'espérance,
> Et ce doux sentiment d'une heureuse existence
> Que ce monde frivole où j'étais entraîné,
> Et son luxe et ses arts ne m'avaient point donné.
> Tout me rit, tout me plaît dans ce séjour champêtre;
> C'est là qu'on est heureux sans trop penser à l'être. (7)

The argument occurs as a *leitmotiv* in all descriptive poems of the time and should not be considered as more than it actually is, namely a poetic style used as an apology for the innocence of country life.

In a number of other poems, the criticism of luxury takes the form of a discourse wherein such criticism is an open condemnation of modern society and a reinstatement of the way of life of the ancient nobles living on their estates. This is the case in Lezay-Marnésia's *Essai sur la nature champêtre*, where he develops the complete argument of the ideology of the nobility.[24] Wealth is not condemned *per se*; rather, what is criticized are the actions of the nobles who have settled at court instead of living on their estates. They are presented as so corrupted by luxury that when they attempt to return to the country, they fail to restore the older values. For them, the country is only a pretext for a new mode of entertainment:

> Le courtisan se lasse aussi de l'imposture,
> Et voudrait quelquefois renaître à la nature;
> Mais esclave, ébloui par l'éclat de ses fers,

Ses yeux sur la nature ont cessé d'être ouverts . . .
Il porte dans les champs son magnifique ennui,
Et se plaît à les voir esclaves comme lui. (34)

Lezay-Marnésia contrasts the description of the courtier with the description of the noble who has left the court of Rome for the gardens of Maecenas:

Libre des passions, des intrigues de Rome,
L'homme était en ces lieux moins étranger à l'homme;
Et le riche, étonné de se trouver un coeur,
D'un regard attendri voyait le laboureur,
Partageait ses doux soins, sa paix, son espérance,
Ses craintes, ses désirs, même son innocence. (36)

Such poetic rhetoric against luxury can be found in the *Essai* of Lezay-Marnésia (73, 77, 79, 80, 101), where it is used as a *leitmotiv* as in most descriptive poems. However, it is most often presented in relationship to the memory of one's ancestors. The modern courtier, for example, is depicted as the shame of his ancestors (48). In a short poem, *Epître à mon curé*, placed at the end of the *Essai*, Lezay-Marnésia gives a description of ancestral and mythic times which can be considered elements in his medieval imaginary:

Ah! ces beaux jours, ces jours si pleins d'appas
Ne luisent plus sur la France éplorée;
L'âge d'or était l'âge où l'or ne régnait pas;
Mais dans notre demeure agreste
Où l'on ne voit ni riches ni seigneurs,
Le crépuscule nous en reste
Et son feu réchauffe nos coeurs. (186)

Behind these words, it is easy to imagine the crenels of the family castle and a life where the power of gold has not yet corrupted amicable relations between lord and vassal.

The medieval imaginary is built around the image of the lord, his good deeds, and a type of personal relationship between master and servant which looks more like paternal love than authority. The monarch is not absent from this imaginary, although he is not a central figure. He is considered a remote form of power, although he conveys the means of regeneration of the kingdom. In his poem *Les Voeux d'un citoyen*, Jean-Baptiste Tschoudi describes the king as "a tutelary God" and the queen as "the mother" (3); their role is to restore justice and happiness throughout the country by taking from the court and giving to the subjects (9). Lezay-Marnésia, in his *Essai*, condemns violently the politics of Richelieu which finally destroyed the castles and crowded the court (67). By way of contrast, he praises the new king, Louis XVI, whom he considers the heir of King Henri IV who had been highly beneficial for his people:

> Du grand, du bon Henri fidèle imitateur,
> Louis aux laboureurs rend des amis, des pères,
> Et redonne aux hameaux leurs Anges tutélaires.
> Nobles, riches, nos champs implorent vos bienfaits! (67)

In actual fact, Louis XVI was, on the eve of the Revolution, the catalyst for all hopes of regeneration and, in certain ways, the expression of the collective medieval imaginary. His series of reforms, although they did not succeed, exhibited a desire to restore the power of the local nobility. The king's interest in country life seemed genuine. On one occasion, he even traveled to the country and used a plow, an action sufficient to depict him as the monarch of the Golden Age. In September 1789, the National Assembly approved the project of a statue by De Varenne in honor of the king. The engraving by Moreau le Jeune represents Louis XVI as the father of the people, standing next to Henri IV who tells him, "My son, the happiness of the people is the source of the happiness of kings." This sentimental relationship between monarch and subject is the same as that existing between lord and vassal.

The medieval imaginary is at its strongest in what may be called the medieval paradigm of protection, a paradigm which may be described as constituting the ideological backbone of Descriptive Poetry. This paradigm is composed of three progressive steps centered on the regeneration of the country: the syndrome, the cure, and the restoration of health. The syndrome's components have been analyzed above. Its main characteristic is the corrupt luxury fostered by the lure of wealth, a theme well served by development of the concept of innocence as related to the state of nature. The simple fieldworker is given as the symbol of virtue:

Ami de l'innocence, honnête agriculteur,
Qu'il est facile et doux de faire ton bonheur! . . .
Le luxe ne vient point lui montrer ses misères
Et le faire rougir de l'état de ses pères.
(Saint-Lambert, 51)

The second component of the syndrome is the condition of the
peasants. However, because of poetic rules, there is no description of
their miserable life. Saint-Lambert (xix-xx) has very clearly set forth
these rules: the poet speaks of peasants but only rarely shows them in
action. The noble is the one who has the duty to ease a burden which
is therefore acknowledged only as the negative of a photograph:

Villageois vertueux! ô mon ami, mon frère!
Je ne te verrai plus accablé de regrets . . .
(Tschoudi, 5)

Du peuple gémissant allégez la souffrance . . .
(Lezay-Marnésia, *Essai*, 128)

The didactic method utilized by the poet is the description of the state
in which happy country people ought to live after the lord restores the
values of order:

Vois-tu l'activité, l'espoir de son bonheur
Eclater dans les yeux du jeune agriculteur?
Content de voir finir les jours de l'indolence,
Il veut par le travail mériter l'abondance;
Il se plaît dans sa peine, il craint la pauvreté,
Mais il craint plus encore la triste oisiveté.
(Saint-Lambert, 8)

The third component of the syndrome is accounted for by means
of the same negative approach and deals with the loss of identity
experienced by the nobility in the cities and at court. While the
"disease" is diagnosed as a shift away from ancestral values, the cure is
simultaneously suggested, namely the return to the country:

Les seigneurs, appelés à des honneurs serviles,
Rampèrent à la cour et dans le sein des villes;

Blessèrent de leurs noms l'antique dignité,
Et perdirent leurs moeurs en perdant leur fierté:
Et les champs délaissés qu'animaient leur présence,
Languissent appauvris par leur funeste absence.
(Lezay-Marnésia, 67)

A footnote to Lezay-Marnésia's *Essai* (172) diagnoses another source of
this crisis of identity, namely the contemporary systematic destruction
of the respect due the national heroes of the past, such as Joan of Arc
whose glory is blemished by Voltaire's book. The rehabilitation of the
great heroes of the past is part of the cure proposed to regenerate
morals.

The means suggested for curing the syndrome revolve around the
figure of the lord. They are of three different kinds: the return to the
country in terms of revival of ancestral values, in terms of *bienfaisance*,
and finally in terms of the new legitimacy of the lord. The main
characteristic of the revival of ancestral values is the reappearance of the
ancient castle protecting its surrounding villages. With the return of
the nobles to their estates, the castle is no longer the impersonal place
of power it had been after the lord left the estate, appointing in his
place an administrator whose sole function was to levy taxes without
offering proper protection: "Ce château, trop longtemps l'effroi du
voisinage, / Est enfin devenu la retraite d'un sage" (Lezay-Marnésia,
140). This concept of the wisdom of the lord is recurrent in
Descriptive Poetry, where it conveys the meaning of personal justice
and loving rule along with that of seigneurial involvement in social
issues: "C'est le château d'un sage aux malheureux ouvert."[25]

It is important not to fall into the trap of adopting a modern
interpretation, as has recently been emphasized by Jacques Heers in his
book *Le Moyen Age, une imposture*.[26] French twentieth-century
representation of the Middle Ages is heavily indebted to the myth of
the Renaissance strengthened by Michelet; it is also heavily indebted to
the tradition of the Enlightenment consolidated by nineteenth-century
republican historians whose opinions are still current. This tradition
succeeded in producing a biased image of the medieval world by
depicting it as a cruel and barbarous period. The eighteenth-century
enlightened nobles, however, were partially free from this imaginary.
In Descriptive Poetry, we find a few allusions to remote periods when
society was not as enlightened as that of the eighteenth century and
authority was not always based on mutual respect:

Par de plus douces lois, la justice répare
La honte et les excès d'un système barbare . . .
Les seigneurs maintenant plus instruits, plus humains,
Désirent d'être aimés et non pas d'être craints.
(Lezay-Marnésia, *Essai*, 141)

A footnote attached to the preceding verses reveals that this passage concerns the *mainmorte*. However, except when dealing specifically with the *mainmorte* and other feudal laws no longer justified in times of peace, references to an authority based only on strength, which ultimately engendered the crisis of identity of the nobility, evoke modern history, when the source of power shifted into the hands of royal administrators who had no personal contact with the subjects. The discussions about feudal privileges which took place in the 1770s and 1780s at the Académie de Besançon prove that although enlightened nobles fought the *mainmorte*, their representation of the Middle Ages, mythic as it may have been, was nonetheless positive and not yet influenced by the general trends of the Enlightenment. In the eyes of a Saint-Lambert or a Lezay-Marnésia, the Golden Age conveyed medieval values, while modern absolutism and bureaucracy had achieved the destruction of the Golden Age.

The castle is not the sole symbol of the revival of ancestral values. As has been seen above, the ancestors themselves are specifically mentioned in relationship to a period when there was no luxury. The castle is the place where the example of ancestral frugality is constantly present in the minds of the new lords: "On y voit les portraits de ses sages aïeux; / Ils vécurent sans faste, il veut vivre comme eux" (Saint-Lambert, 100). The noble who returns to his estates

Habite le donjon qu'habitaient ses ancêtres.
De l'amour des honneurs il n'est point dévoré . . .
Pour juge il a son coeur, pour amis ses égaux,
La gloire ou l'intérêt n'en font pas ses rivaux.
(Saint Lambert, 99)

This reference to ancestors who had lived prior to the time of centralized royal power is a formal condemnation of the vanity engendered by the honors of the court. The ancestors are not only quoted as examples of simplicity, they are also mentioned in relation

to their virtues. In the following example the country is equated with
the return to family land and the graves of former lords:

> Comment abandonner les cendres de ses pères?
> Auprès de leurs tombeaux, par l'amour retenus,
> Nous recueillons encor les fruits de leurs vertus.
> Ils se firent aimer, et pour eux on nous aime,
> Et nos enfants pour nous seront aimés de même.
> Fixons notre séjour, attachons nous aux lieux
> Où tout parle à notre âme, où vivaient nos aïeux.
>
> (Lezay-Marnésia, *Essai*, 69-70)

This latter text gives clear indication that the revival of ancestral values
is closely linked to the question of the legitimacy of the nobility.

If the issue of legitimacy or identity is not theorized as it would
be in a treaty, its connotations are very strong, since the terms used
appeal to the feelings of the readers. Legitimacy is expressed in terms
of love and respect, presented in turn as reciprocation to the duty of
bienfaisance fulfilled by the lord:

> Comme on respectera votre ancienne noblesse!
> Ah! Comme on bénira l'emploi de la richesse,
> Si, brisant vos liens par un choix vertueux,
> Vous savez loin des cours être bons, être heureux!
> . . .
> Le peuple agriculteur, reconnaissant et doux,
> Pour prix de vos bienfaits travaillera pour vous.
>
> (Lezay-Marnésia, *Essai*, 68)

The duty of *bienfaisance* is in effect the main cure, the major
means of regeneration, as well as the foundation stone of the legitimacy
of the noble. It is not modern charity, but rather a duty inscribed in
the charter binding the lord to his subjects. In his *Essai*, Lezay-
Marnésia describes to the local priest the contract between the noble
and his vassals and transforms him into a father fostering life:

> Je leur dois des soins à mon tour.
> Je dois éloigner d'eux la douleur, la misère,
> Les consoler, les aimer, les servir.
> Ainsi que toi, le ciel m'a fait leur père. (190)

The description of *bienfaisance* recurs constantly throughout the poems as a *leitmotiv*, as in this passage from Colardeau:

> Le pauvre, soulagé du fardeau qui l'oppresse,
> En s'occupant pour toi, trouve en toi des secours;
> Et d'un pain légitime alimente ses jours. (2:278)

It is at this point hardly necessary to provide more examples. The results of *bienfaisance* offer the poet opportunity to provide long descriptions of the country people who, having gained better living conditions and regular work, have simultaneously reached happiness. At this point, Descriptive Poetry may well remind the reader of the *Très Riches Heures du duc de Berry*.

However, *bienfaisance* is not only a one-way relationship. The fact that it generates a new aristocratic identity based on the medieval model of protection is only possible because it is a *two*-way relationship. The above quotation from Colardeau shows that if *bienfaisance* may be understood in terms of "duty" for the benefactor, it must also be understood in terms of "salary" for the beneficiary. The contract of *bienfaisance* provides the subjects with work, decent conditions, and potential happiness and protection—and the lords with the products of their subjects' work, the satisfaction of making them happy, and legitimacy in fulfilling the duty of protection. The idea of *bienfaisance* not only signifies the production of good deeds, but also corresponds to the feelings induced by the task:

> . . . soulager le pauvre, inspirer la vertu,
> Est un plaisir plus grand, qui m'était inconnu.
>   (Saint-Lambert, 159)

> Je ne songeai plus qu'à m'entourer d'heureux.
> Titus de mon hameau, son protecteur, son père,
> Je veux que sur ma tombe, on puisse écrire un jour:
> Il sema les bienfaits et recueillit l'amour.
>   (Lezay-Marnésia, *Essai*, 103)

The above quotation reveals, however, that this characteristic of *bienfaisance* should not be taken for the simple pleasure induced by the achievement of good deeds. The task of protection generates love, and on this love is built the new legitimacy of the lord, viewed as the

restoration of the ancient legitimacy of those times when nobles lived
close to their subjects. Hence, the implementation of *bienfaisance* is
both the cure and the restored health: it is the main characteristic of a
regenerated order which, in the eyes of the enlightened noble, informed
medieval authority.

The personal charter which creates the authority of the lord
conveys a paternalistic pattern:

> L'Ami de tes vassaux, et leur Juge et leur Père,
> De leur humble cabane écartant la misère,
> Nouveau Titus, assis sur un trône de fleurs,
> Citoyen couronné, tu règnes sur les coeurs.
> (Colardeau, 276)

In the preface to his essay, Lezay-Marnésia explains that the return of
the nobles to their estates establishes relationships of kindness and
reward between lord and vassal. He further stresses that they are
united with "bonds of love" (42). In his role as protector and guide,
the lord is compared to a "god" (129), and in his role as assistant, to a
"brother" (126). The worker, on the other hand, is compared to a
"friend" (128) who is very much attached to "the seigneurial race" (88).

At this point, it is necessary to analyze carefully how the concept
of *bienfaisance* which emerged in the wake of the Enlightenment met
the medieval imaginary and eventually provided a new identity for the
nobility, an identity corresponding to the paradigm of feudal
protection. The articles of the *Encyclopédie* where *bienfaisance* is
mentioned[27] show that it is neither a form of kindness nor a form of
generosity. It is characterized by the notion of utility and, as such, is
considered a public virtue. Different from charity, *bienfaisance* is part
of a prescriptive order; it does not engender a condescending attitude
but requires a personal involvement and the renunciation of any form
of pride. The behavior of the enlightened gentleman is not based on
a feeling of superiority; it is rather rooted in the feeling he experiences
of being a full member of the community where he lives and in which
he has a significant function to fulfill. *Bienfaisance* itself is the function
of the noble, not a virtue of the commoner, and as such it is the main
component in the foundation of the order of the nobility. The
medieval military environment may have disappeared, but its charter
of protection still exists in the imaginary and has been transformed into
a type of civil protection. *Bienfaisance* is not conceived as a means to

the social promotion of the subjects. It does not question the hierarchy; on the contrary, it reinforces it by aiming at achieving social harmony within the aristocratic system. In that sense, *bienfaisance* becomes an element of the power structure: it achieves its aim of creating harmony and order by using its energy which takes the form of sensibility.

Finally, one could question the role and place of sensibility in the medieval imaginary of the enlightened nobles. As has been shown above, it is not only an aesthetic based on a pastoral dream, but also a didactic means aimed at the restoration of a mythical medieval order. As such, the sensibility most critics describe as a literary characteristic in the eighteenth century is ideological. Ultimately, sensibility appears as that which provides the nobility with the restoration of its identity or legitimacy. From the results of the present research, we might go even further and maintain that sensibility (the energy of the medieval imaginary) is the foundation stone of that legitimacy. Paradoxical as it may be, the ideology of *bienfaisance* transfers the source of the legitimacy of the nobility to the people. The noble is still a noble because he fulfills again his duty of protection. Thus far, this conclusion agrees with the hypothesis of Biou, Galliani, and Sclippa. The enlightened nobility has in effect a modern outlook: it is an order interested only in general welfare. The source of its power is however comparable to that of the medieval lords. The seigneurial charter presupposed to regenerate the country is rooted in a personal link, the nature of which is protection. The proposed model of society follows a paternalistic pattern: the familial spirit of the institution, absence of worries, domination blurred by sensitive harmony and sentimental effusion.

Bienfaisance is in fact the redefinition in modern terms of the medieval contract. It does not advocate the complete maintenance of the feudal contract as such, but it proposes to replace royal absolutism by a form of government in which the noble is protector of his subjects and the soul and life of the local community. Its values are those of an agricultural society where military protection is replaced by a type of protection encompassing all aspects of life. The mode of power relationships is that of a patriarchal society where the modern abstract contract is replaced by the concrete personal and sentimental relationship between the lord and his subjects. One might even be tempted to suggest that the encounter of the medieval imaginary and the thought of the Enlightenment has fostered a new and paradoxical principle: the principle of a nobility based on a legitimacy drawn from the people. In any case, the school of "the return to the country" prepared for the rediscovery of the Middle Ages, a trend which would develop rapidly in France after the Restoration in 1815.

NOTES

1. Michel Baridon, *Le Gothique des Lumières* (Brionne: Gérard Montfort éditeur, 1991), 133.

2. See Jean Starobinski, *L'Invention de la liberté* (Genève: Skira, 1964).

3. See "Gothique," *Encyclopédie ou Dictionnaire raisonné des sciences, des arts, et des métiers*, 7 (1757); "Architecture," *Encyclopédie méthodique*, 2 (1782):457; "Agriculture," *Supplément à l'Encyclopédie*, 1 (1776): 215; "Gloire," *Encyclopédie*, 7 (1759): 718; "Population," Encyclopédie, 13 (1765): 100.

4. *Recueil des opinions de Stanislas de Clermont-Tonnerre* (Paris, 1791), 2:23-4.

5. *Mémoires de M. le comte de Montlosier* (Paris, 1830), 67-8.

6. The word *bienfaisance* has no exact equivalent in English. It is neither charity nor benevolence, neither generosity nor justice. It is rather a social *duty* which seems to have been based on the concept of the innate value and integrity of the community.

7. Quoted in Baldine Saint Girons, *Esthétiques du XVIIIe siècle. Le modèle français* (Paris: Philippe Sers éditeur, 1990), 185.

8. François-Joachim de Pierres, Cardinal de Bernis, *Les Quatre Saisons, ou les Géorgiques françoises* (Paris, 1763).

9. Joseph Alexandre Victor d'Hupay de Fuvéa, *Généralif, maison patriarcale et champêtre* (Aix-en-Provence, 1790), 7, 18, 8-9, 25-7.

10. *Journal de Governeur Morris pendant les anées 1789, 1790, 1791, et 1792*, trans. E. Pariset (Paris: Plon-Nourrit, 1901), 33, 15.

11. Renato Galliani, *Rousseau, le luxe et l'idéologie nobilaire* (Oxford: The Voltaire Foundation, 1989), 194-5.

12. *Journal Oeconomique*, September 1755, 97; March 1756, 81; July 1756, 85.

13. "Moraves," *Encyclopédie* 10 (1765): 704-6.

14. Jean Biou, "Le rousseauisme, idéologie de substitution," *Roman et Lumières au 18e siècle* (Paris: Editions Sociales, 1970), 123.

15. Reproduced in Anthony Vidler, *Ledoux, Architecture and Social Reform at the End of the Enlightenment* (Cambridge: Harvard University Press, 1990), 70.

16. Henri Goyon de la Plombanie, *La France agricole et marchande* (Avignon, 1762), 409-39.

17. Pierre Etienne, *Le Bonheur rural . . .* (Paris, 1788), xviii-xix.

18. Claude-François-Adrien, marquis de Lezay-Marnésia, *Le Bonheur dans les campagnes* (Neufchatel et Paris, 1785, 1788).

19. Roland Bonnel, "Le traitement de la nature dans *Le Bonheur dans les campagnes*," *Facets of the Eighteenth Century*, ed. Roland Bonnel (North York: Captus University Publications, 1991): 109-19.

20. Norbert Sclippa, "*La Nouvelle Héloïse* et l'aristocratie," *Studies on Voltaire and the eighteenth century* 284 (1991): 1-72.

21. Jean-François, marquis de Saint-Lambert, *Les Saisons* (Amsterdam, 1769), x-xii.

22. Jean-Baptiste-Louis-Théodore, baron de Tschoudi, *Les Voeux d'un citoyen, ode au Roi, avec un morceau de poésie champêtre* (Metz, 1775), 4.

23. "Luxe," *Encyclopédie* 9 (1765): 763-71.

24. Claude-François-Adrien, marquis de Lezay-Marnésia, *Les Paysages, ou Essais sur la nature champêtre, poëme*, augmented ed. (Paris, 1800).

25. Charles-Pierre Colardeau, *Epître à Monsieur Duhamel de Denainvilliers*, *Oeuvres de Colardeau* (Paris, 1779), 2:278.

26. Jacques Heers, *Le Moyen Age, une imposture* (Paris: Perrin, 1992).

27. "Bonte," *Encyclopédie* 2 (1751); "Générosité," *Encyclopédie* 7 (1757); "Bienfaisance," *Supplément* 1 (1776).

Ideology and Utopia
in the Medievalism of
Louis de Bonald

W. Jay Reedy

The words "ideology" and "utopia" in my title are meant as an invocation of Karl Mannheim's famous study in the sociology of knowledge.[1] I intend to claim that the medievalism in the writings of the Vicomte Louis de Bonald (1754-1840) holds a twin aspect that is both ideological and utopian. Bonald was France's most prominent reactionary intellectual in the post-Revolutionary decades and a man who also spent fifteen years as an important political figure (he was first a *député* and then a Peer) of the Bourbon Restoration.[2] In his works—which include massive and turgid theoretical tomes as well as brief journalistic essays and parliamentary speeches—images of medieval culture, society, polity, and economy provide the touchstones for his assault on the values of the Reformation, the Enlightenment, and the French Revolution, that nefarious *troika* of changes which dominates his critique of the coming of modernity. But this same, largely imaginary, vision of what was allegedly best about pre-modern Europe's institutions and beliefs is what he quixotically[3] believed could be reconstructed for the future with the help of his "science of society."[4]

It is in this regard that the Vicomte's medievalism was both ideological and utopian, metaphysical and scientistic. This so-called "prophet of the past" (Barbey d'Aurevilly's characterization) from the backward province of the Rouergue, compelled by circumstances to be not a conservative but a reactionary, could remain a traditionalist only by adopting a mode of criticism that is much more subversive in its discourse than one might expect. Even to call him a "Red Tory" is to understate this apparent anomaly. In parts of his *oeuvre*, Bonald's castigations of modernity even bring to mind the attacks of Karl Marx.

Proof that the Vicomte's "modernized traditionalism" possessed this contradictory, or at least double-edged, character can be found in the fact that his writings influenced not only right-wing polemicists—e. g., Louis Veuillot and Charles Maurras—but also those wary of the modern world who were on the political center or left (Tocqueville, Lamennais, *et al*.), as well as theorists involved in the establishment of nineteenth-century sociology such as the Comte de Saint-Simon, Auguste Comte, Frédéric Le Play, and Emile Durkheim.

Though Edmund Burke is well known for having proclaimed the age of chivalry dead in his *Reflections on the Revolution in France* (1790), Bonald was much more enthralled by the medieval world view than was Burke, a political rhetorician content with the limited monarchy guaranteed by the English settlement of 1688-89. What fueled and sustained Bonald's fascination? He gained a good deal of his idealized understanding of medieval civilization, especially of what Georges Duby calls the "chivalrous society," from the antiquarian research of La Curne de Sainte-Palaye and the *Acadèmie des Inscriptions et des Belles-Lettres*.[5] Thanks to rose-colored interpretations like Sainte-Palaye's, Bonald could defend the pre-Revolutionary prerogatives of the Second Estate by portraying the knight of his twelfth- and thirteenth-century "golden age" as the embodiment of courage, fidelity, and lay piety. In short, he was everything that the iconoclastic *philosophe* of the eighteenth century was not. With the aid of an allegory that is as touching as it is naive, Bonald anachronistically imagined how,

> [i]n the days of old, in the century of strength, a gallant knight, mounted on a palfrey, helmet on his head and lance in his hand, persuaded himself in his chivalric dreams that a beautiful princess locked in a tower under guard by a wizard, was going to offer him her hand and lands for freeing her from captivity. Today, in the century of enlightenment, the young literary man, still coated with the chalk dust of school, pen in his hand and the *Contrat social* in his head, imagines in philosophical reveries that a people groaning under despotism will in its primary assemblies confer upon him at least legislative power if he can with speeches and writings break their chains. We have in each case the same passions. But the knight was a generous and brave visionary. The

[modern] literary man is a threatening lunatic. (*Théorie du pouvoir, Oeuvres* 1:755, n. 1)[6]

Depending on J.-F. Michaud's *Histoire des croisades* (1811-1822), Bonald also assumes that the ethos of chivalry was consolidated by the crusading experience.[7] Despite his preference for the rationalistic, indeed, for the pseudo-scientific presentation of his ideas and values, he nurtured a highly nostalgic outlook on the pre-modern past. This nostalgia is apparent where he analyzes the social functionality which the "knightly" *seigneurs* of the lesser nobility offered to European civilization past, present, and future. In a moment of extravagance, he even describes the vocation of the nobleman as a "'sacred flame' [of chivalry] whose faint embers, protected under the ruins of time and passion, could be reilluminated among us if a powerful current fans them back to life" (*Législation primitive, Oeuvres* 1:1331-2). The Crusades, insists this country gentleman who was the son of a military commander, were not an outburst of xenophobia and bigotry as the Enlighteners had charged. Those medieval expeditions to the Holy Land arose from a "humane zeal" to protect oppressed Christians and to "save Europe from Ottoman [*sic*] barbarism" ("Sur l'assassinate de M. Auguste Kotzebue," *Oeuvres* 3:1259; *Théorie du pouvoir, Oeuvres* 1:1288). One consequence of this perspective is that Bonald finds the Crusaders fittingly celebrated in Tasso's epic poem *Gerusalemme liberata* (*Théorie du pouvoir, Oeuvres* 1:307).

What was more, the spiritual dynamism of the Crusades coincided with the gradual ending of serfdom (an institution almost indispensable in the more barbarous early medieval times) and its replacement by less harsh and inflexible forms of feudal tenancy and rent.[9] In the Vicomte's estimation, feudalism—a word derived from "fidelity," he noted—embodied the perfect system of decentralized governance, one in which nobles dutifully served the values of Christian theocracy:

> In fact, the [feudal] institution of public ministry in Christian states is not, like the *Republic* of Plato or the *Utopia* of Thomas More, a dream of a childish imagination that never has been realized. That institution existed in Europe in high perfection. In times which we can regard as neighboring on our own, Christendom saw a whole order of men devoted, in body and fortune, to the defense, and even to the cultivation of society. (*Législation primitive, Oeuvres* 1:1331)

The "abuses of feudalism" denounced by the *philosophes* and then by the Revolutionaries were due not so much to the nature of the institution but to the human nature of a few miscreant individuals whose names bore the *particule*. After all, vices were an inexpungable attribute of fallen human nature. Therefore we should not, Bonald suggests, be too quick in condemning a past social form simply because certain lords and vassals failed to live up to its standards.[10] The feudal institutions in themselves were valid and valuable and demanded admiration. As read by the backward-glancing Vicomte, Sainte-Palaye's research bolstered his own assumption that the feudal monarchism of the Middle Ages was a reciprocal set of relationships that benefited everyone—the sovereigns, the nobility, the clergy, and the common people (*Législation primitive, Oeuvres* 1:1299, 1337, 1341). Bonald, like others on his side of the political fence after the Revolution, looked back with fondness to *La Chanson de Roland* and the honor-bound world of Charlemagne it presumably portrayed. Whatever its literary merits and however romanticized its representation of war, that epic drew Charlemagne as a king highly honored by his counts and his *chevaliers* because he was "incapable of independent action," unable to make decisions of consequence without consulting his nobles. The poem presents an image of royalty that a pre-Revolutionary reformer turned post-Revolutionary reactionary like Bonald could admire despite, indeed because of, the apparent contradiction in its ultra-royalist message.

But the medieval equilibrium in the relationships of kings and nobles in France did not last into the early modern period as far as Bonald was concerned. The postmedieval period saw a decline in the wealth and in the political role of the feudal nobility caused in part by the centralizing monarchs themselves, the Vicomte admits. With the loss of this caste of "public men" who formerly both enforced the commands and limited the ambition of theocratic authority, the kings of France of the sixteenth, seventeenth, and eighteenth centuries "vainly tried . . . to fill the void that was once occupied by that sublime institution [of feudal nobility]" with a merely decorative *chevalerie de coeur*. Moreover, this patriciate of the Court grew more arrogant to the degree that it became politically atrophied. Its pretentiousness accentuated the invidious divisions within the Second Estate of the *ancien régime*. Courtliness distracted nobles from their obligations to theocracy and was no substitute for either genuine political responsibility and social authority or for an ethos of stalwart service to throne and altar.[11] The postmedieval growth of the monarchical state tended to separate the roles of warrior and judge, thereby splitting the traditional elite and—together with the infiltration of Calvinism—setting the stage for both the aristocratic uprisings (i. e., the Wars of Religion, the Fronde, etc.) and ultimately for the nobility's replacement in the Bourbon monarchy's administration by bourgeois functionaries (*Législation primitive, Oeuvres* 1:200). It was the dedicated, uncorrupted, and politically involved nobility of the Middle Ages that Bonald fantasized about and which he wished the Restoration monarchy of the early nineteenth century would help to bring back to authority, prosperity, and privilege.

But the Vicomte's medievalism extended beyond a "feudal" and chivalric image of nobility. Indeed, he maintained that all of the social hierarchies of the Middle Ages provided relational matrices far superior to the unnaturally "mechanistic" system of politics and economics established by the adminstrative state and burgeoning capitalism of the nineteenth century. According to the Bonaldian diagnosis of what ailed the post-Revolutionary West, it was only the modern age that witnessed the bureaucratic power of centralized governments intruding upon the individuals and organic communities already being alienated from each other and from tradition by the artificial needs and ruthless competition which new legal and economic rules warranted. The novel and unchristian type of polity and economy born with the modern age improperly equated license and comfort with liberty:

> In a republic, society is no longer a general body but merely an agglomeration [*réunion*] of individuals. Because the general will is then no more than the sum of particular wills, general conservation, which is its [i. e., society's] object, becomes no more than individual happiness. Thus we notice the consequence in republics that the physical well-being of man is the compensation for his moral degradation and for the sacrifice of his social liberty. Everything is individualized, everything retreats to and is concentrated in private life. The present becomes everything and there is no [notion of the] future. (*Théorie du pouvoir, Oeuvres* 1:200)[12]

By contrast, the pre-modern peasantry of France felt secure and never oppressed by their inherited subordination and interminable toil.

Blind to the coercive extraction of labor value under the feudal and manorial systems, Bonald alleges that medieval peasants lived interdependently and almost always in harmony with those who were their betters and their benefactors, namely the privileged country *gentilhommes* and the village priests. This was because the hierarchical orderings and the religious sentiments which were the traditional rural community's lifeblood dampened competition and softened antagonisms. The traditional social order of things restrained the rich, the powerful, and the "public," encouraged charity, and firmly but fairly kept the unprivileged and "private" members of the Third Estate in their proper place—the place of the laborer and the supplicant. Such selfless devotion to an unwritten constitution mandated by God (and by Nature) was the intangible though "real" essence of medieval theocratic society for Bonald.

Capitalistic society lacked communal ideals—in fact, it was hardly a society at all—and thus could not protect governments or modern civilization as a whole against the perils of ambitious and antisocial individualism. It was not only medieval Catholicism that had combated such pernicious individualism through a device such as the usury laws. The entire corporatist structure which the Revolution tried hard to obliterate—not only the three Estates but also the organization of the "stem" family, of the guilds and of the semi-autonomous communes—are praised without reserve by the theocrat from the Rouergue. Corporatism is portrayed as the main agency of pre-modern socialization and conflict control. In a truly monarchical polity, the tendency of such institutions to fix social roles, rewards, and obligations is pervasive. This anchorage existed even among working-class "families in the mechanical professions through hereditary masterships." Thanks to the trade associations of medieval towns, it was possible to curb people's rising and destabilizing expectations and to inspire "in children a taste for the professions of their fathers and thus assure the perpetuation of the lowliest and most perilous occupations." Corporate bodies, wrote Bonald,

> are, therefore, the essence of a constituted society. [Such a society] tends to make corporate bodies out of individuals, families, and professions. It only sees man within the family, families only within professions, and professions only within the corporate bodies. This is the secret, the mystery, the

interior principle of monarchy. (*Théorie du pouvoir*, *Oeuvres*
1:670, 757)

To Bonald, bringing back the masterships as well as the workers' aid
societies (*compagnonnages*) would be a means of preventing early
nineteenth-century economic liberalism from tearing apart the fabric of
French society and creating more of that unprecedented and highly
dangerous type of poverty known as *pauperisme*. If a country had to
have an urban economic sector—and Bonald, as we might guess,
preferred an autarkic, agrarian economy (cf. "De la famille agricole, de
la famille industrielle," *Oeuvres* 2:236-60)—the market mechanism of the
Smithian economists was insufficient. It could not steer the populace
toward those immaterial though moral and patriarchal ends which
deserved priority over any increase in material production.

The corporations of crafts and trades were for the lower classes a
kind of hereditary municipal nobility which gave importance and even
dignity to the humblest individuals and the least prestigious and
lucrative occupations ("Sur l'économie sociale," *Oeuvres* 3:1279).[14]
Compared with the false "freedom " of the national or international
marketplace, the local bonds and social moralism of the Middle Ages'
intermediate groups permitted people more meaningful liberties and
more meaningful lives.[15] It was the conceited Enlighteners and those
leaders of the Revolution who followed the ideas of Turgot who were
responsible for banishing the corporative layers of communality among
men and between men and the surveillance-oriented state of modern
times:

> [T]he *philosophes* desired a rigorous uniformity in things for
> ease in administering them. But what we need to do is to
> reunite heads and hearts [within and among all individuals]
> while allowing diversity everywhere that nature has placed it
> and custom has introduced it. (*Pensées*, *Oeuvres* 3:1312)

The provinces and towns of pre-modern France had retained a
good deal of independent governance into the seventeenth century and
were residual features of the polity of the medieval kingdoms
appreciated by Bonald. To him, these local entities went back to a
time out of mind and should be allowed to survive indefinitely as
"monads" of the future national community; they were "domestic
states, elements of the public State, Celtic before being Gaulish, Gaulish

before being Roman, Roman before being Frankish." Such microcosms of the royal macrocosm "preceded the monarchy . . . and the State could not exist without them." The Rouergat theocrat was especially exercised about a proposal which the "usurper," Napoleon, made into law in 1813 which stripped towns (and thus the towns' ruling elites) of a residual authority to supervise the common lands supervised since time immemorial ("Opinion sur le budget de 1816," *Oeuvres* 2:1053).[16]

We should not be misled into thinking that because Bonald is frequently considered an "ultra-royalist" that he worshipped the state or even the absolutist conception of monarchy. His notions of government may be imprecisely described as Christian authoritarian, but they are not Machiavellian, Hobbesian, or totalitarian. From principle as well as out of caste interest, he views the pre-Revolutionary "society of orders" and its corporate bodies as functionally indispensable: his monarchical ideal cannot and does not include the characteristic of omnipotence. Indeed, his conception of kingship is more symbolic and passive than active and all-powerful. While strongly upholding a divine-right theory of monarchy, the Jacobins' attempt to totalize the power of the state and to make uniform a society of atomic individuals never spurs Bonald to counteract modernity by advocating a government that is dictatorial or monolithic. A royalist who is also a pluralist, Bonald emphasizes the spiritual mantle and theoretical unity, not the practical powers of the king's office. The best of sovereigns, he declares, "is only, therefore, the secretary of nature and he ought to write only under her dictates" (*Théorie du pouvoir, Oeuvres* 1:393).[17] The Vicomte had no doubt that

> France [before the Old Regime's demise] was more constituted than any other society [on earth] because its *pouvoir générale* was more constituted. That is to say, it was at once better defended and more limited than that of any other monarchy. Public religion, hereditary succession, inherited and permanent distinctions (not only in individuals but in obligations), immunities for the clergy, prerogatives for the nobility, privileges for provinces, cities, and groups, great crown offices, preeminence for a peerage, jurisdictions for sovereign courts, irremovability in the positions of magistrates, all these things . . . were independent of the monarch. (*Théorie du pouvoir, Oeuvres* 1:294)

It was neither Richelieu nor the Sun King who represented the wise ruler, according to Bonald's science of society. Louis XIV, in fact, is criticized for his strident Gallicanism, his disastrous foreign policy, his ruinous taxes, and his administrative interference with local affairs which fell under the purview of the local nobility and clergy. It comes as no surprise that Bonald's favorite monarch, his *exemplum* of kingship, was Louis IX, St. Louis. Tillement's classic *Vie de Saint-Louis* (1847-51) was his prime source of information on that ruler's paradigmatic career.[18] According to the Vicomte, Louis IX was a resourceful sovereign, a brave and devout Crusader, and (his religious intolerance notwithstanding) a king respected as the fairest of judges by everyone in the realm ("De la manière d'écrire l'histoire," *Oeuvres* 3:1064). Under St. Louis, the Catholic religion, the French monarchy, and the noble and clerical agents of throne and altar together achieved an unsurpassed accomplishment—a holistic kingdom which fulfilled Christian principles by reaching that universalist and localist balance that only selfless cooperation among monarchs, nobles, and clergy can produce (*Théorie du pouvoir, Oeuvres* 1:305-6).[19] What is more, the Scholastic intellectual culture that flourished in the days of Louis IX was, especially by comparison with the subversiveness of the *siécle des lumières*, a philosophical movement which (notwithstanding its unwise move away from Platonism) never undermined habits of deference or the consensual religious prejudices of the French.[20]

Unlike his ally turned opponent, René de Chateaubriand, Bonald never sought to redeem the Middle Ages' reputation by waxing rhapsodic about its aesthetic glories.[21] Nor, unlike the apologists for antebellum slaveholding in the American South, did he merely want the modern world of technical progress and productivity softened with a veneer of medieval manners and paternalism.[22] Rather, as an ingenuous proto-sociologist—Robert Nisbet contends he was a sociologist *avant la lettre*[23]—Bonald wrote to bring about a full-scale reconstruction of the valorized structures that underpinned medieval civilization, or at least what his retrospective mind's eye saw as medieval civilization. But it is because of the criticism of modernity highlighted in his now forgotten writings that he deserves to be recognized as the most inflexible and anachronistic but also as the most idealistic of the early nineteenth century's ideologists of medievalism.

NOTES

1. See Karl Mannheim, *Ideologie und Utopie* (Bonn: F. Cohen, 1929).

2. The only intellectual biography remains Henri Moulinié, *De Bonald* (Paris: Presses Universitaires de France, 1916).

3. Bonald even makes a touching attempt to redeem what Cervantes' tragicomic and anachronistic hero—as well as he himself—stood for: "'Don Quixote' possesses so much gallantry; he is intelligent, even spiritual, as concerns everything apart from this [individual] folly. It may even be that his [literary] work has had too much success and that the riddle it directs at excessively generous sentiments should not have been extended to those sentiments themselves. Today, every man who wants to defend interests other than his own personal ones is treated as a 'Don Quixote.' In place of noble enthusiasm and feeling there is now only the somber and sad fanaticism of opinions" (*Pensées, Oeuvres complètes*, ed. A. Migne, 3 vols. [Paris, 1854-7], 3:1406). All translations from Bonald are my own.

4. See my "Language, Counter-Revolution and the 'Two Cultures': Louis de Bonald's Traditionalist Scientism," *Journal of the History of Ideas* 44 (1983): 579-97.

5. Cf. Lionel Gossman, *Medievalism and the Ideologies of the Enlightenment: The World and Work of La Curne de Sainte-Palaye* (Baltimore: Johns Hopkins University Press, 1968). The *Mémoires sur l'ancienne chevalerie* (1759) was reissued in 1781. Kathleen Hardesty has argued ("The Middle Ages in the Encyclopédie Méthodique," *Studies in Medievalism* 2.1 [Spring 1983]: 11-26) that the Enlightenment's contempt for the Middle Ages eased in French intellectual culture at the end of the Old Regime. See also Keith Busby, "An Eighteenth-Century Plea on Behalf of the Medieval Romance: La Curne de Sainte-Palaye's '*Mémoire*,'" *Studies in Medievalism* 3.1 (Fall 1987): 55-70.

6. This opinion about the educated youth of the early nineteenth century reinforces Bonald's almost Platonic view of the virtues of a gerontocratic elite: "Age resists change because it no longer changes. It wants everything to remain at rest around it because it wishes to rest itself and also because changes bring to mind an idea of destruction and death that it wants to repulse. Inflexibility of taste and opinion among the elderly makes it the enemy of all innovations and the strongest rampart of the constitution of societies" (*Théorie du pouvoir, Oeuvres* 1:240, 742-5, 769-73, *passim*).

7. Bonald contended that the French nobility of early medieval times—"essentially conservative on behalf of political society" as long as it was a ministerial agency of kings before becoming "destructive of constituted society when as it was itself an authority"—was "docile and cultivated without ceasing to be brave" thanks to the call of the popes to rescue the Holy Land: "The Crusades were the origin of chivalry, of that religious honor, which produced such heroic and innocent virtues and such frank and courageous men. It was an institution

which people viewed only with respect and which writers of the time only spoke of with enthusiasm" (*Théorie du pouvoir, Oeuvres* 1:597).

8. Cf. P. Rousset, *Histoire d'une idéologie, La Croisade* (Lausanne: L'Age d'homme, 1983).

9. Cf. "De la manière d'écrire l'histoire," *Oeuvres* 3:1063-4.

10. "If men were endowed with angelic perfections which disposed them to practice the most heroic virtues, then neither governments nor laws would be needed" (*Théorie du pouvoir, Oeuvres* 1:374).

11. On the development of the "court-aristocratic figuration" and the sociopolitical context of its obsequious etiquette, see Norbert Elias, *The Court Society*, trans. E. Jephcott (New York: Pantheon, 1983).

12. Or, in Tocqueville's phrasing, modern people show a "cowardly love of present employment [so as to] . . . lose sight of the interests of their future selves and those of their descendants and prefer to glide along the easy current of life rather than to make, when it is necessary, a strong and sudden effort to the higher purpose" (*Democracy in America*, quoted in Roger Boesche, "Why Did Tocqueville Fear Abundance? Or the Tension Between Commerce and Citizenship," *Journal of the History of Ideas* 9 [1983]: 38). Tocqueville, whose father was a staunch royalist, was acquainted with Bonald's works.

13. In attacking Turgot's abolition of the guilds as part of a remonstrance of 1776, *avocat-générale* Séguier had already framed the issue in the same terms: "All your subjects, Sire, are divided into as many bodies as there are different conditions in the kingdom. The clergy, the nobility, the sovereign courts, the law courts, the universities, the academies, the finance companies, they all represent . . . existing bodies which may be viewed as a great chain of which the first is in the hands of Your Majesty, as the sovereign administrator of everything that constitutes the body of the nation" (Flammeront, *Rémonstrance du Parlement de Paris au XVIIIe siècle*, 3 vols. [Paris, 1888-98], 3:293ff.). On corporations before 1789, see Emile Coonaert, *Les Corporations en France avant 1789* (Paris: Gallimard, 1941); François Olivier-Martin, *L'Organisation corporative de la France d'ancien régime* (Paris: Girey, 1938); and Emile Lousse, *La Sociéte d'ancien régime, organisation et réprésentation*, 2 vols. (Louvain: Editions Universitas, 1943).

14. Bonald was far from unique in viewing traditional associations of workers and masters as "chivalrous" in their collective values and symbols. French *companonnage* itself fostered this identity. Sean Wilentz has even found this preference for the trappings of chivalry among industrial working-class fraternities in the United States in the second half of the nineteenth century; cf. his *Chants Democratic: New York City and the Rise of the American Working Class, 1788-1850* (Oxford: Oxford University Press, 1984).

15. This view puts Bonald among those earliest "lamenters" of modernity's erosion of traditional communitarianism treated in Bruce Mazlish, *A New Science: The Breakdown of Connections and the Birth of Sociology* (Oxford: Oxford University Press, 1989).

16. In his *Politique a l'usage du peuple*, the Abbé de Lamennais would state a similar point: "The commune is the state in small; we are more or less free or

more or less enslaved by the [national] state according as the commune is more or less enslaved, more or less free" (quoted in Robert Nisbet, "The Politics of Pluralism: Lamennais," in his *Tradition and Revolt* [New York: Vintage, 1970]), 43.

17. Mona Ozouf correctly observes that the Bonaldian monarch "paradoxically recalls the character of . . . Physiocratic monarchy." The king imagined in Bonald's theory "exercises the most exalted of functions . . . without any need of manifesting it, penetrating [society] with it, or even of carrying out particular activities. . . . In this portrait of the titular king . . . the question of personal royal merits, argued about for centuries, becomes merely rhetorical" ("L'Idée et l'image du regicide dans la pensée contre-révolutionnaire: l'originalité de Ballanche," in F. Lebrun and J. Dupuy, eds., *Les Résistance a la Revolution* [Paris: Imago, 1987], 336).

18. On what St. Louis was like as a monarch—Bonald's image is overdrawn but not wholly unhistorical—see E. R. Labande, "Quelques traites de carctères du roi Saint Louis," *Revue d'histoire de la spiritualité* 1 (1974): 135-46, and William C. Jordan, *Louis IX and the Challenge of the Crusade* (Princeton: Princeton University Press, 1979).

19. Georges Duby writes, "The consciousness of class which gradually caused the French aristocracy to become a homogeneous group was thus crystallized around the knightly ideal, its ethic and the virtues of valour and loyalty. . . . [A] French aristocracy of political equals, largely created about the year 1200 by the growth in princely power which eliminated the castellans, was also based on the recognition in men's minds of an image of the perfect knight." Duby also points out that the late twelfth century was already a period of increasing "economic stress" for the nobility. Bonald's heyday of the nobility—presuming such there really was—was a medieval anomaly! This "stress" was caused by the first economic challenge of the bourgeoisie as well as by the aristocracy's own overspending. See Duby, "The Transformation of the Aristocracy: France at the Beginning of the Thirteenth Century," in *The Chivalrous Society*, trans. C. Postan (Berkeley: University of California Press, 1977), 180-1, 183.

20. Cf. "Si la philosophie est utile pour le gouvernement de la société," *Oeuvres* 3:1383, and "Sur l'histoire de J.-B. Bossuet," *Oeuvres* 3:932.

21. Chateaubriand's great work of Romantic apologetics was, of course, the *Génie du christianisme* (1802).

22. See Eugene D. Genovese, "The Southern Slaveholders' View of the Middle Ages," in *Medievalism in American Culture*, eds. Bernard Rosenthal and Paul Szarmach (Binghamton: Medieval and Renaissance Texts and Studies, 1989), 52.

23. Among other works, see Robert Nisbet, "De Bonald and the Concept of the Social Group," *Journal of the History of Ideas* 7 (1946): 56-74.

(Re)Creating a Medieval Parade: *La Fête historique* in Douai

Jesse D. Hurlbut

Among the printed items of local significance collected in the Municipal Archives in Douai, France, is a thin book with the following lengthy title:

> Notice sur Philippe-le-Bon, duc de Bourgogne et Comte de Flandre, considéré sous les rapports des faits généraux de l'histoire, et principalement des actes particuliers qui intéressent la ville de Douai . . . suivie de strophes, de notes sur le programme de la seconde fête historique, et ornée de lithographies représentant tous les personnages du cortège rangés suivant l'ordre de la marche.[1]

From the title, one might expect to find information or analysis about a medieval ceremony. Instead, it turns out to be a sort of illustrated and annotated souvenir program for a parade that was produced in the middle of the nineteenth century.

This program book was prepared by a municipal officer and illustrated and printed by local artist, Félix Robaux. Included in it are the biographical note mentioned in the title, a set of brief notes establishing the historical authenticity of each component of the parade, three poems, and several fold-out pages with panoramic depictions of the entire parade. The publication gives precious little information about the circumstances of the celebration. Indications of the date, the occasion, and the producers of this event can be deduced only on the basis of one brief note describing two heralds marching near the end of the parade and who were throwing tokens to the spectators:

Les médailles jetées par ces hérauts portent d'un côté cette inscription circulaire: *Société de Bienfaisance*, et au milieu le D gothique, d. Sur le revers est écrit: *deuxième fête historique*, 1840; et au milieu P. Y., initiales des noms de Philippe et Ysabeau. (16)

The gothic D is the heraldic device for the city of Douai (see the banners and arms in Figures 1-4). The P and the Y stand for Philip and the medieval spelling for Isabelle, or Ysabeau. Because of the lengthy biographical note in the program, we know that these are Philip the Good and his wife Isabelle of Portugal. The dominion of this Duke of Burgundy extended from 1419 to 1467 and included this portion of French-speaking Flanders.

We learn that the date was 1840, the event bore the title of "*La Fête historique*," and it was produced in whole or in part by the "*Société de Bienfaisance*." An investigation in the archives about this community organization sheds some additional light. We learn, for example, that the *Société de Bienfaisance* had devised this parade for the purposes of charity. To this end, we read that

[p]endant ces publications et réceptions, ainsi que durant toutes les autres parties de la Fête historique, le groupe des quêteurs, remplissant la noble mission à laquelle il s'est voué, sollicitera la générosité des habitants et des étrangers, en faveur du but philanthropique de la société. (dossier D-5, #48: 1, 3)

This is a quotation from the short booklet of program notes for a similar parade that took place in 1843. In it we also learn that the *fête* had been re-created in 1840, 1842, and in 1843, "sans jamais lasser la curiosité de ses visiteurs" (dossier D-5, #48: 2). There is no evidence of any other parade after 1843. The date of the original *fête historique* remains unknown, but was, in all likelihood, in 1838 or 1839.[2]

The 1840 parade, as it is represented in the program illustrations, was divided into five "tableaux," each of which included several participants. In all, more than seventy-two groups of people are identified.[3] Each of the tableaux focused on a theme or component of a medieval entry ceremony. The first was dedicated to the city and its defenders (Figure 1). The second represented the leadership of the city and the gifts to be given to the visiting duke. The third glorified the chivalric Order of the Golden Fleece, of which Philip the Good was the founder in 1430. In the fourth and fifth tableaux, the duchess and the duke arrived in respective order and accompanied by their retinue.

La Fête historique was not the imitation of a single known historical parade, but was intended to represent the triumphal entries of the fifteenth century in general. A list of historical notes identifies the various sources from which the different components of the parade were drawn. Some of these merely identify the dates that certain municipal bodies, which were represented in the parade, came into existence. For example, one note informs us, regarding the group of *arquebusiers*, that "[q]uelques personnes ont pensé qu'ils n'existaient pas à cette époque. C'est une erreur; car leur existence est constatée dans les armées de la France vers le milieu du 15e siècle" (14). This item is then cross-referenced to the historical note, where the assertion is documented.

The notes chosen to be examined here, however, are those which identify the historical basis for some of the more important floats. From these, we are able to discern to what degree the parade was indeed successful in patterning itself off of its medieval models. Many of the comments regarding these notes are based on research I have conducted on over 130 fifteenth-century entries of the Dukes of Burgundy.

It is easy enough to find discrepancies between *La Fête historique* and its medieval antecedents. For instance, in the second tableau, we find a stretcher loaded with presents of wine for the visiting nobility (Figure 2). The idea for this part of the parade came from the description of the entry of Charles the Bold into Arras in 1469:

> Les présens que l'on fit à ce souverain [à Charles] étaient portés sur une tablette couverte de toile bleue, avec les armes de la ville à droite et à gauche. Aux quatre coins de cette tablette il y avait quatre lions en relief, tenant chacun une bannière aux armoiries de la ville. (15)

I should first like to point out that the description of this *brancard* no longer exists in the medieval records of this event. Presumably, however, it could still be found in the archives in 1840 in preparation for this event. Second, while it is true that the lion on each corner of the display represented the heraldic charge for Flanders, of which Douai was a part, there is no evidence of any representation of lions in any of the medieval entries into Douai. The lion holding a banner was more likely to be associated with the capital of Artois, the city of Arras, whence this decoration originated and where most of the entries of record included representations of lions.

In the same tableau, more "presents" were displayed on a larger float (Figure 3). Two sources for this presentation are cited in our notes. First, at the 1355 entry of John, King of France, into Douai, two beef cows, each one with a castle on its back, were offered as presents to the king. The second source is from Duke Philip's Feast of the Pheasant in 1454, where an elephant entered the banquet hall with a castle on its back. Both of these are verifiable historical occurrences, but it should be noted that the organizers of *La Fête historique* drew from two events nearly a hundred years apart, one of which was not even a ceremonial entry, but a banquet. In addition, in both instances, the symbolism originally associated with these presentations had been completely lost. The cows delivered to King John in 1355 were not beasts of burden. Rather, they represented the prosperity of the king's domain and were intended to be cooked and eaten by the king and his household during his visit in the good city. The elephant, led by a Saracen, originally served as the vivid reminder of the Turkish invasion of the Holy Land in the days of Philip the Good. A disheveled Lady Church appeared in the castle on the elephant's back and implored the duke to come to her rescue by organizing a crusade.

Similar issues may be raised about each of the other displays in the parade. The third tableau included the canopy, which was traditionally carried over kings at their first entry (Figure 4). There are three mistakes here. First, there is no one under the canopy.[4] Second, the use of the canopy in secular celebrations was restricted to the entries of the king and was an honor that Duke Philip never enjoyed. Third, it was always carried by the highest municipal dignitaries, but the notes to *La Fête historique* indicate that this canopy was carried by mere pages.

The most notable distinction between the medieval entries and this historic re-creation is that in the fifteenth century, stages were prepared along the side of the parade route where *tableaux vivants* and mime plays were performed for the entertainment of the duke or duchess. This gave rise to the peculiar situation of diffusing the focal point of the event: not only were the spectators admiring the pomp of nobility, but the attention of the nobility, and presumably of the public as well, was drawn towards the different stages. These stages often allowed for the interaction of the Duke with the city, a process which reinforced the political social values that the bringing together of the city and its lord overtly signified.

In the 1840 parade, there was an attempt to preserve the theatrical element of these stages on the floats, as we see with the staging of Jason's conquest of the Golden Fleece (Figure 5). The interactive socio-political dynamics, however, were more difficult to transfer onto a float. For example, the dialogue, or exchange between the duchess and the city is missing from her float (Figure 7). This float was based on the historical account of the entry of Queen Isabella of Bavaria into Paris. Speaking of the queen and her company, the Chronicles of Froissart relate the following:

> Et puis [ils] passèrent oultre et vindrent à la seconde porte de Saint-Denis, et là avoit ung chastel ordonné . . . et ung ciel nué et tout estellé très-richement, et . . . dedens ce ciel jeunes enfans de coer, lesquels chantoient moult doulcement en fourme d'angèles, laquelle chose on veoit et ouoit moult voulentiers. Et ad ce que la royne passa, dedens sa littière, dessoubs la porte, le paradis s'ouvry, et deux angèles yssirent hors en eulx avalant et tenoient en leurs mains une très-riche couronne d'or garnie de pierres précieuses, et la mirent et assirent les deux angèles moult doulcement sur le chief de la royne en chantant.[5]

We can see from the illustration how the details of this interactive event between the city's angels and the celebrated queen have been transposed into an attractive display. The float, however, lacks the social intercourse of the original event.

At this point, there is no reason to continue to question and to refute the authenticity of this nineteenth-century celebration. It seems clear that this parade performed a distinctly different function from its medieval predecessor. Unlike the entries of the Duke, La Fête did not accomplish any socio-political, or "ritual" function needed to preserve the social order. It was, rather, a celebration of history with philanthropical designs.

The selection of historical sources given in the parade notes could not possibly have lead to a successful re-creation of a medieval event. They include only one brief reference to a fifteenth-century entry into Douai. The other references are for entries into Arras or Paris, or in the fourteenth century. Other sources are not even from ceremonial entries. For example, the Duke's float (Figure 8) was designed on the basis of images from wax seals, a painting of the council of Mechelen and, as one note informs us, "le reste est dû à l'heureuse imagination de M. Wallet"—one of the local professors of architecture.

This is not the result of any lack of local documentation. There were five important entries into Douai in the fifteenth century. Each of these included impressive stage presentations and municipal decorations.[6] It may be argued that in 1840, the archival descriptions of these events had not yet been discovered. Still, two of these events are cited in the *Note sur Philippe-le-Bon*, yet very little of this "*Fête*" is based on either of these. Instead, the choice of documentation reflects a kind of selective authenticity.

In spite of this, we need not conclude that the parade was unsuccessful, unprofessional, or lacking in sophistication. Its creators concluded that it was among those activities which demonstrate "*le bon goût, l'élégance et la fidélité des traditions historiques*" (*Notice* 11). There is no need to deride this claim of fidelity to historic traditions. If the parade was not part of an effort to restore social order, as the medieval entry was, neither was it a point-by-point historically accurate re-creation of a particular event. The parade was created as a reminder of local history, and, in fact, successfully identified in the series of tableaux the fundamental components of the medieval entry: the glorified city (tableau 1), the extraordinary gifts (tableau 2), praise of the Duke and his accomplishments (represented in tableau 3 by the celebration of the Order of the Golden Fleece) and, finally, (in the fourth and fifth tableaux) the splendor of nobility. *La Fête historique* was not a historical re-creation, but was the creation from history of a modern celebration of local heritage.

NOTES

1. H. Pilate-Prévost, *Notice sur Philippe-le-Bon* . . . (Douai, 1840).

2. It is of some interest that all of these parades took place during the reign of King Louis-Philippe. Was the choice of historical subjects for the parades (and in this case, monarchical) inspired by an effort to nurture the stability of the current regime, or was it simply an innocent return to the local historical heritage?

3. There is evidence that the first page of the illustrations is missing, suggesting that there were in fact one or two more groups. One presumes that the

dozens of participants involved in this production were local volunteers. There is, unfortunately, no surviving record of the direction or organization of this anonymous crowd of performers.

4. The same thing happens with the *Litière de la Souveraine* (Figure 6). The duchess was usually conveyed about the city in one of these, but as we see here, it is being carried around empty!

5. Froissart, *Oeuvres*, ed. Kervyn de Lettenhove (1867-77; Osnabrück: Bibio Verlag, 1967), Tome 14:9-10.

6. Interestingly enough, there is no documented account of Isabelle of Portugal ever celebrating an entry into Douai.

Modern Approaches and the "Real" Middle Ages: Bertrand Tavernier's *La Passion Béatrice*

Laurence de Looze

The greatest witness to the events of the fourteenth century is undoubtedly Jean Froissart, whose massive *Chronicles* have often been seen rightly or wrongly as one of the first pieces of vernacular historical scholarship. Detailing the happenings of the Hundred Years' War (which began about 1336, hence within about a year or so of Froissart's birth), the *Chronicles* provide a tapestry of the political events of the period.

Remarkable events there certainly were. It is perhaps this last of medieval centuries—the fourteenth—that Umberto Eco was thinking of when he remarked hyperbolically that "All the questions debated during the sessions of the Common Market originate from the situation of medieval Europe."[1] The century saw the first appearances of national armies and nation states, of merchant cities and competitive capitalist economies (banks, checks, prime rates), of a unionized work force (the guilds), and of new machines (for example, the mechanical clock which parceled time out mathematically). In the fourteenth century the vernacular European languages became set in roughly the forms they still have today. The century also witnessed pogroms against the Jews. The plague passed through Europe several times (the worst being the epidemic of 1347-1349). And while the Hundred Years' War might not have been a "World War," it was certainly international in character, dragging in most of the Western European kingdoms in one way or another.

It is therefore no overstatement to say that the fourteenth century was a difficult period for Western Europe, and for France in particular. In the long string of conflicts that would finally culminate in the battle of Agincourt, French knights were repeatedly brought down by English longbows, perhaps most disastrously at the Battle of Crécy in 1346 and at the Battle of Poitiers in 1356 when the King of France (as well as a host of his noblemen) was taken prisoner and carted off to England to await ransom. In the interim the economy of France was ruined, cultivated lands reverted to wilderness, and bands of *écorcheurs* or bandits, many of them warriors for either the French or English who were regularly put into unemployment by truces, ravaged major parts of France.

Given these many calamities, it has often seemed surprising to students of the period that many of the great fourteenth-century writers, though they occasionally acknowledge the major upheavals, neither discuss them very much nor seem terribly concerned about them. For example, the greatest French poet of the century, Guillaume de Machaut, mentions the plague of 1349 almost in passing in his *Jugement dou roy de Navarre* before he gets to his real subject, which is whether or not he insulted the female sex when he claimed in an earlier work that a knight whose lady has gone off with another man suffers more than a lady whose lover has died. Somewhat similarly, Geoffrey Chaucer refers only briefly to the Peasant Uprising of 1381 and not at all to other important events. To be fair, however, we should keep in mind that in our own day many bestsellers come and go with hardly a peep about AIDS or the threat of annihilation from nuclear weapons or the fact that fifty to sixty million lives were lost during World War II alone. Certainly we should not require medieval writers to have had more of a social conscience than we do. Still, seeing the fourteenth century from our standpoint as a period of extraordinary upheaval, it is mildly surprising to our sensibilities for a writer to have declared, as Froissart did in his *Chronicles*, that his work would be devoted in the main simply to showing magnificent deeds (*grans merveilles*) and feats of arms (*faits d'armes*) carried out by glorious knights.[2]

Now the fourteenth century has been a topic of choice for modern filmmakers to "re-view," surpassed in popularity only by the many films about Joan of Arc or King Arthur and his knights. In part this popularity has been due to the rich literature from the period, as in the cases of Pier Paolo Pasolini's films of *The Canterbury Tales* (1972) and

The Decameron (1971). But because it seems to provide a distant mirror for our own modern world, to use Barbara Tuchman's famous phrase, the fourteenth century has also been the setting for several cinematic representations which are not based on medieval literary works *per se*. Ingmar Bergman's *The Virgin Spring* (1960) and *The Seventh Seal* (1956) powerfully blend historical recreation with Bergman's personal mythology. The recent box office success *The Name of the Rose* (1986) from Umberto Eco's novel of the same name combines the medieval quotidian with the modern detective story. And the French production of a few years ago *Le Moine et la sorcière* (1988) attempts to recreate the daily life of peasants.

In one of the most powerful recent films about the fourteenth century, *La Passion Béatrice* (Clea Productions, 1987), Bertrand Tavernier, filming a scenario written by his ex-wife Coco Tavernier O'Hagan, has also taken up the fourteenth century's day-to-day existence—this time that of the petty French nobility—and mixed it self-declaredly with modern psychological approaches (Freudian and Jungian above all).[3] In so doing Tavernier has also filmed what might be seen as the repressed counter-story to Froissart's *Chronicles* and to much of the literary froth of the period; for Tavernier's fourteenth century is a world from which *grans merveilles* and *faits d'armes* are entirely absent. In fact, the titular protagonist's father, François de Cortemart, when asked to recount his exploits against the English on the field of battle, responds tellingly that there were none: "Faits d'armes?" he continues scornfully, "Formidables bêtises!"

If I have insisted on the historical developments of the fourteenth century, it is because what takes place in Tavernier's film becomes more intelligible when seen in the shadow of the political and literary history of France in the period. In the negation of precisely what Froissart so loved—those feats of arms—Tavernier clearly sets himself up as a counter-Froissart, determined to tell not of the courtly behavior of the fourteenth century but, as it turns out, of the monstrous.

Since Tavernier chooses to delve into the *un*courtly, the *anti*social, and the *ir*rational, the tools of modern psychoanalysis are equally useful for understanding this film. Tavernier states at the beginning of the film that though the film is even more one of emotion than of psychology, the characters are nevertheless "guided only by their interior drives" ("n'y sont guidés que par leurs pulsions intérieures") and that "they are what we still are at night and in our dreams. They are our unconscious" ("Ils sont ce que nous sommes encore la nuit, dans

nos songes. Ils sont notre inconscience"). Taking my cue from
Tavernier, then, I intend to use Freudian, Jungian, and neo-Freudian
(Lacanian) psychoanalytic approaches to elucidate this film. In
particular I will concentrate on the distribution and construction of
sexual roles. Basing my observations on the Freudian/Lacanian
observation that sexuality is not innate but acquired, I shall consider
the ways in which social power is marked as masculine and masculinity
is defined as symbolic possession of the phallus.[4] Béatrice, I shall argue,
must become a "man" during the course of the film in order finally to
defeat her deranged father. Then, in the second part of this essay, I
shall move to a consideration of what it "means" to film a distant age
from such a consciously and even self-consciously modern stance. Does
the structuring of a historical film on historiographical and
psychoanalytic models that stress what has been repressed by the
culture or by the psyche move us closer to or make us more distant
from an understanding of what the Middle Ages were?

La Passion Béatrice begins with François de Cortemart killing his
mother's adulterous lover with his father's dagger when he discovers
the couple in bed immediately after his father has left for war. The
boy then spends three months atop the manor's tower, coming down
only when the priest announces that his father is dead and François is
now the new lord. François holds the dagger to the sky and
announces, "Mon Seigneur Dieu, je vous hais" ("My Lord God, I hate
you").

Next, a voice-over narrator that turns out to be François' future
daughter describes how weak, small, and wounded her father must have
felt as a boy, all alone on the tower. Many years have passed. We see
Béatrice, François's daughter, an adolescent now, yearning for her
father who left for battle at least four years prior with her brother
Arnaud. The two were taken prisoner by the English and have been
held for ransom ever since. In her effort to raise the necessary ransom
money, Béatrice sells off much of the family land to a wealthy young
merchant named Bertrand Lemartin.

Béatrice's father and brother return during a full moon more than
half a year later. On the return journey François comes across a
peasant woman who has just given birth to a baby in the snow; he
claims the woman as his possession ("c'est ma propriété"), abandoning
the baby girl without burial because "girls have no souls." Once
reinstalled in his manor, François humiliates his son for being a

coward, comes close to blasphemy in the priest's presence, and reproaches his daughter for having sold the lands too cheaply and for having ransomed her brother at all. He and his band of *écorcheurs* terrorize the surrounding countryside, pillaging and then splitting up the booty and women they take. When the son kills a bird with an English longbow, François orders that it be thrown to the pigs as food ("Animals have no souls," it is pointed out, "and anything without a soul is edible").

The daughter who so adored her father in his absence finds herself beginning to hate him. Meanwhile, François suffers from an "impure love" for his daughter, and one night after crossing himself backwards he rapes her in the women's sleeping chamber.

Béatrice makes an attempt to have her father killed through witchcraft, but the only result is that the sorceress she consults is captured and burned at the stake. Increasingly mad and blasphemous, François conceives a project to marry his own daughter and orders the local priest to perform the ceremony. Then he decides to wed Béatrice to the merchant Lemartin instead. Lemartin at first addresses her in the terms of courtly love, but when François informs him that his daughter is not a virgin, Lemartin withdraws his marriage offer. Finally François organizes a hunt in which his band chases his son as its prey. For the hunt he dresses his son in a dress and Béatrice in his son's clothing. This echoes a comment he made to Béatrice shortly after returning from captivity: "C'est toi qui aurais dû être le fils" ("You're the one who should have been the son"). After the hunt Béatrice returns to the castle. Finding François in bed, Béatrice stabs her father with the same dagger he used to kill his mother's lover many years before.

Béatrice's father, François de Cortemart, is the prime mover for most of the film and his role in the film is crucial. Initially defined by the murder of his mother's lover, François suffers thereafter from a loss of maternal love and a lasting identification with the masculine ethic of the medieval *miles*. François's terms for girls and women are inevitably "garces" or "putains," including both his mother and Béatrice herself. Béatrice is a whore, he says, because she has been possessed by him. In one scene he challenges his son to become a man by possessing sexually a girl named Nicolette he has taken in a raid. Women are property, analogous to land. I have already mentioned that François claims as his property a woman who has just given birth. More strikingly, he proposes to Lemartin that he will resew his own daughter's maidenhead repeatedly so that Lemartin can keep purchasing her "virginity" until every acre of the familial lands has been bought back. In the most gruesome fashion, François's actions restate two common medieval notions: first is the analogy, articulated in such medieval literary works as *The Romance of the Rose*, that associates the plow sowing in the field with the penis that "sows" its seeds in the vagina;[5] and second is a view of woman as an economic signifier in a series of relations between men.[6] In François's proposal to sell and resell his daughter sexually, Béatrice is made the "field" and part of the family land to be possessed by a lord.

But the feminine is both the engenderer of life and the life engendered, is both a field to be cultivated and the potential fruit of the field, is—in François's life, at least—both the lost mother (engenderer) and the daughter (engendered) he cannot have. Since Béatrice has "wrongfully" sold off the family property, according to François, he tries to "recover" his debt in blasphemous fashion by exploiting her as (sexual) property. But in his deliberate frustration of Lemartin's marriage proposal, François passes from the "rational" sexual economic system of the Middle Ages, which consciously exchanged women for land through marriage, to a mad economy in which the feminine is at one and the same time the land that produces, the product to be consumed, and the object to be bought back. The metaphor for this circle that bites its own tail is incest. That the feminine is a product to be consumed as much as a land to be plowed is the syllogistic conclusion to be derived from two separate premises carefully articulated in the film:

A) Everything that has no soul is edible.
B) Girls (like birds) have no soul.

C) Therefore girls are edible.

It is this view of the feminine as the hunted, the to-be-consumed, that justifies in artistic terms, if not in terms of fidelity to history, the cross-dressing of the final hunt. The dual role of woman as representing both ends of the fertility cycle is similarly evoked when François lays Nicolette across an eating table in the scene in which he exhorts his son to prove his manhood: symbolically woman is again both the land in which one sows as well as "edible" product/produce. Like many a madman François takes to horrific lengths a logic that is implicit already in the culture. In this instance it is the cultural view of woman as coinage whose value is controlled (i. e., owned) by men.

Furthermore, this monstrous attempt to join the two ends of the life cycle, thereby smashing chronology,[7] represents an attempt on François's part to return to the mother via the daughter. François, as I have suggested, becomes a "man" when he stabs his mother's lover with a dagger. In so doing, however, he also cuts himself off from all maternal love and thereafter seeks (symbolic) reunion with the feminine element. If the rape of Béatrice is the most shocking incidence of this desire, this urge also characterizes what I might call the "elemental" metaphors in the film. For François's yearning for union with the lost feminine is also evident in his reiterated desire to be buried at sea when he dies. Carl Gustav Jung has called attention to the fact that the sea represents both the unconscious and the feminine in the Western psyche. Moreover, for the medieval world water was specifically designated along with the earth as a feminine element. If we bear in mind that in French *la mer* ("the sea") and *la mère* ("the mother") are virtual homonyms, especially in the spoken language, then François's repeated desire to die and be laid to rest "à la mer" is an unmistakable allusion to his desire to return to the lost mother and to the feminine.[8]

What is most monstrous about all this is that François forces Béatrice to live literally an incestuous love for the parent that François only experienced symbolically when he killed his mother's lover in bed. The morning after the rape, Béatrice bars the door to her bedroom and will admit no one. The room replaces the body in Béatrice's attempt to close herself off from her father after not having been able to resist his literal transgression of her body. When François forces open the door and pushes his way into the room, yelling all the while "Ouvre-moi!" ("Open up for me!"), he is restaging not only his intrusion into his mother's adulterous bedchamber but the rape of the night before.

As for the other principal character, Béatrice, she echoes in name the more famous Beatrice celebrated by Dante Alighieri as his beloved in both the *Vita Nuova* and the *Divine Comedy*. Dante's Beatrice was made the object—or rather the mediatrix—of an increasingly spiritual love in *The Divine Comedy*, and the close association of the name with spiritual love has continued to this day. Here again, however, Tavernier is telling his story "against" the dominant models of the fourteenth century; he is, in the Greek sense of άντί, *anti*-Dante just as he was *anti*-Froissart. To give the same name to the protagonist of Tavernier's film is to invite the spectator to contrast the Dantean love—one that moves from physical to spiritual fertility—with a love that gradually degenerates into incest and deliberate blasphemy. If Dante's Beatrice "suffered" to refine Dante's love and make it productive spiritually, Tavernier's Béatrice is forced to suffer an entirely carnal and degrading love. Tavernier's film is therefore a counter-text not only to chivalric chronicle literature *à la* Froissart but also to that of both Christian and courtly love—a kind of *dolce stil nuovo alla rovescia*, if you will.[9]

Now if sexual identity is indeed predicated on the symbolic possession of the phallus, as Lacan has argued, and not on anatomy, the stage is set in Tavernier's film for a certain plasticity regarding gender. I have already alluded to a switch in gender roles in the final "hunt." The son Arnaud, seen as effeminate, is made the hunted feminine object. Béatrice by contrast is cast as masculine. Indeed, the symbolic masculinity of Béatrice resurfaces a number of times during the film. While François has been in captivity, Béatrice has taken on the man's role of running the manor.[10] François' mother complains several times that Béatrice cavorts around the countryside like a boy rather than staying home and sewing like a girl.[11] And François laments that Béatrice should have been the son in the family.

I wish to go further, however, and argue that in Lacanian terms Béatrice *does indeed* become the son. If she has had to "become" her mother *vis-à-vis* her father by sharing his bed, her only way out is also to "become" François and avenge a parent's wrongful love. This is what follows on the cross-dressing in the hunt scene. Just as her father did after the opening scene of the film, she returns—dressed now in masculine clothing—to the manor where she will take vengeance. She uses the same dagger her father used. She even repeats virtually the same line François uttered as a boy: "Seigneur Dieu, je vous hais" ("Lord God, I hate you"). She then stabs her father in his bed, assumably the same bed in which François stabbed his mother's illicit lover. Béatrice therefore becomes the avenging son. Like the fourteenth-century writer Christine de Pizan who declared that in order to succeed as a professional writer she had to become a man, Béatrice becomes masculine at the level of the signifier.[12] As if to underscore this link between Béatrice and the full assumption of the masculine when she stabs her father with the dagger, the "t" of "Béatrice" in the title as it appears at the beginning of the film has been turned into a representation of the dagger, the phallic signifier and instrument of power and revenge.

What are the implications of this assumption (in both senses of the term) of masculinity? On the one hand we might see this gender crossing as a response to the few options open to girls in medieval society as it is depicted in Tavernier's film. After all, in the film the inventory of the women includes wife, recluse, sorceress, and Béatrice herself. Of these, the wife/mother is shut inside sewing; the recluse is slowly shut into her hut where she will have to remain until she dies ("even if it makes her go mad," one young girl explains); the sorceress is burned at the stake; and Béatrice, until she takes on the role of avenger that should have fallen to the son Arnaud, is forced into an incestuous relationship. Furthermore, we might wish to ask whether this gender switch purges the evil that is in François' nature. Does it break the cycle of a cursed family—or merely continue it?

Though this last question is probably unanswerable, it is clear that Tavernier's film contains many elements that betray modern as much as or more than medieval concerns. Most reaction to the film has dealt in an impressionistic way with this strange mix. Certainly there has been no clear consensus on whether *La Passion Béatrice* is a good film, nor even on whether it is valid in its depiction of the Middle Ages. Some critics have complained about its anachronistic elements, among them Antoine de Baecque and David Denby. At the other end of the spectrum is Patrick Schupp's claim that the film represents "un quotidien qui est certainement très proche de la vérité" (50). In a sense both views are correct, for Tavernier has deliberately combined naturalistic elements with elements that cannot be historically or logically "real." He has described the equilibrium he sought to achieve as follows:

> Faire un film historique, c'est une manière de comprendre la réalité. Michelet a écrit une phrase sublime: 'Pour traiter l'Histoire, il faut désapprendre le respect'. . . Le but, c'est de faire douter le spectateur d'une version officielle de l'Histoire. C'est la meilleure façon de le faire douter de la réalité contemporaine. (quoted in Douin, 88)

Tavernier apparently believes that this skeptical and even self-doubting approach permits him to combine naturalistic reconstruction with a story so extreme as to be nearly incredible. How, then, should we evaluate his combination of minute quotidian *realia* regarding dress, eating, and hygiene, manners, and what we would now call "lifestyles" with a self-consciously anachronistic methodology derived from the *Annales* school of historiography and (neo) Freudian psychoanalytical currents? In a sense everything depends on what we label as the "real" Middle Ages. Is it possible, for example, to film the alterity of the Middle Ages without, in fact, compromising that alterity?

A first problem is that we have no way to judge how close a film comes to conveying the reality of medieval experience, since our notions of what is "realistic" are defined above all by conventions of realism formulated in the nineteenth century. It has become a commonplace of film theory to argue that the intrusive camera "violates" its object, then tries to cover this violation by erasing the signs of its presence. In the case of a distant historical period, this trespass is even greater since the camera necessarily imposes a uniquely modern sensibility. Furthermore, this modern view has been reinforced by the development of a cinematic grammar based largely on nineteenth-century narrative models, regardless of the period being depicted.[13] Most film editing, like most film theory, implicitly assumes that a very different world can be (re)created using fundamental tenets of mimesis and narratology to which a modern audience subscribes.

Medieval aesthetics, however, were radically different from our own. In art, for example, a "hierarchy of size" rather than linear perspective dominated for most of the medieval period, so that a figure's size in proportion to the whole of a scene was an indication not of distance from the viewer but of relative importance. The very real possibility exists, therefore, that precisely when a film about the Middle Ages looks most "real" to us, it has in fact most distorted the Middle Ages in the direction of our artistic and literary conventions. Moreover, in medieval times narratives were also often formally non-linear, doubling back on themselves (as in the case of epic *laisses parallèles* and *similaires*) or mysteriously jumping around (as in some romances). "Repeating scenes" of this type have characterized some modern fiction (Robbe-Grillet's *nouveaux romans*, for instance) and some films (in particular those of Alain Resnais), but they are not a common feature of the current narrative lexicon.[14]

Every film about the Middle Ages must therefore inevitably negotiate some accord with the alterity of the medieval world. Even minimizing or treating it as non-existent is a way of coming to terms with it. Hollywood productions, in particular, which commodify the Middle Ages for a mass audience, have generally reduced the alterity of the medieval world to exotic (and vaguely medieval) dress and decor. As for other aspects of Hollywood treatments, modern ideologies and manners effectively supplant anything smacking of an "other" mentality.

Nevertheless, outside California there have been several attempts to recreate for the camera the extraordinary (and disconcerting) alterity of the medieval world. One thinks immediately of treatments of the Arthurian material by Robert Bresson and Eric Rohmer. Bresson attempts to recreate the fragments of perception which would have characterized the experience of knights themselves. In so doing he captures something of the mystery of the medieval view of the world, while also making the lack of diegetic integrity a fitting metaphor for the disintegrating Arthurian realm. If Bresson tries to see the medieval world as medieval people saw their daily lives, Rohmer, by contrast, tries to see the Arthurian text as medieval artists depicted things. Reproducing Chrétien de Troyes's *Perceval* almost word for word (in modern French translation), Rohmer "sees" (i. e., "films") it according to the iconography of medieval manuscript illuminators, using for instance the medieval hierarchy of size I have mentioned.

The problem, of course, in the cases of both Bresson and Rohmer is that the very elements that would have been self-evidently part of the world-construct for a medieval person appear strangest to modern sensibilities. The paradox is therefore that the more genuinely medieval the cinematic recreation is in that it attempts to portray either how the medieval world looked to medieval people or how it was depicted as looking by their artists, the more a modern person is barred from experiencing it as a medieval person would have—that is, as at all "normal." Furthermore, the very notion of filming in a manner such that the result would be intelligibly "medieval" to a medieval person is paradoxical in itself, since only a twentieth-century person could possibly conceive of capturing any "world" on a strip of film. Everything about the celluloid experience is so violently unmedieval in every way that the Middle Ages is "always already" transformed by the very act of filmmaking. The more intelligible the film is to a modern person, the more it has compromised any genuine medieval mentality; and the more "medieval" it is, the more it must betray the accepted grammar of cinematography. Those films that have tampered with the logic of cinematic discursivity—Andrei Tarkovsky's *Andrei Roublev*

(1966) for example, or Carl Theodor Dreyer's *La Passion de Jeanne d'Arc* (1928)—have been considered confusing and hard to follow by the general public, even despite their extraordinary beauty as pure image.

Obviously no filmmaker can resolve all these paradoxes in a single film. Tavernier opts for a third approach: modern in terms of approach and overall structures (*Annales* school, psychoanalytical theory, linear narrative), yet medieval in terms of quotidian details. Tavernier's approach visually in this film is one of an almost ruthless naturalism which presents an unromanticized view of the fourteenth century. As a result the scenes are replete with many accurate and petty details of daily life (food preparation, eating habits, bathing methods, delousing, entertainment, etc.).[15] In the manor itself—and at some of the most disturbing moments, as for instance when a nude Béatrice barricades her door the morning after the rape—recourse is made to a hand-held camera, increasing the viewer's sense of immediacy.[16]

At the same time, the methodology, like the technology of filmmaking, is resolutely modern. In self-consciously acknowledging his Freudian and historiographical models, Tavernier signals the intrusion of his most unmedieval interests in the aspects that, culturally and psychologically, have been repressed. Fourteenth-century authors by and large did not take up for their own sake the problems of women, children, petty lords, or incest as Tavernier does.[17] Moreover, when the *Annales* school or Freudian critics dig up these elements as repressed aspects to which the extant shards of medieval culture unknowingly bear witness, they are uncovering a latent content in genuine medieval artefacts. Tavernier consciously decides to make these elements—quite anachronistically—his manifest content. In uttering overtly what medieval culture didn't want to speak, Tavernier's film becomes paradoxically modern and medieval. The more his film tells a story that is modern rather than medieval in its overt interests, the more deeply, paradoxically enough, he can dig into certain niches of medieval culture.

This tradeoff of modern and medieval in *La Passion Béatrice* characterizes not only the visual but the aural field as well. In fact, the film's soundtrack provides an excellent opportunity to see this delicate balancing act at work. In resolving the question of what music should accompany the Middle Ages, Tavernier was faced with the inherent problem that genuinely medieval music sounds highly foreign to our ears now, with the result that we cannot "hear" it as they did—hear it, that is, as "natural" and self-evident. By contrast, the music which sounds most normal to our ears is all from more recent periods and therefore has little in common with medieval harmonies and habits.

For *Béatrice* Tavernier hired the jazz bassist Ron Carter to produce a soundtrack. Jazz, as part of our everyday world and yet, in its more experimental forms, a challenge to our ears, is both modern and yet "other" *vis-à-vis* dominant cultural models. Now Tavernier's love of jazz is well known, and his *Round Midnight* (1986) stands as a tribute to jazz music. Carter's music, to which are added one air by the greatest composer of the fourteenth century Guillaume de Machaut[18] and a "Pié Jesu" by Lily Boulanger, strikes a workable balance between modern idioms and fidelity to medieval forms. In *La Passion Béatrice* one is hard pressed at many moments of the film to say whether the musical sounds seem primarily fourteenth-century or twentieth-century. There are many medieval and medievalesque melodies in the soundtrack, but there are also moments of dribbling bass notes or harmonic runs up the strings that could have come straight from one of Ron Carter's improvised solos in a live concert. The rhetorical effect of this musical blend is one of "real life" at a mid-fourteenth century manor in the Pyrenees, while acknowledgment is made at the same time to the fact that one inevitably sees and hears with modern eyes and ears.

Any attempt to decide in a yes or no fashion whether *La Passion Béatrice* actually shows us what fourteenth-century life was like is doomed to failure. That we feel it as realistic during the two hours that the film runs is no certain guide. We might do well to keep in mind that Froissart too in his *Chronicles* seems to relate events as they really took place. He inflates somewhat, it is true, though historians to this day must rely on him for much basic information. Certainly he does not seem to discover such stories as Tavernier's taking place in the manors he visits. Yet as a caveat it is worth mentioning the extent to which his ideology of *grans merveilles* and *faits d'armes* in fact determines what he comes out with. In a recent book George Diller has studied Froissart's account of Edward III's love for the Countess of Salisbury—a tale full of courtly love and noble sentiment (in the Amiens manuscript version, at least) and which includes a chess game between the two in order to determine whether the countess will accept the king's ring.[19] Froissart's source, Jean le Bel's *Chronicle*, tells a very different story, claiming that Edward sent the Count of Salisbury to do battle in Brittany, then appeared at the countess's castle and brutally raped her. According to Jean le Bel the countess was too traumatized from the events ever to sleep with her husband again. Froissart's tale of course makes Edward III over according to the mold of a courtly lover from literary sources. Jean le Bel's account, by contrast, designed in fact to spread propaganda harmful to the Plantagenets, is equally "literary" in its tale of the king who covets and possesses the wife of one of his top counselors.

In the final analysis, then, one cannot really label either Froissart's or Tavernier's visions of the fourteenth century as decidedly "true" or "false." What one can say is that Tavernier shows himself as much a student of Foucault as of Freud, a debt he has freely admitted.[20] In conclusion, then, I submit that Tavernier's film artfully combines that which is repressed by the psyche with that which has been repressed culturally through the writing of History and Literature of the capital "h" and capital "l" kinds. The result is a conglomeration of what may have happened historically, even down to very small details, and what may have happened in the psyche, right down to our most repugnant and hidden selves.

NOTES

1. Umberto Eco, *Travels in Hyperreality*, trans. William Weaver (London: Pan Books, 1986), 65.

2. These are the terms of the Rome Reg. Lat. 869 manuscript, whose prologue begins: "Afin que les grans mervelles et li biau fait d'armes, liquel sont avenu par les geres de France et d'Engleterre . . . soient notablement registré . . . je Jehans Froissart . . . me voel ensonniier de metre en prose et ordonner selonch la vraie information que je ay eu des vaillans honmes, chevaliers et esquiers" (*Chroniques: début du premier livre*, ed. George T. Diller [Geneva: Droz, 1972], 35). Other manuscripts mention only "li grant fait d'armes" (*Oeuvres de Froissart: Chroniques*, ed. Kervyn de Lettenhove [Brussels, 1867], 2:1).

3. Reaction to Tavernier's film has been very mixed, with some reviewers declaring it his finest film, others his worst. If Patrick Schupp, writing in *Séquences* (June 1988, 50-1), found that Tavernier's film is "l'un des sommets de son oeuvre," David Denby of *New York Magazine* (28 March 1988, 97-8) found it "anguished, clotted, hard to follow, and generally a failure." Laurie Stone, in a review of several Tavernier films in *Ms.* ("Medieval Rights and Wrongs," April 1988, 30), found *Béatrice* "surpris[ing] and enthrall[ing]." But Stanley Kauffmann, in the *New Republic* ("Bloodshed Then and Now," 14 March 1988, 32-3), found *Béatrice* to be "gauche," Antoine de Baecque in *Cahiers du cinéma* (December 1987,

52) felt it was simply a patchwork of "*tous les clichés*" about the Middle Ages, and Katherine Dieckmann, writing in the *Village Voice* ("Time and Punishment," 5 April 1988, 72, 89), felt the film merely piled "scenes of ugliness and torture one on top of the other." One of the aspects which clearly disturbs many critics is the combination of historical naturalism with elements that cannot be logically or historically "real." *La Passion Béatrice* is not alone in having been attacked for failing to tell a neat, chronological tale in which cause and effect are always discernible: Andrei Tarkovsky's *Andrei Roublev* (1966), Robert Bresson's *Lancelot du lac* (1974), and Eric Rohmer's *Perceval le gallois* (1979) have all been criticized on the same grounds.

4. Jacques Lacan, "Le stade du miroir comme formateur de la fonction du Je," *Ecrits I* (Paris: Seuil, 1966), 89-97.

5. For example, Genius's exhortation to procreate: "Mar leur ait Nature doné / au faus don j'ai ci sarmoné, / greffes, tables, marteaus, anclumes, / selonc ses lais et ses coustumes, / et sos a pointes bien aguës / a l'usage de ses charrues, / et jaschieres, non pas perreuses, / mes plantëïves et herbeuses, / qui d'arer et de trefoïr / ont mestier, qui an veust joïr, / quant il n'an veulent labourer / por lui servir et honourer, / ainz veulent Nature destruire / quant ses anclumes veulent fuire, / et ses tables et ses jaschieres, / qu'el fist precieuses et chieres / por les choses continuer, / que Mort ne les peüst tuer" (*Le Roman de la rose*, ed. Félix Lecoy [Paris: Champion, 1965-73], vv. 19513-30).

6. See, for example, Georges Duby's *Medieval Marriage* for a discussion of how marriage was deeply enmeshed in economic transactions (*Medieval Marriage: Two Models from Twelfth-Century France*, trans. Elborg Forster [Baltimore: Johns Hopkins University Press, 1978]). Tavernier has acknowledged his debt to the historians Duby and Jacques Le Goff (see Jean-Luc Douin, *Tavernier* [Paris: Eidelig, 1988], 88).

7. This goes back at least to Sophocles, whose Oedipus, for example, laments in *Oedipus at Colonus* that one of the horrors of incest is that father and child, who should be hierarchical and vertical in time, are made siblings and therefore horizontal.

8. François's family name may also allude obliquely to this estrangement from the sea. His name, "Cortemart," ending in a silent *t*, is pronounced "Cortemar." Just across the Pyrenees from the department of Aude where *La Passion Béatrice* was filmed and the story evidently takes place, this compound would immediately be recognized as composed of *corte* (from *cortar*, to cut) and *mar* (sea). We should also bear in mind that the play on *mer* and *mère* characterizes one of the most famous of French films, and hence one well known to Tavernier. François Truffaut's *Les Quatres cent coups* ends with a shot of the protagonist, who has been estranged from his mother (*mère*), running suddenly into the sea (*mer*) after his escape from a reformatory. I propose that Tavernier makes an intertextual wink back at one of the greatest of French films, while at the same time integrating the loss of the mother into a medieval ideology.

9. Bertrand Lemartin's short-lived courtship of Béatrice can also be discerned as Tavernier's bitter critique of another stock-in-trade of canonical

medieval literature, *fin'amors* discourse.   One minute Lemartin is declaring to Béatrice that he wants to venerate her, to inhabit "l'espace qui délimite votre âme"—words which she repeats to herself in a kind of love-trance—and the next he has dumped her.

10. As Duby demonstrates, it was quite common for women to undertake these functions when men were absent.

11. Learning to sew was a standard part of medieval socialization for women, and exhortations to young girls to sew well occur in a number of Old French literary texts.

12. In her *Livre de trois vertus*, Christine de Pizan also advises widows (she herself was one) to "take the heart of a man" if they wish to have success. See *A Medieval Woman's Mirror of Honor: The Treasury of the City of Ladies* by Christine de Pizan, ed. Charity Cannon Willard (New York: Persea Books, 1989), 199.

13. There are some exceptions, as for example the didactic parallel cuts Eisenstein favored.   But these have come to be used very little.   French "New Wave" directors of the 1960s and 1970s also rebelled against the "narrativization" of the medium; Tavernier, however, is part of a post-New Wave generation that has rebelled in turn against Godard *et al.* by returning to narrative modes.

14. Some critics' complaints about a lack of "coherency" in *La Passion Béatrice* have also been due to nothing more than a limited understanding of the givens of the age.   Stanley Kauffmann, for example, wonders why François Cortemart attacks and burns a nearby settlement (32), for which the information given that he leads a band of *écourcheurs* was evidently conceived as sufficient explanation for the French public, more likely to be familiar with events of the fourteenth century than are Americans.

15. One should also note the determined "medievalness" of the title *La Passion Béatrice*, meaning "the passion *of* Béatrice." In Old French—and still in the fourteenth century—a noun followed immediately by a singular name, pronoun, or noun designating a person indicated possession.   No preposition, in other words, was needed.   Thus *les noces le roi* ("the king's wedding"), *li fils Gerald* ("Gerald's son," whence our "Fitzgerald"), etc.   See Guy Raynaud de Lage, *Introduction á l'ancien français*, 9th ed. (Paris: SEDES, 1975), 24-5.

16. Cf. Douin, 72. Douin stresses the way the camera work emphasizes the sense of life *en directe*.   Some reviewers (for example, Kauffmann [32]) have objected to what they see as over-use of the hand-held camera; Dieckmann, by contrast, finds the camera work "imaginatively vital" (89).

17. Medieval literature did however often evoke these issues in the course of didacticism or allegory; what they were not generally given was treatment as important social issues in their own right.

18. The use of Machaut's rondel "Ce qui soustient moy, m'onneur et ma vie" is surely bitterly ironic.   The refrain, like the whole poem, is fully within the conventions of *fin'amors* poetry: "Ce qui soustient moy, m'onneur et ma vie / Aveuc Amors, c'estes vous, douce dame" (*Guillaume de Machaut: Poésies lyriques*, ed. V. Chichmaref [Paris: Champion, 1909], 573).

19. George T. Diller, *Attitudes chevaleresques et réalités politiques chez Froissart* (Geneva: Droz, 1984).

20. Naomi Greene, in her article "'Dominer et Punir': The Historical Films of Bertrand Tavernier" (*French Review* 64 [1991]: 989-99), has provided an overview of the Foucauldian nature of Tavernier's historical films. I would stress, however, that in *La Passion Béatrice* it is important to recognize the synthesis of Foucault and Freud.

Spain's Medievalist Project in the New World

Theresa Ann Sears

Although relatively little has been written on the topic, Spain is perhaps the paradigmatic medievalist culture. From the religious (and to a certain extent, racial) propaganda that consciously shapes the figure of El Cid already in the epic, to Don Quijote's mad but methodical determination to revive the order of knight errantry in the seventeenth century, to the critics and historians of the late nineteenth and early twentieth centuries who reconstructed a sort of Ur-Spain—folkloristic and tied to the earth of medieval Spain—Spain is periodically marked by a desire to return to the glory days of the *Reconquista*, the seven hundred-year reclamation of Spanish land from the Moors that culminated in 1492. In no other historical effort do we see this more clearly than in her adventure in the New World.

It is a paradoxical project, for we might expect that seeking out the new would preclude the attempt to hark back deliberately to the old. Yet in the voices of Columbus and Cortés, in those of Philip II and Bernal Díaz del Castillo, we hear the exploration and conquest conceptualized as a conscious revival of the Reconquest and the Counter-Reformation, a desire to draw the line against the new, in (of all places) the New World. In fact, this should not surprise us, for Spain has always seen progress as something of dubious value. The idea that each succeeding century, each named period brings about an improvement in human life and culture is a rising metaphor for human history that has seldom gained much currency in Spanish thought, whether popular or academic. Instead, Spanish history is more frequently seen as a *decline*, from the glorious moment that encompasses the final triumph of the Reconquest and the first inklings of a new world to conquer. The lack of attention, as it were, that the stern satisfaction of the goal laboriously reached produces, briefly opens the door to the visiting Renaissance Humanism.[1] The result is that the greatest achievements of both the Middle Ages and the Renaissance seem to occur simultaneously in Spain, mocking the notion of historical periods calmly succeeding one another in an orderly fashion.

For this reason, the late fifteenth and early sixteenth centuries—the reign of *Los Reyes Católicos*—are often seen through, and in many cases at least partially obscured by, a halo of nostalgia for puissant and intellectually challenging times whose like has never been seen since.[2] What makes the oppression of the sixteenth century possible is precisely this idealization of medieval forms and values. The nostalgia for the reign of Ferdinand and Isabella is a nostalgia for the "Castilian virtues of an idealized middle ages," when "Spaniards had lived sober, hard-working lives, practising frugal virtues, and dedicated to religious and martial arts" (Elliot, 250-51). As Spain's decline accelerated and became more alarming in the seventeenth century, reformers looked, not for progressive change, not to move ahead, to be in fact reborn, but behind, to the past. They preached "a message of return. Return to primeval purity of manners and morals; return to just and uncorrupt government; return to the simple virtues of a rural and martial society" (Elliott, 252).

The period of the Reconquest become Spain's moral, as well as political, touchstone. It also served as "Spanish medieval preparation for empire." Spanish mariners' navigational successes constituted "a continuation of traditions and achievements of medieval Castilian sea power." Even the ferocity with which Spain undertook the Counter-Reformation in order to protect her citizens from the heresies of Protestantism and uncertain conversions models itself on the Reconquest, where Spain first put to use "the crusading spirit which so uniquely appeals to the best and worst in human nature."[3]

Perhaps the spirit of the Reconquest might have folded back upon itself and imploded were it not for the opportunity to extend its energies afforded by the conquest of the New World. Although it developed motifs wholly its own, the new conquest bore a striking resemblance to the old.[4] Institutions developed on the Reconquest frontier found a home in the New World (Kamen, 56). Even the geographical principles upon which Columbus based his dubious identification of the Caribbean Islands as the Indies are "the most classic expression of the imprecise Ptolemeic and medieval notion of geography."[5] More importantly, Columbus defended the use of inaccurate calculation of the circumference of the earth based on those concepts, in spite of the existence of other, more accurate figures and descriptions.

Geography was not the only field in which the deliberate recourse to the medieval marked the New World enterprise. Columbus, as well as historians writing while Columbus still lived and soon after his death, placed the discovery within a providential discursive framework, part of "the religious philosophy inherited from the Middle Ages" (Bataillon, 452).[6] Columbus's recourse to such a conceptual framework, however, implies revival, and not continuity. In the first place, he is clearly aware that "este presente año de 1492" ("this present year of 1492")[7] represents the end of an era. The Catholic Monarchs have "dado fin a la guerra de los moros, que reinavan en Europa, y . . . acabado la guerra en la muy grande ciudad de Granada" ("given an end to the war with the Moors, who used to reign in Europe, and . . . finished the the war in the very great city of Granada"). This being the case, Columbus feels it appropriate to revive an older quest, to win the "Great Khan" to Christianity (*Diario*, 15). The plan represents, moreover, a new version of the old, not only because the old Reconquest has clearly ended,[8] but also because Columbus intends to approach his destination in what he believes is a new way:

> ordenaron que yo no fuese por tierra al Oriente, por donde se costumbra de andar, salvo por el camino de Occidente, por donde hasta oy no sabemos por cierta fe que aya passado nadie.

> (you [i. e., the monarchs] ordered that I not go by way of the East, in the direction of which it is customary to go, but rather by the Western route, by way of which we do not know for certain that anyone has ever gone). (*Diario*, 16)

Thus, the medieval purpose of religious crusade is to be revived in a new era and a new direction, now that the peninsula has been reclaimed for Spanish Christians, cleansed not only of the hated Moors, but also of "todos los judios de todos vuestros reinos y señorios" ("all the Jews from all of your kingdoms and holdings") (*Diario* 16).[9]

Although most historians speak of Columbus's medievalist tendencies in terms of the persistence of the medieval,[10] then, Columbus's own words in the "Prologue" to the diary of his first voyage, which we have seen above, emphasize a clear awareness of an ending and a new beginning. The result, as Kadir suggests, is a peculiar "edginess" in Columbus's writing: "To dwell in/on prophecy is to dwell nomadically. Always at the junctures of discontinuity, the prophetic ethos shades out of time and place" (20). The enigmatic quality that Columbus the man and his enterprise have always possessed may grow out of just this attempt to bring forth the past into the future—history into prophecy—without the connection provided by the present. For Columbus, the present becomes only the empty space between "was" and "will be."

Columbus never learned to live comfortably in the present. When events overtake him that he cannot control, his mind shifts out of the practical present and into a past reimagined in the future. On the 26th of December, 1492, in the midst of the confusion caused by a ship lost to carelessness, internecine disputes among the crew, and increasingly resistant natives, Columbus occupies his mind with the reconquest of Jerusalem. Forced to leave some men behind due to lack of space, he dreams of returning some day to find

la mina de oro y la espeçeria, y aquello en tanta cantidad que los Reyes antes de tres años emprendiesen y adereçasen para ir a conquistar la Casa Sancta . . . < <*que toda la ganançia d'esta mi empresa se gastase en la conquista de Hiersulem* . . . > >

(the gold mine and the spices, and that in such quantity that the Monarchs before three years could undertake and prepare to go to conquer the Holy Land . . . < < that all the earnings from this my enterprise be spent on the conquest of Jerusalem . . . > >) (*Diario*, 101)

Even Ferdinand and Isabella, who "laughed and said it pleased them" ("se rieron y dixeron que les plazía"), seem to have found Columbus's vows and claims less than credible. Much more effective governors and conquerors than he, the Catholic Monarchs entirely lacked what Stephen Greenblatt calls Columbus's "craving for something that continually eluded him, for the kingdom or the paradise or the Jerusalem that he could not reach," which made him such an uneasy time traveler.[11] If and when Columbus's claims of wealth panned out, the king and queen would put it to far more practical and immediately rewarding a use than a new crusade to the Holy Land.

Although Columbus is perhaps the most mystical of the chronicler-conquerors, all of them share to a certain extent his inability to live in what a modern sensibility would call the empirical present. Greenblatt correctly explains that

> practical knowledge, the actual observations and recorded events, serve to confirm what Columbus already believes. If they do not, they are not made to serve as the bases for new, radically different hypotheses; they are for the most part simply demoted from signification. (89)

This tendency accounts in part for the displacement of medieval ideas of the marvelous from such sources as bestiaries and chivalric romances to the discovery chronicles. Unwilling or unable to accept and understand the true marvels that they encountered, Columbus and those that followed quite literally in his wake expected the medieval world of make-believe to appear in the lands that they explored. Columbus believes he is being told of islands populated only by women, of dog-snouted cannibals and one-eyed men, ideas that come not from the natives, but from Columbus's own imaginary repertoire, fed as it was on such tales as *Mandeville's Travels* (1322-1356) (Greenblatt, 157), now recognized as pure fiction. Although it becomes increasingly important to emphasize one's reliability as a chronicler as the Crown begins to receive conflicting accounts of events, the nature of those events also challenges the understanding of those who experience them. This conflict plays itself out most clearly in Bernal Díaz de Castillo's *True History of the Conquest of New Spain*.[12]

By the time that Cortés (who is Díaz del Castillo's principal subject) begins his operations in Mexico, the New World has become, from the perspective of even twenty years earlier, a very crowded place. Cortés's own narrative, *The Letters of Relation*, take shape in this atmosphere of political tug-of-war, in which Cortés defies his own commander in setting off for the interior. Castillo, who writes his "true history" many years after the events that he recounts, has decided to do so in order to provide the story with the authority of an eyewitness: "lo que yo oí y me hallé en ello peleando, como buen testigo de vista, yo lo escriberé" ("that which I heard and found for myself fighting in it, as a good eyewitness, I will write") (*Historia*, 25).

Although Castillo claims that "otra elocuencia y retórica mejor" ("another eloquence and better rhetoric") would be required to do Cortés's "heroic deeds" justice, Castillo attempts to accomplish more than simply setting the record straight. As his reference to "heroic deeds" suggests, he intends to place the story within a rhetorical context that will legitimize Cortés's actions. He argues by the very structure he chooses—that of the romance of chivalry[13]—that it is not a narrative of insubordination, destruction, plunder, and self-aggrandizement, but rather one of "muy buenos y leales vasallos servidores de Su Majestad" ("very good and loyal vassals, servants of Your Majesty"), "valerosos capitanes y fuertes" ("valiant captains and strong") (*Historia*, 26). If Europe is no longer a place where such heroism could take place, then New Spain, "Spain" and yet "not-Spain," provides a space where chivalry once again reigns.

To this end, where Cortés's own presentation focuses firmly on himself, Castillo's embraces a much more numerous cast of characters. He gives us his own circle of brave knights. He names and describes those who would bring down his hero by fair means or foul (mostly foul). Moctezuma himself becomes a kind of courtly prince, whose dealings with Cortés, even under the duress of house arrest, are carried out with honor and courtesy on both sides until the very end: the Duc d'Orléans in Aztec dress. As in romances of chivalry, women have a role to play. If we know anything of "Doña Marina," Cortés's famous mistress and translator (known and despised in Latin America as "Malinche"), it is because Castillo (unlike Cortés) makes a point to note her presence in every conversation with Moctezuma. The undoubted rapine and careless appropriation of Aztec women, even those of royal blood, by the conquerors becomes, in Castillo's rendering, a courtly *mise en scène*, in which Cortés grandly gives the ladies Spanish names and bestows their hands upon his men. King Arthur was never more courteous to his valiant knights and virginal damsels!

When Jacob Burckhardt undertook his seminal formulation of the concept of the Italian Renaissance, he warned, "It is the most serious difficulty of the history of civilization that a great intellectual process must be broken up into what seem arbitrary categories, in order to be in any way intelligible."[14] Part of Burckhardt's difficulty lies in his negative evaluation of the Middle Ages: it is perhaps easier to describe if one does so without prejudging the relative value of that described. Because Burckhardt finds himself unable to regard the medieval in anything but the harshest light, he also finds himself forced to demonize Spain, whose hegemony in Naples brought with it the decline of his beloved Renaissance. But Spain never saw either herself or her Middle Ages the way Burckhardt did. Along with her triumph, there was an air of melancholy about the end of the Reconquest: the glory had passed; what would cause it to return? The merciless repression that followed the official end of the war revealed "the profound social conflicts taking place in Spanish society" (Kamen, 59). Spain was not a culture to look ahead or outside for solutions: as Elliott comments, "Innovation was not easy to justify in a world which instinctively tended to assume that all change was for the worse" (257). In such a context, the discovery came as an astonishing blessing. It *was* possible to reanimate the crusading spirit; possible, too, to transport an idealized, revived version of ourselves to that new place, from which threatening influences would be excluded by sheer distance, and in which our own lapses would be forgotten. America, in the conquerors' chronicles, becomes "a doubly blessed utopia: a dream come true and a place to recapture a lost cosmic ideal," the greatest and most elaborate medievalist project of all.[15]

NOTES

1. J. H. Elliott (*Spain and Its World 1500-1700: Selected Essays* [New Haven: Yale University Press, 1989]), sees Spain in the period as "a reorganized and re-articulated medieval society." He also suggests that this constitutes less a continuation than a revival of the Middle Ages: when Cortés first returned to Spain in 1528, he encountered "Erasmian Spain—a country peacefully adjusting itself to a new heroic role under the leadership of men fired by ambitious ideas of universal empire." In contrast, in a visit just twelve years later, the explorer finds that "the humanist Spain of his first visit had become deeply tinged by the sombre hues of the Counter-Reformation" (28).

2. Henry Kamen writes, in *Spain 1469-1714: A Society in Conflict* (New York: Longman, 1983), "Looking back from their age of crisis, Spanish writers directed their nostalgia to the good times preceding the discovery of America and the coming of the Habsburgs. Without exception, they located Spain's 'golden age' in the reign of Ferdinand and Isabella" (255). The great Spanish historian Ramon Menéndez Pidal, while noting the inescapable ambiguities of the period, still calls it "a reign, finally, which for all Spaniards represents a happy golden age, remembered nostalgically as incomparable by one and all." See his "The Significance of the Reign of Isabella the Catholic, According to her Contemporaries," trans. Frances M. López Murillas, in *Spain in the Fifteenth*

Century: Essays and Abstracts by Historians of Spain, ed. Roger Highfield (New York: Macmillan, 1972), 402.

3. John Fraser Ramsey, *Spain: The Rise of the First World Power*, Mediterranean Europe Series 1 (University, Alabama: University of Alabama Press, 1973), 85-6, 112.

4. "The attitudes of the new expansion were so unprecedented that it is difficult to see it simply as an extension of the old Reconquest. Already, it was a new age" (Kamen, xiv).

5. Marcel Battaillon, "The Idea of the Discovery of America among the Spaniards of the Sixteenth Century," in Highfield, 438.

6. J. P. Oliveira Martins also maintains that "Columbus's reception in Spain carries us back to the 'Middle Ages'" (*A History of Iberian Civilization*, trans. Aubrey F. G. Bell [New York: Cooper Square, 1969], 224). Djelal Kadir argues (*Columbus and the Ends of the Earth: Europe's Prophetic Rhetoric as Conquering Ideology* [Berkeley: University of California Press, 1992]), "In his *Book of Prophecies* and dire epistles, Columbus articulates a number of topoi that throughout the Middle Ages, to which he so inextricably belonged, shaped millenarian expectations into conventional form" (29).

7. I quote from "Diario del primer viaje," in *Textos y documentos completos*, ed. Consuela Varela (Madrid: Alianza, 1989). All translations are my own unless otherwise indicated.

8. Columbus notes that "por fuerça de armas vide poner las vanderas reales de Vuestras Altezas en las torres de la Alfambra . . . y vide salir al rey moro a las puertas de la ciudad" ("by force of arms I saw the royal banners of Your Highnesses placed on the towers of the Alhambra . . . and I saw the Moorish king leave through the city gates") (*Diario*, 15), a ceremony that clearly marks the termination of seven hundred years of struggle.

9. Kadir sees it slightly differently: "But for Columbus' frame of mind, engendered as it was by the typological mindset of the Medieval ethos, *all* past was but a premonitary sentience that augured his providential calling" (3-4).

10. William D. Phillips, Jr., and Carla Rahn Phillips, for example, speak of the first voyage "as an extension of the militant Christianity that had launched the Crusades against Islam in the eleventh century" (*The Worlds of Christopher Columbus* [New York: Cambridge University Press, 1992], 12).

11. Stephen Greenblatt, *Marvelous Possessions: The Wonder of the New World* (Chicago: University of Chicago Press, 1991), 81.

12. References are to *Historia verdadera de la conquista de Nueva España*, ed. Carlos Pereyra (Madrid: Espasa-Calpe, 1983).

13. Many have noted this element of Díaz de Castillo's history. Greenblatt, for example, goes further than most: "In the face of the undreamed, and consequently in a crisis of representation, Bernal Díaz turns to the language of medieval romance, with its dream images, its magical castles and temples, its rhetoric of amazement. . . . The absolutely other cannot be conveyed at all, cannot perhaps be even perceived, but the romance can at least gesture toward this other, marked with the signs of fantasy, unreality, enchantment" (132).

14. Jacob Burckhardt, *The Civilization of the Renaissance in Italy*, 3rd ed. (London: Allen and Unwin, 1950), 1.

15. José Promis, *The Identity of Hispanoamerica: An Interpretation of Colonial Literature*, trans. Alita Kelley and Alec E. Kelley (Tucson: University of Arizona Press, 1991), 6. With 1992's quincentenary, books on Columbus and the entire period of conquest are being published faster than one can read them. The works cited in this article in no way encompass the complete bibliography on the topic, but since most cover much of the same ground, it is to be hoped that those cited here are representative of what is available.

Medievalism in Serbian Painting of the Nineteenth Century

Ljubica D. Popovich

While the nations of Western Europe continued their social, economic, cultural, and artistic evolution almost without interruption, developments of this nature came to a virtual halt in all countries under the Byzantine sphere of influence, Serbia included, with the Ottoman conquest. This upheaval during the late fourteenth and the first half of the fifteenth century had a devastating effect on the region, and among all the institutions, only the church survived.[1] The feudal class was eradicated and the common people became virtual slaves. Such conditions were not conducive to creative efforts, and those which occurred were directed toward religious art and a careful preservation of tradition.

During the course of the Austro-Turkish wars of the second half of the seventeenth century, the Serbian people and church sided with the Austrians. Defeat of the Austrian forces had repercussions that further altered the course of Serbian history, life, culture, and art. When the Serbs, led by the patriarch Arsenije Čarnojević, crossed the Danube and Sava rivers in 1690, a new, although difficult, era began.[2] As the mode of life changed, so did the canons of art. Originally, the Serbs fiercely guarded their tradition-bound art because of its strong ties to their religious and ethnic identity. Yet this time-worn art could not withstand the force of the fully developed Baroque style it confronted in Vojvodina and elsewhere north and west of the old Byzantine *limes*. In spite of the fear of the Baroque style, identified with Catholicism by the Orthodox Serbs, this new and powerful western style started a slow amalgamation with the traditional orthodox iconography.[3] This process signified the re-entrance of the Serbs living in the diaspora into the European cultural and artistic evolution. From the eighteenth century onward, this process can be followed in art, first in the regions across the Sava and Danube rivers, and later, beginning in the nineteenth century, in the liberated territories of Serbia proper.

Historical subjects, although painted during the Baroque period for documentary and didactic purposes,[4] became popular during the Biedermeier phase (1815-1848) of Neoclassicism, a phase known for its sentimentality which reflected the taste of the new, growing, and prosperous bourgeois society. Thus, the Biedermeier-style painters heralded the advent of thematically specific medievalism in Serbian painting. For example, the historical compositions of Katarina Ivanović (1811-1882), the first significant Serbian woman painter, represented interesting subjects inspired by medieval history.[5]

Among the Serbian people of the diaspora, as well as those within the liberated homeland, the next historical style, Romanticism, was enthusiastically accepted. Its repertory included interest in utopian, mystical, oriental, and medieval subjects. By making people aware of the importance of national tradition and their historical past, and, in the case of the Serbs, the wealth of their epic poetry, Romanticism raised national consciousness. In Vojvodina, Romanticism flourished between 1848 and 1878 and, in Serbia proper, its spirit lasted well into the twentieth century.[6]

Twentieth-century art historical research interest in Serbian art of the modern era, and under this term one includes art of the Baroque and the subsequent periods, started with the 1927 publication of V. Petrović's and M. Kašanin's study of Serbian art in Vojvodina (see note 2). In this work, the authors discussed the inception of modern art among the Serbian people of the diaspora, i. e., within the domains of the former Austro-Hungarian empire, and outside the Turkish-held territories of Serbia proper. Since that publication, many art historians have explored various *isms* in Serbian art, starting with Neoclassicism.[7] To the best of my knowledge, medievalism as a phenomenon has not received monographic attention, although some of its aspects have been explored within different contexts. For example, D. Medaković examined historicism in Serbian painting,[8] and L. Trifunović studied, from the formal and the ideological points of view, some of the old and new aspects of the twentieth century artistic movements in Serbia, which owe this type of inspiration to art of the Middle Ages.[9] My own work has approached the question of medievalism in Serbian art so far only indirectly, focusing on literary sources of inspiration and on the resulting images in painting and sculpture.[10]

Knowing historical circumstances particular to the Serbian people helps one understand why medievalism in art was strong and persistent. It should be taken into consideration that there was a sudden break with past in 1459, with the fall of Smederevo, and what followed was not a natural evolution of a society, but a mere existence of people who were split and living under the *aegis* of foreign empires. However, with the renewal of political and cultural life, medievalism started manifesting itself in various ways during the course of nineteenth and twentieth centuries. The impact of medieval inspiration is felt from architecture to the minor arts,[11] and from sculpture to painting, although its scope was much broader than just medieval themes. Nevertheless, medievalism left its memorable, but often disguised imprint on both the form and the content of painting (see Popovich, "Battle of Kosovo," 244, 239-43). Furthermore, revered medieval sites, such as Kosovo Polje (the Field of Kosovo) or monuments of architecture, and above all famous monastic churches, were a direct source of inspiration for painters from the second half of the nineteenth and throughout the twentieth century.[12]

Since it is impossible to explore, even in a most perfunctory manner, all of these manifestations of medievalism in Serbian art, the focus of this study will be on selected examples of Serbian paintings, specifically of single figures representing historical personalities created primarily during the second half of the nineteenth century. These should document the impact of medieval texts and of subseqently written histories upon these historical pseudo-portraits. Besides their subject matter, these representations contain certain formal features which can be characterized as medievalism. Above all others, the formal frontality dominates these depictions. Such a point of view can be tied directly to the formal tradition of medieval images.

In the long history of art, it is interesting to observe the dynamics between the word and the image. At times these two co-exist in harmony, at others they are either divorced from each other, or one can dominate the other. This was the case with nineteenth-century Serbian painting, when literary sources became a rich mine for popular subjects. Only certain categories of literary sources will be explored here, together with some of their visual realizations in painting. The first to be examined are medieval biographies of Serbian kings and archbishops,[13] whose lives were popularized through their cult in the Serbian church. These, together with the publication of works such as J. Rajić's *History* in 1794-1795 in Vienna,[14] provided a veritable treasury of textual and illustrative information about medieval personalities and the episodes from their lives. Thus, a close relationship between the illustrated text and the painting is established and it can be documented by examining several typical cases. For example, the representation of *Tzar* Dušan (ruled 1331-1355), done by Jakov Orfelin (died 1803)[15] to illustrate Rajić's *History*, served as a direct source of inspiration for the pseudo-historical portrait of the same ruler painted by Djura Jakšić (1832-1878) in 1857 (Kusovac, no. 323; also Jovanović, 208-61). Orfelin depicted *Tzar* Dušan in bust contained within a medallion, framed by various symbolic objects, such as standards, spears, and a trumpet (Figure 1). Dušan's head is in profile, turned to the left-hand side. The *Tzar* is crowned and shown with a prominent nose, short curly beard, and long mustache. For his painting of *Tzar* Dušan, Jakšić used the iconographic type for the face and the crown from Orfelin's illustration, but he turned the figure's profile to the beholder's right (Figure 2). The dark eyebrows, long curly black hair, and beard with moustache, as well as the strongly implied movement of the body, contribute to the illusion of a powerful ruler. This painter also added other insignia of royal power, such as a shoulder sash and ermine cape, held together with a jeweled chain over a romantically conceived medieval garment.

This facial type is perpetuated through the representation of *Tzar* Dušan by amateur painter Dimitrije N. Petrović (born c. 1840), dated in 1862 (Kusovac, no. 772). In this work, however, the artist turns the figure to the left side in a three-quarter view (Figure 3). Because of that, it resembled in part the illustration by Orfelin (Figure 1), and in certain other details, such as the position of the left arm and hand, that of Jakšić (Figure 2). However, Petrović does not have either the artistic ability nor the romantic temperament to emphasize the monumental or dramatic character of *Tzar* Dušan's historical *persona*. The slender features of the face appear sweet rather than powerful, despite the crown which implies absolute power. The body is dematerialized through the surface decoration of the jewel-encrusted pseudo-medieval costume. However, the painter adds some new symbolic details to his image, such as the Serbian coat of arms inserted in the back of the throne.

Especially popular were the pseudo-portraits of those rulers and churchmen canonized by the Serbian Orthodox church.[16] Although the tradition of portraits for some of those figures, such as Stefan Nemanja (St. Simeon, ruled 1167-1196), or St. Sava (c. 1173-1235), his son and the first archbishop of the *autokephalos* Serbian church, survived in an almost uninterrupted sequence from the Middle Ages,[17] the modern era gave such representations new forms. These Romantic and even "realistic" depictions of St. Sava and others, or the scenes from their lives, continue to be painted primarily as a part of church decoration. These representations of single figures and scenes formed an integral part of the iconographic programs of huge iconostasis, so characteristic for the churches from the eighteenth century onward.[18]

A pseudo-icon of Stefan Nemanja painted by Stevan Todorović (1832-1925) for the Serbian Orthodox Church in Idvor (Banat, Vojvodina) in 1879 is a good representative of this type of work (Figure 4) (Jovanović, 243). The image of Stefan Nemanja, who ruled Raška (Serbia) as a Grand *Župan* from about 1167 to 1196, shows an interesting iconographic dichotomy: Nemanja is depicted as a powerful middle-aged secular ruler, with a dark beard and hair, wearing a royal crown and a cloak fastened by a bejeweled fibula over his tunic. At the same time, he is identified by an inscription above his head as St. Simeon. This is his monastic name, taken upon his becoming a monk toward the end of his life, and the title "saint" was granted posthumously by the Serbian Orthodox church when he was canonized (Domentijan, 295-6). In this manner, the painter simultaneously represented a ruler and a saint, and combined an iconographic element of medievalism with his own contemporary norms in painting.

Possibly one of the most popular subjects of pseudo-historical portraits was *knez* Lazar (1371-1389), a Serbian leader who died a martyr's death in the Battle of Kosovo with the Ottoman Turks in 1389 (Bogdanović, 34-46). The stylistic and conceptual transformation of his image is very illuminating, since it can be followed through all the stylistic periods of Serbian art, from the Middle Ages to the modern era (Popovich, "Battle of Kosovo," 236-47, Figures 1, 15-23, 29-33). *Knez* Lazar's contemporary fresco image painted before 1389 survived in the donor's composition in his foundation, the *katholikon* of the monastery Ravanica (Figure 5).[19] His posthumous portrait, also in fresco, dating from 1403 is preserved in the monastery Ljubostinja, the foundation of Lazar's wife, *knjeginja* Milica (Figure 6).[20] In both instances the standing, crowned frontal figure of the *knez* wears an imperial dalmatic with loros. His hair falls to his neck, and his medium-length dark beard is divided in two distinct strands. In spite of artistic convention of that time, it seems that *knez* Lazar had characteristically prominent cheekbones. In the earlier of two representations he holds a long cross in his right hand, while the left hand supports the model of his foundation. This task he shares with his wife. Therefore, this is a true *ktitor*'s portrait. In the latter representation in Ljubostinja, *knez* Lazar is depicted in the processional family group, as the founder of the Lazarević's line. Very little descriptive material remains about the physical appearance of *knez* Lazar in medieval literature. Constantine the Philosopher, in his Life of *Despot* Stefan Lazarević, provides a short biographical sketch of *knez* Lazar. In it, he does not offer the reader any specific description of the *knez*'s appearance. Rather, like the fresco painters, Constantine emphasizes those characteristics which should be ideally typical for a leader: "This land here [Serbia] bears the fruit [Lazar] worthy of herself and of whom she was proud during many years, not only as a ruler, but also as a gentle father and courageous comrade-in-arms, who was wise and most humble in everything" (57). Such a text provides a feeling about the man's character, but not about his physical appearance. Therefore, the artists of subsequent generations were free to search for an ideal image which would be befitting this ruler.

A woodcut representation of *knez* Lazar, c. 1700, stands on the crossroads of medieval and modern, but still belongs to the former.[21] From the fact that it was a woodcut, which could produce multiple images, one can deduce that it was used by the Orthodox church to continue with the popularization of the cult of *knez* Lazar. At this time, his cult emanated from the monastery Vrdnik-Ravanica in Srem, where *knez* Lazar's body was translated from his original burial place in his foundation Ravanica, in Serbia.[22] In the woodcut, a standing *knez* Lazar is flanked by two tall, stylized religious edifices representing the buildings over the tomb of Christ in Jerusalem (Figure 7). He is bearded, but rather young-looking and still dressed in a Byzantine imperial garment, decorated with double-headed eagles. The *knez* is crowned and nimbed, the latter indicating his status as a saint. His sainthood is confirmed by the identifying inscription in Old Church Slavonic, "Holy *Knez* Lazar the Serbian," which is placed above his shoulders. In his right hand he carries the usual attribute of both a ruler and a martyr, a cross. In his left, he carries, as a symbol of his martyrdom, his own nimbed and crowned head. This iconographic type is known as *kephalophoros*, and is comparable to some of the representations of St. John Prodromos.[23] By turning barely perceptively to his left, *knez* Lazar, still looking toward the beholder, seems to offer his haloed head to the blessing hand of Christ, which emerges from a segment of light, depicted in the upper right-hand corner of the image.

The visual iconographic detail of the decapitated head has its verbal parallels in two literary sources. In the above mentioned biographical sketch, Constantine the Philosopher writes the following about the death of *knez* Lazar: "because God thus allowed, the great one [Lazar] and those who were with him, were crowned with the martyr's wreath. What happened after that? [Lazar] achieved the death of the blessed because he was decapitated . . ." (60). It is obvious that the nimbed head offered to Christ in the woodcut representation can be clearly connected with the verbal description of the decapitated head of Lazar "crowned with the martyr's wreath." The nimbus, as the luminous circle around the head, has the same iconographic meaning as "the martyr's wreath." Furthermore, the detail of the detached head can be also related to a second literary source, an epic poem entitled *The Finding of Knez Lazar's Head.*[24] In this poem, the anonymous bard tells how the "shining head" of *knez* Lazar was united with Lazar's body after a separation of forty years. Once again, the nimbed head from the woodcut and the "shining head" from the epic poem represent the same symbolic detail, depicted in one case visually, and in the other verbally. In analyzing this poem, Z. D. Zimmerman provides the following insights: the unification of *knez* Lazar's head (which is equated with the spirit of the nation) with the body (which is equated with the nation itself), symbolizes, in a metaphorical sense, the reunification and the preservation of the Serbian nation.[25] Thus, the texts from the medieval biography and the epic poem contribute to a better understanding of the iconography of *knez* Lazar's representation.

During the Baroque period a definite break occurred from the medieval art forms, but not from the medieval subject matter. As a good example, once again, a representation of *knez* Lazar can serve well to illuminate this point (Figure 8). An engraving from 1773 by Zaharija Orfelin (died 1785) (Davidov, *Fruškogorski*, 80, and Figure 274, with the older bibliography) depicts *knez* Lazar and his setting visually closer to a formal portrait of Louis XIV by Hyacinthe Rigaud (1659-1743), represented in all of its baroque splendor,[26] than to Lazar's images in medieval frescoes or on the postmedieval woodcut (Figures 5-7). In the Z. Orfelin engraving, the face of *knez* Lazar, although generalized, still resembles that from the frescoes. Unlike the French king, the Serbian prince does not wear a wig. *Knez* Lazar's standing pose, with his left hand on his hip and his right holding a scepter which rests on a elaborately carved table, almost duplicates that of Louis XIV from Rigaud's portrait. Although only a *knez*, Lazar is provided with all the imperial insignia which are laid on the table: the crown, the orb, and the sword. His long brocade garment, sash, and cloak, together with the backdrop of an elaborately folded curtain, a column with spiral fluting, illusionistically rendered depth of an interior setting, and the rich frame denote the artist's time, rather than harking back to the medieval era. What is introduced of medievalism here is primarily in the subject matter and not in the style. Within the overwhelming pre-eminence of the baroque features, there are two small details in this engraving which can be categorized as medievalisms: a clearly delineated nimbus, which encircles the head, and an inscription written within the halo, stating in Old Church Slavonic "Holy Lazar, the Grand Prince of Serbia."

Knez Lazar continued to be a popular subject during the Romantic as well as the subsequent periods (see Popovich, "Battle of Kosovo"). Undisputedly the greatest Serbian painter of the Romantic style, Dj. Jakšić, created an intense, almost usettling representation of *knez* Lazar between 1857-59 (Jovanović, 242 and Plate 7). The figure seems to surge forward from the dark curtained background, as if trying to break through the picture plane (Figure 9). The impression is that of an actor on a stage, reaching for his audience. The dramatic lighting touches the ermine of the cloak, making the gold and the gems on the crown and on the garment glitter. The right hand, placed against the chest and gathering the folds of the mantle, glows with the warmth of living flesh. The head, however, is the focus of this painting. Long white hair and a medium-length beard frame the face, whose left side is almost obscured by the deep shadows. The thin face is that of an ascetic, which is suggested by the sunken cheeks, slender long nose, and an unearthly pallor of the forehead. The eyes, however, mesmerize the beholder. Sunken, red-rimmed as though the figure were crying, framed by gently curving brows and deep rings underneath, the eyes glisten with the inner fire, almost emanating the inner spiritual strength of *knez* Lazar. Perhaps by focusing upon the eyes the painter brought into this image not only the subject matter, but consciously or unconsciously, a touch of medievalism as well.

The representation of *knez* Lazar, attributed to Novak Radonić (1826-1890) and painted in the late 1850s, belongs to the category of the romantic-style images created to be used as icons for the iconostasis.[27] The *knez* stands in a frontal pose, suitable for a ruler, a bishop or a saint (Figure 10). A long dark blue tunic is bound by a loros, and a red ermine-lined mantle frames the figure. A gold encolpion is suspended from his neck. The bony fingers of the right hand make a gesture resembling a blessing, and those of the left hold a scepter. The face is long and thin, infused with a gentle expression. It is framed by a rounded gray beard. An elaborate gold crown surmounts the tall forehead. The eyebrows are dark and thick, the gaze directed toward the left-hand side, seemingly without a focus. This romantic, and above all, sentimental rendering of *knez* Lazar appears at first glance devoid of any medievalism, except for its subject matter or the encolpion. However, even in this painting, the strength of tradition can be felt. For example, although not outlined, the nimbus is suggested by a luminous spot in the background and behind the head of this ruler. Furthermore, choices of colors used for the garment, such as the lapis lazuli blue, gold, and red are very similar to the chromatic schema applied in fresco depictions of *knez* Lazar's dress in his already discussed portrait from the monastery Ljubostinja (Figure 6) (Djurić, Plate 4).

The artist S. Todorović has already been mentioned in connection with his pseudo-portrait of Stefan Nemanja for the church in Idvor (Figure 4) (Jovanović, 243). For the same church, he also painted in 1879 a representation of *knez* Lazar (Figure 11). Typologically, it shows a clear dependency on the painting attributed to N. Radonić (Figure 10), and due to that fact, does not contribute anything new to the iconographic development of the images of that ruler. Yet there is a single surviving traditional element which constitutes medievalism in this work. Above the head of Lazar, there is an identifying inscription which does not designate him as the *knez*, his actual title, but as the *Tzar*. The latter was the title accorded to *knez* Lazar in epic poetry.[28]

These were some among many typical pseudo-portraits of historical personalities, popular during the nineteenth century, and in which one can find various manifestations of medievalism.[29] Equally numerous were the compositions inspired by the primary sources, such as above-mentioned medieval biographies, as well as by secondary sources, such as histories (see Rajić). The scenes illustrating specific events based on such sources were created for both religious use and private comsumption. As the tradition dictated, such images were produced as cyclical episodes. Their medievalism lies primarily in the subject matter and in very romanticized superficial details on garments, weapons, horse harness, and similar objects. The most frequently painted scenes were selected for their didactic value and dramatic effects. Popular were the scenes from the lives of the first members of the Nemanjić dynasty: Stefan Nemanja, Rastko (St. Sava, the first Serbian archbishop), Vukan, and Stefan the "First Crowned." When the chosen episodes deal with the lives of the fourteenth-century Serbian rulers, preference seems to be given to the moments of miracles or tragedy.[30]

Besides the above-mentioned phenomena of medievalism in painting, one might mention artistic anachronism, which transmits the the medieval traditions in a very primitive way. Such anachronisms manifest themselves most clearly in the iconographic solutions. For example, in the year 1848, which marks the beginning of the Romantic movement, Zoograph Anastas painted "The Funerary Mass for Stefan Dečanski" on the inside lid of this king's sarcophagus in the monastery Dečani (Vujović, 263, Figure 88). The death of king Stefan Dečanski is described in "The Life of King Stefan Dečanski" given in two versions, one written by Archbishop Danilo (156-61) and the other by Grigorije Camblak.[31] The death scene is based on the representation of the Dormition of the Virgin.[32] Also, the same type of composition is used in Serbian art of the thirteenth century to represent the death of the Serbian queen Anna Dandolo in Sopoćani (V. I. Djurić, 133).[33] Although Zoograph Anastas reverses the position of the figure on the funerary bier and augments his scene with the greater number of participants, the essential iconographic element of the dormition scene remains: the angels holding the personified psyche of the deceased within the radiance of light, in order to uplift it in heaven and into the presence of the Lord.[34] This is not the only case in which a Byzantine iconographic schema is used in Serbian painting of the nineteenth century. These traditional iconographic solutions found in religious art were readily explored for other subjects, especially by lesser artists, since such compositions were easily read and understood by the generally unsophisticated public in Serbia of that period (Popovich, "Battle of Kosovo," 240).

An interesting example of medievalism in literature and art is found in another death scene. The original source of inspiration was the medieval source "The Life of *Tzar* Uroš" by the patriarch Pajsije.[35] This in turn was a source of inspiration for the drama of the same name, written in 1826 by Stefan Stefanović. This drama about the life and death of the last Serbian *tzar* was frequently performed and it was popular at the time. Such a theatrical performance must have been the source of inspiration for the painting of the same subject by N.

Radonić, dated in 1857 (Jovanović, 164, Figure 42). Radonić's Romanticism is evident is his work through dramatic lighting, depiction of pseudo-medieval garments, compositional arrangement of the figures posed theatrically, and finally in the rendering of the landscape itself. The traces of medievalism are found in his painting in the grouping of the participants. The scene resembles the Lamentation of Christ;[36] the three women on the left (*Tzarica* Jelena and her ladies) resemble the Virgin Mary and her companions in the Lamentation, and the three male figures on the right resemble St. John the Evangelist, Nicodemus, and Joseph of Arimathaea, although their role in the drama is of a very different nature. Radonić's image probably served as a source of inspiration for another painting of the same subject. It was done by the primitivist Petar Čortanović (1800-1868), and postdates N. Radonić's work by four years (Jovanović, 250). In the later version, the position of *Tzar* Uroš's body was reversed, but the grouping of all other figures remains the same. The works of this nature document very well the interest of the artists in events from the medieval period and their popularization through words and images among the general public.

Yet there existed another source of literary inspiration which also enhanced medievalism as a phenomenon in Serbian art. That source was found in the rich heritage of oral literature, and more specifically in the epic poetry. Collected and published by Vuk Stefanović Karadžić (1787-1864) between 1814 and 1862, epic poetry became known to all, recited by heart by many. Therefore, the medieval and other subjects that it inspired in the visual arts were easily comprehended by the people, and immensely popular. Although Vuk's first publications, such as *Mala prostonarodna slavenoserbska pesnarica*[37] (1814), predate by several decades the beginnings of Romanticism in 1848, the nature of Vuk's work in general had close affinities with the interests of the Romantic movement. Consequently, Serbian painters, Romanticists above all others, visually explored the rich subjects of the epic poetry made popular by Vuk. The greatest part of these epic poems cover the medieval and Turkish-rule periods. The picturesque decasyllabic verses lend themselves very easily into visual transcriptions. Regardless of the varied artistic capabilities of Serbian painters, a close correlation between the image and the text continues, proving that the artists, like their public, must have known these epic poems by heart. The iconographic repertory of these paintings with medieval subjects far exceeds the scope of this study. It is sufficient here to signify their existence and their basic categories: pseudo-portraits of historical personalities and legendary heroes as well as the scenes representing their deeds.[38] In general, regardless of the ability of the artist, these images are always illustrative, and they document, together with all the others, the popular taste in Serbia during the nineteenth century. For the Serbs in the diaspora, paintings representing themes from the Middle Ages evoked a heroic past. In this manner they served to keep alive the ethnic heritage and the national identity. In Serbia proper, just liberated from the Ottoman rule, such paintings served as visual documentation and a reminder that during the Middle Ages the Serbs had powerful leaders, a strong and independent state, and all the institutions which marked the accomplishments of a medieval culture.[39] Through these subjects, the painters found sponsors for their works, and the popular medieval themes served to link the past with the present in the minds of those nineteenth-century religious and secular Serbs who patronized this type of painting.

NOTES

1.   George Ostrogorsky, *History of the Byzantine State* (New Brunswick: Rutgers University Press, 1957), 475-91; Dimitrije Bogdanović *et al.*, *Istorija srpskog naroda* (Beograd, 1982), 2:36-389.

2.   Veljko Petrović and Milan Kašanin, *Srpska umetnost u Vojvodini od doba despota do ujedinjenja* (Novi Sad: Matica srpska, 1927), 70-2.

3.   Dejan Medaković, *Putevi srpskog baroka. Nacionalna istorija Srba u svetlosti crkvene istorije našega doba* (Beograd: Nolit, 1972), *passim*.

4.   Pavle Vasić, *Doba baroka* (Beograd: Umetnička akademija, 1971), 10-13; Dejan Medaković, *Tragom srpskog baroka* (Novi Sad: Matica srpska, 1976), 193.

5.   Although these representations are stylistically and chronologically behind the development of Central Europe, one can still mention here "Serbian Queen Jelena" ("Doček srpkinje Jelene urgarske kraljice," 1865-9), "The Patriarch of Constantinople Condemning the Luxury of the Court" ("Patrijarh carigradski anatemiše raskoš," 1865-73), a theme from Byzantium imbued with heavy moralization, or "Betrothal of Olivera-Mara" ("Turski poklisari prose Maru," 1870-79), the daughter of *knez* Lazar, who was sent to the harem of the Ottoman sultan after her father was killed at the 'Battle of Kosovo. See Ljubica D. Popovich, "Katarina Ivanović (1811?-1882): The First Significant Serbian Woman Painter," *Serbian Studies* 1 (1980): 17-28; also Nikola Kusovac, *Srpsko slikarstvo XVIII i XIX veka*, nos. 294, 298, 300 (Beograd: Narodni Muzej, 1987).

6. Miodrag Jovanović, *Srpsko slikarstvo u doba Romantizma 1848-1878* (Novi Sad: Matica srpska, 1976), *passim*.

7. Miodrag Kolarić, *Klasicizam kod Srba 1770-1848* (Beograd: Prosveta, 1965), *passim*.

8. Dejan Medaković, "Istoricizam u srpskoj umetnosti," *Prilozi za kniževnost, jezik, istoriju i folklor* 33.3-4 (1967): 197-211; Nenad Simić, *Odnos izmedju srpske književnosti i slikarstva*, Diss. University of Belgrade (unavailable in the USA).

9. Lazar Trifunović, "Stara i nova umetnost," *Zograf* 3 (1969), 39-52.

10. Ljubica D. Popovich, "The Battle of Kosovo (1389) and Battle Themes in Serbian Art," in *Kosovo: Legacy of a Medieval Battle*, eds. W. S. Vučinić and T. A. Emmert, Minnesota Mediterranean and East European Monographs 1 (Minneapolis: University of Minnesota Press, 1991): 227-66; Ljubica D. Popovich, "Some Common Themes in Writings of Vuk Stefanović Karadžić, Serbian Epic Poetry, and the Nineteenth Century Serbian Painting," presented at the Symposium on Vuk Stefanović Karadžic, University of Illinois-Chicago Circle, 1987 (publication of these proceedings is forthcoming).

11. Dejan Medaković, *Srpska umetnost us XIX veku* (Beograd, 1981), 256-73, especially 258; also Ljubica D. Popovich, *Serbian Art*, Vol. 2 of *Serbian Americans*, Cleveland Ethnic Heritage Studies (Cleveland: Cleveland State University, 1976), 256-8, Figure 32; on the minor arts, see Hristina Lisičić, "Dragutin Inkiostri-Medenjak," *Zbornik za likovne umetnosti* 1 (1965), 337-49.

12.For examples, see the following collections. Jovanović, Figure 44: Novak Radonić, "Manastir Hopovo"; Figure 69: Stefan Todorović, "Manastir Manasija" (1857). *Zadužbine Kosova: spomenici i znamenja srpskog naroda*, ed. Atanasije Jevtić (Prizren-Beograd: "Delo" [Ljubljana], 1987): Djordje Krstić, "Kosovo Polje" (1881), 222-3; Milan Milovanović, "Gračanica" (1908), 231; Pedja Milosavljević, "Pećka Patrijaršija" (1943), 231; Nadežda Petrović, "Prizren" (1913), 233, and "Kosovski božuri" (1913), 235; Petar Omčikus, "Visoki Dečani" (1950-86), 252. In Kusovac, see no. 229: Vasilje Daskalović, "Pećka Patrijaršija" (1874); no. 269: Svetozar Zorić, "Soko Grad" (1909); no. 394: Pavle-Paja Jovanović, "Manastir Sopoćani" (c. 1898); nos. 407-10: P. Jovanović, "Skice za kompoziciju Rade Neimar predaje model Manasije" (c. 1905). For works by Djordje Krstić, see Kusovac, no. 626: "Manastir Blagoveštenje" (1881-83); no. 628: "Sveti Nikola kod Kuršumlije" (1881-83); no. 636: "Manastir Žiča" (1881-83); no. 643: "Unutrašnjost manastira Žiče" (1881-83); no. 646: "Manastir Studenica" (1881-1830); and no. 652: "Manastir Voljavča" (1881-83). Even the naive artists of the second half of the twentieth century seem unable to resist the visual lure of monuments from the medieval past. See Miroslava Bošković and Milica Maširević, *Naifs Artists in Serbia* (Torino: Eskanaziarte, 1977), no. 46: Milan Rašic, "Žiča" (1970); no. 81: Dobrosav Milojević, "Koze u manastiru" (1973); no. 49: Budimir Rajković, "Kula" (1959).

13. Domentijan, *Životi Svetoga Save i Svetoga Simeona*, trans. Lazar Mirković (Beograd: SKZ, 1936) XLI, v. 282, *passim*; Archbishop Danilo, *Životi kraljeva i arhiepiskopa srpskih*, trans. Lazar Mirković (Beograd: SKZ, 1935), XXVII, v. 257, *passim*; Konstantin Filosof, *Život Despota Stefana Lazarevića*, in *Stare srpske*

biografije XV i XVII veka, Camblak, Konstantin, Pajsije, trans. Lazar Mirković (Beograd: SKZ, 1936), XXXIX, v. 265, 43-125; Milivoje M. Bašić, ed. and trans., *Iz stare srpske knijiževnosti* (Beograd: SKZ, 1911), v. 137, 95-167.

14.   Jovan Rajić, *Istorija raznih slavenskih naradov najpače Bolgar, Horvatov and Serbov*, 4 vols. (Vienna, 1794-95), *passim*.

15.   Jakov Orfelin, "Stefan Dušan Silni," heading from Chapter 12 of Jovan Rajić's *Istorija* (Beograd: Istoriski Institut, SAN).

16.   The Serbian Orthodox Church commemorates in its calendar nine canonized Serbian rulers and eight Serbian archbishops and patriarchs.

17.   For the scenes connected with Serbian rulers, see Gordana Babić, "Painting," *Studenica Monastery* (Beograd: Jugoslovenska Revija, 1986), 82-6, and Figures 72-3; Vojislav I. Djurić, *Sopoćani* (Beograd: SKZ i Prosveta, 1963), 78, and drawing on 133. For portraits, see Svetozar Radojčić, *Portreti srpskih vladara u srednjem veku* (Skoplje, 1934), *passim*. For the image tradition specifically of Stevan Nemanja, the following can be mentioned: the partially preserved fresco depiction of Nemanja as the monk Simon, c. 1128-1234, in the monastery Milaševa, painted barely more than three decades after his death, and within the living memory of those who knew him. See Svetozar Radojčić, *Mileševa* (Beograd: SKZ/Prosveta, 1963), Plate 4. However, this type of image was disseminated more readily through portable objects, for example, one small icon of a standing St. Simeon (Stevan Nemanja) with St. Sava, dated from the early fifteenth century. See Svetozar Radojčić, *Staro srpsko slikarstvo* (Beograd: Nolit, 1966), Plate 50. These kinds of images survived into the nineteenth century, helping the transmission of iconographic types from the Middle Ages into the modern era. See Branko Vujović, *Umetnost obnovljene Srbije 1791-1848* (Beograd: Prosveta, 1986), Figure 66, an icon of St. Simeon (Stevan Nemanja) and Stefan Prvovenčani, by Zoograph Aleksije Lazović, dating from 1818; and Figure 29, a woodcut of St. Simeon of Hilander and St. Stefan, by an anonymous artist, about 1820.

18.   Dinko Davidov *et al.*, *Fruškogorski manastiri* (Beograd: Galerija SAN, 1990), nos. 040, 044, 048, 050, 058, 060, 062; also Petrović and Kašanin, Figures 21-24 and 187-202.

19.   Branislav Živkovic, *Ravanica. Crteži fresaka* (Beograd, 1990), drawing on 51; also Mirjana Ljubinković, *Ravanica* (Beograd: Jugoslavija, 1966), Figure 2.

20.   Srdjan Djurić, *Ljubostinja: crkva Uspenja Bogorodičinog* (Beograd: Prosveta, 1985), 90-2, Plate 4 and Figure 104.

21.   Dinko Davidov, *Srpska grafika XVIII veka* (Novi Sad: Matica srpska, 1978), 245, 246; Jevtić, Figure on 238.

22.   Dejan Medaković, "Kult kneza Lazara u srpskom baroku," *O knezu Lazaru: Naučni skup u Kruševcu* (1971; Beograd, 1985): 321-35; Popovich, "Battle of Kosovo," 237 and n. 56.

23.   For the image of St. John Prodromos as *kinokephalos*, see Radojčić, *Staro srpsko*, Plate 63; Vujović, Figures 72, 98, 103, 110, 112, and 113; Davidov, *Fruškogorski*, plate 033.

24.   The title of this poem in Serbian is "Obretenije glave kneza Lazara" (see Jevtić, 212-13).

25. Zora Devrnja-Zimmerman, *Serbian Folk Poetry: Ancient Legends, Romantic Songs* (Columbus, OH: Kosovo, 1986), 205-6.

26. Julius S. Held and Donald Posner, *17th and 18th Century Art. Baroque Painting, Sculpture, Architecture* (New York: Prentice-Hall and Abrams, 1979), Figure 168.

27. For the question of the attribution of this work, see Jovanović, 163).

28. For the title *Tzar*, given to *knez* Lazar, see Vojislav Djurić, *Antologija narodnih junačkih pesama*, 7th ed. (Beograd: SKZ, 1973), no. 14, 251-60: "Car Lazar i Carica Milica."

29. Serbian zoographers of the eighteenth century continued with the medieval tradition of royal portraits in monumental paintings. As good representatives of this trend, the images of "*Tzar* Uroš" and "*Knez* Lazar" can be mentioned. They were painted between 1737-39, most likely by Andeja Andrejević and his workshop in the church of St. Stefan ("Lazarica") in Kruševac; see Vujović, 188 and Figures 1-2.

It should also be mentioned that the first known Serbian copper-plate engraver, Hristofor Žefarović (died 1753), made frontal portraits of Serbian medieval rulers for his *Stematografija* (1741). A typical example of these representations is "*Kralj* Vladislav," grandson of Nemanja and the founder of the monastery Milaševa. The style of this engraving is a hybrid one: it contains anachronistic elements from the romanticized past, such as the pseudo-dalmatic tht the ruler wears, the loros, the nimbus, and the cross that the king carries. These are mingled with the illusionistic space, swags of drapery, and architectural details, such as stairs and columns, typical for the Baroque style. See *Enciklopedija likovnih umjetnosti* I-V, dir. Miroslav Krleža (Zagreb: Leksikografski Zavod, 1959-66), s. v. "Žefarović, Hristofor."

Due to the popularity of St. Sava, representations of this Serbian saint are too numerous to attempt to discuss within the limits of an article. It is sufficient to mention here that the iconographic tradition of depicting St. Sava was continued from the Middle Ages to the twentieth century. As usual, St. Sava is depicted in a frontal pose, dressed in the garment of a hierarch. For a characteristic medieval representation, see Rajojčić, *Mileševa*, Plate 2; as a typical Romantic-style portrait of St. Sava, one can cite the painting now in the Gallery of Matica srpska in Novi Sad (see Nikola Kosovac, "Adam Stefanović," *Zbornik za likovne umetnosti Matice srpske* 2 (Novi Sad, 1966): 329-40.

Furthermore, representations of the Serbian kings even had unexpected applications. The image of Stevan "the First Crowned" (*Prvovenčani*) (1196-c. 1228), attributed to the painter Stefan Gavrilović, decorated the second preserved flag of Karadjordje. This banner dates from 1804, the year Karadjordje led the First Serbian Insurrection against the Ottoman Empire. The iconography of this king conforms to the type already discussed: an idealized face, long hair and beard, an imperial dalmatic, loros, ermine-lined cloak made of brocade, a scepter and a cross, a crown, nimbus, and inscribed name identification. There are also elements of medievalism found in the application of this royal portrait. Like an icon from the Byzantine period, which guarded a city or protected an army, the image of the first Serbian king assumes on this standard the meaning of a sign (*znamenje*). On the other side of this flag, the Serbian coat of arms completes the symbolism. See Vujović, 226, Figure 52 and Plate 13.

30.   A good example for the miracle is a representation of the eyesight restoration to Stefan Dečanski at the time of his coronation. See Jovanvić, 199, 202, 206, and Figures 72, 73. An example of the depicted tragedy is provided by the scene of "The Murder of *Tzar* Uroš"; see Jovanović, 167, 170, 172, 250, 267, and Figure 42.

31.   Grigorije Camblak, *Zivot kralja Stefana Dečanskog*, in *Stare srpske biografije*, 28-30.

32.   Ludmila Wratislaw-Mitrović and Nikolai Okunev, "La Dormition de la sainte Vierge dans la peinture médievale orthodoxe," *Byzantinoslavica* 3.1 (Prague, 1931): 134-80.

33.   See also Vladimir Petković, "La mort de la reine Anne à Sopoćani," *L'art byzantin chez les Slaves*, 1.2 (Paris, 1930): 217-221.

34.   Ljubica D. Popovich, *Personifications in Paleologan Painting (1261-1453)*, Diss. Bryn Mawr College 1963, 123-30.

35.   Patrijarh Pajsije, *Život cara Uroša*, in *Stare srpske biografije*, 138-41.

36.   Gertrud Schiller, *Iconography of Christian Art*, 2 (Greenwich, CT: New York Graphic Society, 1982), "The Lamentation," 174-9, Figures 594-6.

37.   Vuk Stefanović Karadžić, *Mala prostonarodna slavenoserbska pesnarica* (Vienna, 1814), *passim*, and *Srpske narodne pjesme*, Vol. 4 (Vienna, 1862), *passim*.

38.   For a partial list and discussion of such subjects, see Jovanović, 162-7, 197-202, 245-61, and above, n. 10.

39.   Dragoslav Srejović *et al.*, *Istorija srpskog naroda* (Beograd: SKZ, 1981), 1: 273-96, 328-40, 389-433, 476-95, 603-16, 641-63.

Kazantzakis: Dante's Translator and Rhapsodist

Andreas K. Poulakidas

In the summer of 1932, Nikos Kazantzakis—well known for such novels as *The Last Temptation of Christ* and *Zorba the Greek*—translated into verse *The Divine Comedy* of Dante. The first draft was completed in forty-five days in France at Boulogne-sur-Seine, at Avenue de Moulineaux, 93. Nearby was also living his closest friend and confidant Pantelis Prevelakis, with whom he had hoped to work on common literary projects at the time. There are several reasons why Kazantzakis undertook to translate Dante's *Divine Comedy* and to write a canto in *terza rima* in praise of Dante. Both his parents had died that year, his mother in March and father during the latter part of the year. He was very distressed at their deaths, for he had been away from Greece for nearly a year and a half. It is understandable that in focusing on Dante, Kazantzakis, who looked upon himself in his self-imposed exile as a kind of Dante, would benefit from Dante's religious consolation to overcome his grief at the loss of his parents. Personally this may have been the reason why he undertook to read and study Dante's *Divine Comedy*. Professionally, however, there was a more important reason.[1]

In the spring of 1932 Kazantzakis, after many drafts and revisions, had finished his *magnum opus*, his epic poem *The Odyssey*. He copied out clearly and legibly this manuscript of some 1984 pages that he presented on June 1, 1932 as a gift to Prevelakis. All other manuscripts would deal only with changes and corrections on the various parts of his monumental epic that he had basically already completed. Kazantzakis wrote the following on the cover page of this manuscript:

> I have copied this *Odyssey*
> for the favor of
> P a n t e l i s   P r e v e l a k i s
> and I present it to him;
> and for his favor—and with the secret hope—
> I copied for him these following verses of
> Dante:

Credette Cimabue nella pintura
tener lo campo, e ora ha Giotto il grido,
sì che la fama di colui è scura.
Così ha tolto l'uno all'altro Guido
la gloria della lingua; e forse è nato
chi l'uno e l'altro caccerà del nido.

Purg. [XI] 94-99   N. Kazantzakis
Gottesgab-Paris, 1932[2]

The following year Kazantzakis apparently had seen this manuscript and had written in pencil on its second page Dante's lines taken from *Paradiso* 1:34-6:

Poco favilla gran fiamma seconda:
forse di retro a me con miglior voci
si pregherà perchè Cirra risponda.

It is obvious that at this time Kazantzakis, while focusing on his *Odyssey*, had Dante also very much in mind. Prevelakis, an art historian and Italophile, responded to these two courtesies by adding the following lines from Dante immediately after those that Kazantzakis had penciled in:

Non è il mondan romore altro ch'un fiato
di vento, ch'or vien quinci e or vien quindi,
e muta nome perchè muta lato.
(*Grammata*, 326 [*Purg.* 11:100-3])

In his great epic poem of 33,333 lines, Kazantzakis attempted to do what Dante did for the Italian language. Like many other Greeks of the last two centuries, Kazantzakis had dedicated his efforts to promote the modern Greek language, i. e., the spoken, demotic language of the Greek people that had been subordinated by conservative, established circles and institutions under the purist, classical Greek parlance (*kathareuvousa*), despite the fact that the Greek language in its present form had evolved and developed from antiquity and the classical period to the Hellenistic and Byzantine periods into the language that it had become. Kazantzakis's vigorous efforts to advance the demotic language, to establish it as the official language in all of the institutions of modern Greece, made him a prominent and acknowledged advocate of the language, and he had acquired the conviction that his mission recapitulated that of Dante and Luther, since they had also advocated and promoted the vernacular language of their people. Consequently, his *Odyssey* was his culminating endeavor to preserve the language, a language that for many Greek people, even for the educated and learned, was not too understandable. In fact, in 1939, a year after his *Odyssey* was published, he published his *Lexilogio tis Odysseias*, a glossary of nearly fifteen hundred words defined and explained so that the modern Greek reader could understand the poetic text. As expected, this work became and still is a cause of much controversy regarding the nature of the demotic Greek language.[3] It becomes now apparent why he then translated Dante's literary epic.

Kazantzakis had acquired a reasonably strong background in Italian during his junior high school years (1897-1899) at the Franciscan-sponsored French Commercial Academy of the Holy Cross on the island of Naxos and later by his trips to Italy where he spent many days. In his library at the Historical Museum of Herakleion, texts can be found that he very likely relied on at different times in translating Dante's *Divine Comedy* into demotic Greek.[4] Since Kazantzakis's initial translation of Dante took place in Paris, it stands to reason he may not have immediately relied on any of these sources if they were in his library in Greece at that time. He may also have acquired some others at that time, using in addition the libraries in Paris for his translation. He may, however, have referred to some or all of them once he returned to Greece. For example, in Kazantzakis's letter of 11 October 1932 to Prevelakis, he writes: "I have found here an excellent translation of Dante (1931): *terza rima*, rhyme, fidelity. An excellent edition (which also contains his *Vita Nuova*), but it costs 25 *pesos* and I didn't buy it. Maybe later" (*Grammata*, 330). It must be noted that the commentary and notes appended to the *Divine Comedy* were not written until October 1933 at his home on the island of Aigina. Ultimately, this translation was published in December 1934, two and a half years later, at Athens by the publishing firm Kyklou (Prevelakis, "Symboli," 18-19).

Through his letters to Prevelakis we can learn of Kazantzakis's lifelong interest in Dante. Kazantzakis often quoted Dante's verses in Italian orally or in writing. Apparently in 1932 when he had completed the first draft of this translation, he managed to publish the first three cantos from the *Inferno* in the Athenian periodical *Kyklos* (2 [1932]: 145-54). The general response was that his translation was anachronistic and its language vulgar, *malliari*, i. e., hairy, beastly. Among those very critical of the language of these cantos was his former brother-in-law Lefteris Alexiou, who concurred with the judgment that Kazantzakis's translation was very slangy. Later on, Alexiou undertook his own partial translation of *The Divine Comedy* and published it in his periodical *Kastro*. Kazantzakis did not think highly of Alexiou's translation and felt it did very little justice to the original text. He had some harsh words for Alexiou and was bitter toward him, because he had sent him three letters on this matter and never received a reply. Yet in his letter of 21 January 1933 from Madrid, when he believed that it would take at least five to six years before his translation would be published, he expressed his hope that Prevelakis would write the introduction and Alexiou the notes to his translation. Of course it was published sooner than that, and he ended up writing both introduction and notes. At this time when critical discussions were going on regarding these two translations of *The Divine Comedy*, reference was also made to the Mavilis translation of Dante's epic.

At the end of September 1933, Kazantzakis indicated to Prevelakis that he would begin revising and rewriting his first draft; thus, at Aigina he then must have had access to all his books noted on Dante and to those dictionaries indicated. After trying to find people who would finance the publication, towards the end of October 1933 he began negotiating the publication with Melachrinos, a man Kazantzakis described as lethargic and sluggish. Though Kazantzakis was exasperated by Melachrinos, he announced to Prevelakis that the publication would begin on 1 January 1934. Finally, after an agonizingly slow process, Prevelakis was informed on 20 November 1934,

> Dante any day now will be published completely. Thirty-three different printings took place, and it will be selling for 350 drachmas. It cost me 65,000 drachmas, and I feel obligated to give complimentary copies to many who worked hard for its publication. The Italian Embassy will confer about this work and will recommend it in Italy, etc.; it plans to send a copy to Mussolini. The Italian professor Biagi spoke about this translation here at the university. The

[Greek] intelligentsia was divided into two groups: those few = [*sic*] enthusiastic, the multitude raving against its language. I'll be able to rest, however, once this work is behind me. (*Grammata*, Item #213, 442)

The following recorded item in Prevelakis's letters is the acknowledgment of the receipt of this most anticipated book, on whose third page Kazantzakis wrote: "May our God always make it possible in this hell of Greece for them to yell out to us: '*O voi, che siete due dentro ad un foco.*' 15-12-34" (*Inf.* 26: 79).

With this Kazantzakis set Dante aside and prepared to travel with the coming of 1935 to the Orient. It was not until his letter of 12 August 1941 from Aigina that Kazantzakis wrote to Prevelakis: "I have started to make a drastic revision of Dante with many and significant changes." Towards the end of March 1942 he informed Prevelakis that his revision of Dante's *Inferno* was ready for printing, and he considered this revision far superior to his first edition. Almost a decade later, after he had served as UNESCO'S first appointed dirctor of translations, he wrote to Prevelakis on 24 July 1950 from Antibes: "I often read Dante, especially each morning before I start on my work, and I find that I'm breathing the air that is so vital to me. I certainly would like to re-examine my second translation, but I don't have the manuscript with me. I've never been so ready for Dante" (*Grammata*, 628).[5]

The translation of Dante's *Divine Comedy* contains two appendices: the detailed comments and extensive clarifications on the various allusions in this epic, followed by a four-page glossary of demotic words that the reader might not comprehend. This work is introduced with a biographical sketch on Dante and then an analysis of his *Divine Comedy*, consisting of an external diagram of this epic, i. e., of the plot and Dante's journey through the three spiritual spheres of man. The next pages of this introduction pertain to the "*esoteriko diagramma*," as he refers to it, in which Kazantzakis critically evaluates Dante's thought and creative genius and relates it to his own understanding of literature and the world. It is interesting to note what he writes about Dante:

He established an order within his soul. Hell, Purgatory, Paradise can be found within us, a mystical, fearful human Trinity, and the entire song of Dante is nothing else but the ascetic, tenacious ascent from beast to God. Damned, Agonizing, Liberated: these are now the three levels of the complete human being. If one of the three ever is missing—even that of the Damned, above all of the Damned—humankind becomes a miserable, half-being.[6]

Kazantzakis could not resist applying to this analysis one of his most prevailing themes: his concept of *metousiosis*, his philosophical-theological belief in transubstantiation. In Dante he senses this process, this evolutionary process at work that testifies in behalf of this ascension. The supernatural is found very much within the natural, thus his admiration for Dante.

Even though it may have been feasible to translate this poem into the *terza rima* stanzaic rhyme scheme in which it was written, since the Greek language in general is phonetic, extremely flexible in its syntax and even in its grammar, Kazantzakis apparently did not feel obliged to do so. Undeniably, it would have taken him much longer to translate this work if he had been more faithful to Dante's rhyme scheme. Each rhapsody of this poem is an uninterrupted stanza that most consistently carries in every line the rythm of his *hendeka-syllabos*, eleven-syllabic line that ends throughout, without exception, in a penultimate (feminine) accent and that usually but not consistently follows the beat of an iambic hexameter. In his introduction Kazantzakis comments on the great passion this great Italian poet had toward the word, the perfect verse, and the perfect form. "Dante chose his words as a merciless general selects his soldiers for a dangerous mission" (xxix). Both had a great concern for the native, spoken tongue that they wanted to save and serve. In this introduction as well, Kazantzakis mentions Dante's essay *De Vulgari Eloquentia*, whose title Kazantzakis translates as *Gia tin euglottia tis demotikis glossas* (deliberately interpreting *vulgari* as "demotic").

The most classic reference that Kazantzakis makes in his other works to Dante can be found in his novel *Zorba the Greek*, where the employer, Kazantzakis himself, is absorbed in reading Dante's *Divine Comedy*, particularly his *Inferno*. In this novel the weak, ascetic, otherworldly employer, a contrast to Zorba the vitalist and activist, is shown to live vicariously by reading about hell via Dante rather than wanting to plunge into it in all its risks and turpitudes as does Zorba:

Out of my pocket I drew a little edition of Dante—my travelling companion. I lit a pipe, leaned against the wall and made myself comfortable. I hesitated for a moment. Into which verses should I dip? Into the burning pitch of the Inferno, or the cleansing flames of Purgatory? Or should I make straight for the most elevated plane of human hope? I had the choice. Holding my pocket Dante in my hand, I rejoiced in my freedom. The verses I was going to choose so early in the morning would impart their rhythm to the whole of the day.[7]

As was earlier indicated, in November of 1932, the same year that Kazantzakis translated Dante's epic, he wrote a canto in honor of Dante dedicated to his former brother-in-law, who had also visited him that year in Paris and who ironically later on became so negative about Kazantzakis's translation. In fact, in his letter of 18 October 1932 to Prevelakis from Madrid Kazantzakis told him that on that sunny day after his long walk to the park around the Prado, he was seized by the need to write a canto to Dante as soon as he returned home—"I wrote them quickly so I wouldn't forget them, I may need them"—and he copied down several random verses in this letter, some of which were included in his final draft (*Grammata*, 331-2). This canto, as was true of the many other cantos that he wrote in demotic Greek in honor of great personages such as Shakespeare, St. Teresa, Buddha, Christ, Moses, Nietzsche, and others[8] that comprised his work *Terzines*, followed the strict, cohesive *terza rima* form (aba,bcb,cdc—) and copiously observed the eleven-syllabic, feminine line that he used in translating Dante's *Divine Comedy*. He stated on the forefront page to this work that he dedicated these verses, i. e., these twenty-one cantos in *terza rima*, to the two sublimest words that the pride and bravery of man has, as of now, created: "DESPERADO, NADA."[9]

I have translated this canto on Dante. Through it we are able to ascertain the great admiration that Kazantzakis had for the greatest of Italy's poets and for one of the world's greatest masterpieces.

DANTE
for
Lefteris Alexiou

Coarse souls that understand all things about love
and blossom a rose in the fires of the brain,
3   watch from afar our leader passing by of
bent back in this sun-scorched divided domain
in the humid autumnal rain's drip-and-drop,
6   entering Ravenna palely with slow pain.
On horseback the honorable gentry's gents crop
out with the curly hawk on top of their wrist;
9   the bells proclaim aloud on the very top
Of large belfries the desire of prayerful mist;
and he, with Daphne's bitter leaf on his lips,
12   · biting it, chewing it to his soul talks: "List
to this, soul, how your last frosty evening nips!"
Two rouge golden cherubim at left and right,
15   the yes and no like dogs stood by him as pips,
mute, of the hunter death, the almighty mite.
His wayward innards opened up like old graves,
18   and deep in him a hoarse voice was raised to fight:
"May I not die, my God, till in the pitch," it raves
"and sulphur I throw my enemies and foes;
21   God can not ever save what the mind enslaves!"
Curses, revenge, hatred, and myriad woes,
a sack of catepillars his heart would shake
24   and like an adder his slim soul hisses and blows.
One by one all his enemies would he bake
inside his mind's nine kettles of melting pitch
27   and his entire black innards would he awake—
barking at frauds, phonies, pimps, and sons-of-a-bitch,
at cheapskates, animal-copulators, scamps,
30   and haughty friars, male-bedding with an itch!
Bent, mute, in his ardent, smoking, burning camps,
he turned them over, slowly roasted them like crabs;
33   his nostrils would steam like gluttonous lamps
as earth and hell would be built on brand-new slabs.
Most cheap, cool was the tar, a thousandfold long,

36   it seems, that sinners seethingly nabs and grabs,
   and he would lean on the wall whinnying his song.
       With sneering smile, the harpoon, his pen he lifts
39   and plunges headfirst into verse this sad throng.
   His hatred, a yellow-eyed hawk, flies and drifts
       an archangel of virtue, guardian true,
42   and perches upright, dropping poisonous gifts
   into our leader's brain that damns this damned slue.
       As long as God stands, so stands his sweetest hate,
45   an usher to the doors of Paradise New;
   "I forsake not virtue nor justice negate:
       if they break your tooth, I will smash their jaws!"
48   Like a brave man he talks fearless of his fate,
   and armed with invisible visions and laws,
       secretly his bitter lips smile as he sees
51   the holy damsel behind him without flaws.
   The towers at sunset shine in the breeze,
       warmly, softly, raindrops in the fields do fall,
54   the owl sighs, the fragrant earth weeps, heaves, and frees
   slowly the night to her wild embracing call—
       and he on earth, bending over, drags his feet
57   lightly, worn over strange stairs past all recall.
   His eyes lorn bid farewell to the lambs that bleat,
       to cattle returning from the yoke in pairs,
60   to pomegranates and maidens in the street,
   to figs, to grapes in the marketplace, to prickly pears.
       He smells the fruit of the earth, he curls his ears
63   to catch the words of people at countryfairs.
   The freshest parlance, the richest tongue he hears
       how it pours round his innards and makes them gay;
66   how from the people's lorn, brooding hen appears
   the word—a swan that's hatched and makes its own way
       into the peaceful, pure waters of the verse!
69   His eyes he shuts, sees the bleeding, dying day
   in the West, and hears the gulf that does immerse
       his soul with evening echoes: Firenze stirs.
72   Towers, palaces, and churches, all so terse,
   he knows by heart her holy charms; his mind blurs
       now in his memory's shadowy upper suite
75   like a Second Coming that right now occurs.

Oh, my! nowhere has he heard such words of wheat
            and has he ever eaten such tasty bread;
78   Alas! he shall not see her again, his sweet.
The accursed clans have set a price on his head;
            but his omnipotent soul her dear soul brings
81   one last time to his mind's mirror, alive yet dead.
Like a thirsty, lost guide at some desert springs,
            he cools his parched lips in his beloved's deep founts
84   and softly from his bereaved heart's coldest things
drips the one last salty, burning tear that counts.
            Standing near him, an old village woman views
87   his pure cheek, wet eye, for her so naught amounts,
his worn sandals, his life's sorrowful blues;
            she feels sorry for him, a sorry, sore sight
90   that a grape from her basket to him ensues.
His sad hands rejoice holding this fall's delight;
            Leaning on a rock, he nibbles grape by grape,
93   and the world becomes more blissful, blessed and bright.
He freshens up and takes off his black old cape.
            It's a heavy burden to make the flesh soul,
96   to calm down the flame to light—and man from ape.
The earth becomes now a grape, the blood's made whole,
            a climbing vine of God that leads to heaven.
99   Man's back and shoulders did tremble like a mole
always toiling wings of freedom to leaven;
            His tears did glitter and did shine in the air,
102   and in a conscious flash he snatched his seven
rags; and into the azure ether saints stare
            to behold him now angelic and to hold
105   a lily white in the light, and they declare;
"My God! how suddenly the pains grow so cold,
            and pity's sake sprouts a snowy bloom.
108   It's a nightingale, not a heart sold for gold,
that does warble on the vine and that does boom
            from earth to heaven as rhapsodists ascend!"
111   The cantos jolt inside the grave's deadly doom
the wings of his mind and him do condescend;
            his trembling fingers he pushes deep inside
114   his wounded heart to search and transcend
beyond his verses of pain that can not hide.

His verses creaked like dried, shriveled leaves,
117 storm-tossed by an autumnal weathervane's tide;
Of thyme, incense, sweat they smelled, under the eaves
  of exile, poverty's breath, stinking and rank;
120 His thick, burning tears turned pale, as he perceives,
his twisted script's blackness from its inky tank,
  and scribbled and niched deeply scratches of rage,
123 swordthrusts between candle drops guarding his flank.
With his slender, fine fingers the debauched page
  he slowly turns, draws near with love, faith, and awe,
126 say, as if he slipped into some other age.
Woven rhymes, following an unbending law,
  three by threes, tightly they are nestled like rocks;
129 and his thoughts, in the mind of the builder, draw
sturdy columns that arise with iron locks;
  and some harmonious voices in the dark
132 like lawmakers designate a nation's stocks.
Like a tall building the true song of the lark
  glittered ever so damply in the rain-soaked night;
135 Demons from Hell have clambered up in this ark
—dull roots—the gracious, wild flower in God's sight,
  before the holy mothers' oil-burning lamp,
138 arose, like virginal fluff, and flickered light.
Deeply and calmly the bells awoke the camp,
  and silent, the spiteful, coarse blacksmith of ink,
141 who did versify man's self, this little tramp,
freed now of time and space, would happily sink,
  with flesh and with spirit renewed and whole and sound,
144 into his plots, dancing-stories on the brink.
A cool breeze of grace and truth blew all around,
  and like an illustrated beautiful veil
147 the horsemanlike mind was suspended unbound:
an emerald-sapphirine throne he senses, hail,
  descending ardently from the earthly sun
150 haloed by our most genuine show-and-tale:
a bull, lion, eagle, archangel—the Son.
  The rose unfolds the old secrets of the mind,
153 the light shines entirely through dark death undone,
a soft voice entwines his innards most confined,
  and with secret rejoicing and horror new,

156   with light as a whip he sees four beasts resigned,
        driven like a victory now overdue,
             as a wild-eyed, bellicose, unsmiling, austere
159   Beatrice descends on him in a hallowed hue.
        Myriad-rose heaven and the angels dear
             harvest the grapes, like a busy swarm of bees,
162   the honey of dark immortality here.
        On earth white cypresses swayed on their knees,
             the flaming chariot stood perfectly still,
165   sweetly a tiny voice larked up in the trees
        that all of life's sorrow becomes now a thrill,
             and the mind has melted in the sun like snow:
168   "Dear friend, a thousand welcomes may you feel."
        Quickly he sets his palms for a shade to show,
             he smiles to love, his life's invisible crutch;
171   a stream his tears run, and down his cheeks they go;
        he struggles for support which his hands can touch
             and with his innards' flow tender words of art
174   to know, how sweetly to welcome her as much.
        But the holy eyes of his beloved sweetheart,
             like calm nets in a dreamlike state e'er so nigh,
177   haloing his breathless body-mind, depart.
        The night softly unveils all the star-lit sky,
             the crossed hands of the fierce athlete become cold;
180   and the bargain-hunters found Dante did lie
        dead, as the first stars peeped out all to behold.

NOTES

I wish to express my appreciation to Professor Emeritus Dimitri Sotiropoulos (formerly of the Foreign Language Department at Ball State University), a well known authority in the Greek demotic language, for hours of consultation with him.

1. Pantelis Prevelakis, "Nikos Kazantzakis: Symboli stin Chronographia tou Biou tou" ("A Contribution to the Chronography of his Life"), *Nea Hestia* 46 (Christougenna, 1959), 18.

2. Pantelis Prevelakis, *Tetrakosia Grammata tou Kazantakis ston Prevelaki* (Athens: Ekdoseis Helenis N. Kazantzaki, 1965), item #155, 325. All translations mine.

3. The following studies enable one to understand more fully the problems and issues surrounding the demotic language of Kazantzakis: N. P. Andriotis, "He Glossa tou Kazantaki," *Nea Hestia* 46 (Christougenna, 1959), 90-5; Peter Bien, *Kazantzakis and the Linguistic Revolution in Greek Literature* (Princeton: Princeton University Press, 1972); Amilios Chourmouzios, "He *Odysseia* tou Nikou Kazantzaki," *Knosos* (Maios, 1958), 27-30; I. Th. Kakrides, "To Chroniko mias Synergasias," *Nea Hestia* 46 (Christougenna, 1959), 115-20.

4. During my 1973-1974 sabbatical in Greece, I spent some time at the Historical Museum of Herakleion that houses the library of Kazantzakis and recorded in my notebooks those significant books pertaining to Dante. Some had been given a numerical identification by those in charge of his library collection. The sources on Dante and on the Italian language are as follows:

DANTE'S WORK:
Dante Alighieri. *La Divina Commedia.* G. A. Scartazzini, G. Vandelli, L. Polacco. Milano: Ulrico Hoepli, 1914 [B144].

Dante Alighieri. *La Divina Commedia* a cura di Carlo Steiner. Torino: G. B. Paravia, 1947 [B147].

Dante Alighieri. *La Divine Comedie: L'Enfer,* traduction nouvelle et notes de L. Espinasse-Mongenet. Paris: Nouvelle Libraire Nationale, 1920 [B145]. Kazantzakis made some notations in the text.

Dante Alighieri. *Vita Nova.* Paris, n. d. There is an inscription that reads: "For your birthday. 21 (?) 1934."

La Divina Commedia di Dante Alighieri. Nell'Arte del Cinquecento (Michelangelo, Raffaello, Zuccari, Vasari, ecc.), a cura di Corrado Ricci. Fratelli Treves, Editori, 1908. An immense, illustrated edition of Dante's *Divine Comedy*: a collector's item.

Le Opere di Dante Alighieri a cura del Dr. E. Moore, 4th ed. Oxford, 1924 [B146]. This contains all the works of Dante, his poetry and prose, i. e., *De Vulgari Eloquentia*, etc.

CRITICAL STUDIES ON DANTE:
Cossio, Aluigi. *Sulla Vita Nuova di Dante: Studio Critico-Letterario.* Leo S. Olschki, Editore. Firenze, n. d. Bears the following inscription: "Nikos'Angelo 20/5 - 2-915." Most likely this book was given to him as a gift by his friend and most promising fellow poet, Angelo Sikelianos, when they both traveled together throughout Greece, a trip that started around 15 November 1914, three days after they met, and lasted until the latter part of March or early April 1915. They toured Mount Athos and various other parts of Greece, searching for "the conscience of the earth and of their race." (Prevelakis, "Symboli," 8).

Gmelin, Herman. *Dantes Weltbild.* Leipzig: Verlag von Quelle & Meyer, 1903.

La Grande Encyclopedie. Inventaire Raisonne des Sciences, des Lettres et des Arts. Paris: H. Lamirault et Cie. Editeurs, 61, Rue de Rennes, n. d.

Olivero, Federico. *Literaturas Inglesa e Italiana.* Madrid: Editorial-America. A collection of essays on authors such as Dante, Coleridge, etc. It contains the following inscription: "5-6 Avril 1933, la nuit, de Paris a Marseille"].

Eleutheroudaki Encyclopaedikon Lexicon. Athinai: Ekdotikos Oikos Eleutheroudaki, 1927.

ITALIAN DICTIONARIES:

Italiano-Español y Español-Italiano, Nuovo Diccionario. Paris: Garnier Hermanos, n. d..

Lexicon Italo-Hellinikon Epitomon hypo K. Barbati. Typographeion "He Karteria," 1861.

Vocabolario Diamante della Lingua Italiana. Compilato di Giuseppe Rigutini, G. Barbera, Editore, Firenze, n. d.

5. See also *Grammata*, 259, 298, 325, 326, 327, 330, 331, 335, 352, 353, 355, 357, 368, 369, 394, 397, 399, 400, 401, 405, 406, 410, 412, 413, 415, 418, 421, 422, 425, 429, 431, 436, 437, 438, 442, 443, 489, 499, 505, 513, 520, 585, 604, 606, 610, 615, 628, 639, 643, 663, 664, 666, 667, 673, 675.

6. Dante, *He Theia Comodia*, sta Hellinika apo ton N. Kazantzaki. Athens, 1962, xxviii. "It is dedicated to the memory of Anglo Sikelianos, '*il miglior fabbro del parlar materno.*'" All translations mine.

7. Nikos Kazantzakis, *Zorba the Greek*, trans. Carl Wildman (New York: Simon and Schuster, 1964), 9, 12. It is disappointing to note that in his very last work, published posthumously, his autobiographical *Report to Greco*, Kazantzakis does not mention Dante at all even though he enumerates so many others who left their mark on him.

8. The "others" included John Psycharis (1854-1929), philologist, folklorist, linguist, and noted demoticist, who inspired Kazantzakis's interest in the modern Greek language.

9. N. Kazantzakis, *Tertsines* (Athina: Typographeio Ph. Konstantinidi kai K. Michala, 1960), 11-183.

Notes on Contributors

THOMAS BARBIERO is Professor and Chair of the Department of Economics at Ryerson Polytechnical Institute. He has published numerous articles in the *Journal of European Economic History* and is the author, with Campbell McConnell and Stanley Brue, of *Economics: Principles, Problems, and Policies* (1993).

DAVID E. BARCLAY is Professor of History and Director of the Center for Western European Studies at Kalamazoo College. In recent years he has written a number of articles on conservatism and the Prussian monarchy in the mid-nineteenth century. His next book, *Frederick William IV and the Prussian Monarchy, 1840-61*, will be published in English by Oxford University Press and in German by Siedler Verlag, Berlin. He plans a biography of Frederick William II, King of Prussia from 1786-97, and will edit the papers of conservative politician Leopold von Gerlach (1790-1861).

ROLAND BONNEL is Assistant Professor of French at Dalhousie University and Visiting Professor at the University of San Miguel de Tucuman, Argentina. A specialist in eighteenth-century French studies, he is General Editor of the series Eighteenth Century French Intellectual History, published by Peter Lang, and is currently investigating the concept of Utopia in the period. His book on the identity of the French nobility before the Revolution is forthcoming in 1994.

HILARY BRAYSMITH is Assistant Professor of Art at the University of Southern Indiana. Her ongoing research on Caspar David Friedrich has been supported by a Fulbright Fellowship and a Germanistic Society of America Scholarship.

LAURENCE DE LOOZE is Assistant Professor of Comparative Literature at Harvard University. Author of articles on fourteenth-century English, French, Icelandic, and Spanish literature, he is currently completing a book on the medieval pseudo-autobiography and an edition and translation of Froissart's *Prison amoureuse*.

JESSE D. HURLBUT is Assistant Professor of French and Honors at the University of Kentucky. His dissertation documented and studied fifteenth-century ceremonial entries of the Duke of Burgundy; current research interests include late medieval drama, allegory, and patronage, as well as medievalism in popular culture.

LISBET KOERNER recently earned the Ph. D. in history from Harvard University, where she has accepted a lectureship in the History of Science Department. Her dissertation, "Nature and Nation in Linnaean Travel," directed by Simon Schama, discusses the impulses behind Enlightenment voyages of discovery. She has published articles on the early modern history of science and on the Scandinavian welfare state.

MICHAEL LAVIN recently received the Ph. D. in Italian Studies from the University of Toronto. His dissertation is titled "Censorship, Academic Freedom and Literary Studies in the Tuscany of the Last Medici." His research interests include Vico, literary theory, and ideological discourse.

DOMENICO PIETROPAOLO is Associate Professor of Italian and Academic Coordinator of the Graduate Centre for the Study of Drama at the University of Toronto. He is the author of *Dante Studies in the Age of Vico* (1988), editor of *The Science of Buffoonery: Theory and History of the Commedia dell'arte* (1988), and co-editor of *The Enlightenment in a Western Mediterranean Context* (1984) and *Pirandello and Modern Theatre* (1992). Author of numerous articles on Vico, literary theory, and eighteenth-century Italian literature, Professor Pietropaolo is also Corresponding Editor for *Studies in Medievalism*.

LJUBICA D. POPOVICH, Associate Professor of Art History at Vanderbilt University, studied art history at the University of Belgrade before coming to the United States. Her research has been supported by grants from the National Foundation on Arts and Humanities, the American Philosophical Society, the Dumbarton Oaks Fulbright Program, and the Resource Center for Medieval Slavic Studies at Ohio State University. She has published some twenty articles on Byzantine and Slavic art and is also the author of *A Survey of Serbian Art from the Late 12th to the Early 20th Centuries* (1976).

ANDREAS K. POULAKIDAS, Associate Professor of English at Ball State University, has published articles on Kazantzakis in *Comparative Literature, Philological Quarterly, Symposium, Folia Neohellenica,* and other journals. He is currently at work on a book on the fiction of Kazantzakis.

W. JAY REEDY is Associate Professor of History at Bryant College. He has published numerous articles in *The Journal of the History of*

Ideas, Historical Reflections, Proceedings of the American Philosophical Society, and *Studies on Voltaire and the Eighteenth Century.*

CAROL L. ROBINSON is a member of the Department of English at Gallaudet University and is currently completing a dissertation titled "The Schizophrenic Object of Desires, Fears and Whims: A Study of the Sorceress/Lady of the Lake in American and British Film Adaptations of British Medieval Literature." She has presented papers and organized seminars on medievalism in film, and her article on Godard's *Hail, Mary* appeared in the Summer 1989 issue of *Post Script.*

THERESA ANN SEARS, Associate Professor of Spanish at the University of Maine, Orono, has published articles on Spanish literature in *Medieval Perspectives, Fifteenth Century Studies, Romanic Review,* and other journals. In press from Peter Lang is her book *A Marriage of Convenience: Ideal and Ideology in the 'Novelas Ejemplares.'* She is now at work on a book entitled *Calypso's Song: Spain and the Medieval Ideal.*

RICHARD J. UTZ, Assistant Professor of English at the University of Northern Iowa, received the Doctor of Philosophy degree in English and German philology from the University of Regensburg; he taught formerly at that institution and at the Pädogogische Hochschule of Dresden. His book *Literarischer Nominalismus im Spätmittelalter* was published by Peter Lang in 1990. "Nominalist Perspectives in Chaucer's Poetry: A Bibliographical Essay," co-authored with William H. Watts, will appear in *Medievalia et Humanistica* this year.

GERD-H. ZUCHOLD is director of a research project on historical preservation at the Technical University of Berlin. He is also chair of the Ferdinand-von-Quast-Gesellschaft and President of the Landesheimatbund Brandenburg. He is the author of numerous publications on responses to antiquity in European art since the Middle Ages and to Byzantine art in the nineteenth century, as well as on art in Prussia in the eighteenth and nineteenth centuries. His most recent book is *Der Klosterhof des Prinzen Karl von Preußen im Park von Schloß Glienicke* (Berlin, 1993).

Figure 1. Peter von Cornelius, *Greeting of the Two Queens. Nibelung Cycle* (Berlin, 1817).

Figure 2. *Hagen.* Marmorpalais, Potsdam. 1848.

Figure 3 *above. The Dead Siegfried.* Marmorpalais, Potsdam. 1848.

Figure 4 *left. Hagen and Gunther.* Nationalgalerie, Berlin. 1871.

Figure 5. *Scene from the Nibelungenlied.* Nationalgalerie, Berlin. 1871.

Figure 1. Carl Russ, *Rudolph von Habsburg Reprimands the Watch for Denying the Entry of the Poor*. 1811. Oil on canvas. Reproduced by kind permission of the Muzeum Mesta Brna, Czech Republic.

All illustrations to this article are reproduced from Willi Geismeier, *Die Malerie der deutschen Romantik* (Dresden: Verlag der Kunst, 1984).

Figure 2. Ludwig Kohl, *Gothic Hall with Knights of the Holy Feme*. 1812. Oil on canvas. Reproduced by kind permission of the Narodni Galerie, Prague.

Figure 3. Josef Wintergerst, *The Reconciliation of Ludwig of Bavaria with Frederick the Fair, 1325*. 1816. Oil on canvas. Reproduced by kind permission of the Museen für Kunst und Kulturgeschichte der Hansestadt, Lübeck.

Figure 4. Heinrich Olivier, *The Holy Alliance*. 1815. Gouache on paper.
Reproduced by kind permission of the Staatliche Galerie, Dessau.

Figure 5. Caspar David Friedrich, *Hutten's Tomb*. 1823. Oil on canvas. Reproduced by kind permission of the Kunstsammlung, Weimar.

Figure 1. Wilhelm Kreis's plan for a *Totenburg* in Noyers Pont Maugis, France. 1943. Pen drawing. Reproduced from Kreis, *Soldatengräber und Gedenkstätte* (Munich: Callwey, 1944).

Figure 2. Wilhelm Kreis's plan for a *Totenburg* in Warsaw. 1943. Pen drawing. Reproduced from Kreis, *Soldatengräber und Gedenkstätte* (Munich: Callwey, 1944).

Figure 3. Wilhelm Kreis's plan for *Totenburgen* in Norway (left), Africa (upper right), and Greece (lower right). 1943. Pen drawing. Reproduced from Hans Stephan, *Wilhelm Kreis* (Oldenburg: Gerhard Stalling, 1943).

Figure 4. Wilhelm Kreis's plan for a Soldiers' Hall in the Berlin Army Headquarters. 1939. Pen drawing. Reproduced from Hans Stephan, *Wilhelm Kreis* (Oldenburg: Gerhard Stalling, 1943).

Figure 5. Anselm Kiefer, *To the Unknown Painter (Dem unbekannten Maler)*. 1982. Watercolor and pencil on paper. Private collection. Reproduced by kind permission of the owner and photographed from Mark Rosenthal, *Anselm Kiefer* (Philadelphia: Philadelphia Museum of Art, 1987).

Figure 1. Char de la Ville et des Defenseurs du pays.

Figure 2. Presens offerts au Souverain.

All illustrations to this article are reproduced from H. Pilate-Prévost, *Notice sur Philippe-le-Bon* (Douai, 1840).

Figure 3. Char des présens.

Figure 4. Char du Souverain.

Figure 5. Char de Jason et la Toison d'or.

Figure 6. Litière de la Souveraine.

Figure 7. Char de la Souveraine.

Figure 8. Char du Souverain.

Figure 1. Jakov Orfelin, *Tzar Dušan*. Late eighteenth century. Reproduced by kind permission of the Serbian Academy of Arts and Sciences, Belgrade Historical Institute.

Figure 2. Djura Jaksić, *Tzar Dušan*. 1857. Reproduced by kind permission of the National Museum, Belgrade.

Figure 3. Dmitrije N. Petrović, *Tzar Dušan*. 1862. Reproduced by kind permission of the National Museum, Belgrade.

Figure 4. Stevan Todorović, *Stefan Nemanja*. 1879. Serbian Orthodox Church, Idvor. Reproduced by kind permission of the Museum of the Serbian Orthodox Church, Belgrade.

Figure 5. *Ktitor*'s composition with *Knez* Lazar. Fresco, before 1389. Monastery Ravanica. Drawing by Branislav Živković and reproduced by his kind permission.

Figure 6. *Knez* Lazar and *Knjeginja* Milica. Fresco, 1403. Monastery Ljubostinja. Photograph courtesy of Srdjan Djurić.

Figure 7. *Knez* Lazar. Woodcut, c. 1700. Monastery Vrdnik, Ravanica. Reproduced by kind permission of the Museum of the Serbian Orthodox Church, Belgrade.

Figure 8. Zaharija Orfelin, *Knez Lazar*. Engraving, 1773. Reproduced by kind permission of the Gallery of Serbian Art, Novi Sad.

Figure 9. Djura Jakšic, *Knez Lazar*. 1857–59. Reproduced by kind permission of the National Museum, Belgrade.

Figure 10. Novak Radonić, *Knez Lazar*. 1850s–1863? Reproduced by kind permission of the Gallery of Serbian Art, Novi Sad.

Figure 11. Stevan Todorovic, *Knez Lazar*. 1879. Serbian Orthodox Church, Idvor. Reproduced by kind permission of the Museum of the Serbian Orthodox Church, Belgrade.